Four Weddings
and a Kiss

Other Novels by These Authors

A Bride for All Seasons

Margaret Brownley

THE BRIDES OF LAST
CHANCE RANCH SERIES

Gunpowder Tea

Waiting for Morning

Dawn Comes Early

ROCKY CREEK ROMANCE

A Vision of Lucy

A Suitor for Jenny

A Lady Like Sarah

Log Cabin Christmas
Collection

A Pioneer Christmas
Collection

Robin Lee Hatcher

A Promise Kept

WHERE THE HEART
LIVES SERIES

Beloved

Betrayal

Belonging

Heart of Gold

A Matter of Character

Fit to Be Tied

A Vote of Confidence

Mary Connealy

TROUBLE IN TEXAS SERIES

Swept Away

Fired Up

Stuck Together

KINCAID BRIDES SERIES

Out of Control

In Too Deep

Over the Edge

A Match Made in Texas

Debra Clopton

Her Unforgettable Cowboy

Her Homecoming Cowboy

Her Lone Star Cowboy

Her Rodeo Cowboy

Her Forever Cowboy

His Cowgirl Bride

The Trouble with Lacy Brown

Four Weddings and a Kiss

A WESTERN BRIDE COLLECTION

MARGARET BROWNLEY
ROBIN LEE HATCHER
MARY CONNEALY
DEBRA CLOPTON

THOMAS NELSON
Since 1798

NASHVILLE   DALLAS   MEXICO CITY   RIO DE JANEIRO

Published in Nashville, Tennessee, by Thomas Nelson. Thomas Nelson is a registered trademark of HarperCollins Christian Publishing, Inc.

Thomas Nelson books may be purchased in bulk for educational, business, fund-raising, or sales promotional use. For information, please e-mail SpecialMarkets@ThomasNelson.com.

Scripture quotations are taken from the King James Version of the Bible.

Publisher's Note: This novel is a work of fiction. Names, characters, places, and incidents are either products of the author's imagination or used fictitiously. All characters are fictional, and any similarity to people living or dead is purely coincidental.

Library of Congress Cataloging-in-Publication Data

Four Weddings and a Kiss : a Western bride collection / Margaret Brownley, Robin Lee Hatcher, Mary Connealy, Debra Clopton.
   pages cm
  ISBN 978-1-4016-8854-7 (softcover)
1. Weddings—Fiction. 2. Love stories, American. 3. Christian fiction, American. I. Connealy, Mary. Spitfire sweetheart II. Hatcher, Robin Lee. Love letter to the editor. III. Clopton, Debra. A Cowboy for Katie. IV. Brownley, Margaret. Courting trouble.
  PS648.L6F755 2014
  813'.08508—dc23   2013049755

Printed in the United States of America

14 15 16 17 18 RRD 5 4 3 2 1

Margaret Brownley: *I dedicate my story to Robin, Mary, and Debra. Working with these three terrific ladies was a joy, a privilege, and an honor.*

Robin Lee Hatcher: *To my readers. Thanks for joining me in the adventure.*

Mary Connealy: *To my newest grandbaby. A little boy whose name I don't know yet because he's going to be here right about the time this book comes out.*

Debra Clopton: *For my Taycie, Kyelie, and Paige—I love you sweet girls to the moon and back and then endlessly around and around and around . . . What beautiful gifts of God you are to me. What joy you bring my days. May each of you grow up loving the Lord and knowing that for as much as I love you, your Heavenly Father loves you even more.*

Contents

Fort Worth, Texas, 1885

REVEREND GREGORY MILLER DREADED GOING HOME. THE weeklong revival meeting had been a resounding success with more than a thousand in attendance. Tomorrow he would board a train bound for Phoenix. With the thought came the memory of big blue eyes and a sweet curving smile.

He clutched his hands into a ball, praying, *Why, God, why? I've been a faithful servant and served my church well. So why do You feel the need to test me? Actually,* punish *would be a more apt description.*

Breaking up with Elizabeth was the hardest thing he'd ever done, but it was also the most necessary. The marriage would have been doomed from the start.

"But how can I go on without her?" he railed. "Will You tell me that, God?"

Realizing he'd spoken aloud, Gregory's eyes flew open. His heated face had less to do with the campfire blazing beneath the star-studded sky than the disapproving stares from the other four preachers. Talking aloud during silent prayer was frowned upon. The other campfires scattered about the grove seemed to dim in light of his blunder.

He mopped his forehead with a handkerchief and ran a finger along his stiff collar.

"Please accept my humble apologies."

One preacher lifted a monocle to his eye. "Who exactly is this woman causing you such distress?"

Before Gregory could answer, the preacher next to him shifted his weight on the fallen log and slipped his Bible into his frock coat pocket. "I told you he had calico fever," he drawled in a Texas twang. "Why else would a young man mope around like a tick-fevered doggie?"

"I wasn't moping." Okay, so he'd kept pretty much to himself during the revival, interacting with the other ministers only when necessary. So what? "And her name is Elizabeth Princeton."

His response brought a chuckle from the minister who hailed from Wyoming.

"This woman, Elizabeth . . . Do you love her?"

Gregory sucked in his breath. Such a nosy question. But having spoken during silent prayer, he felt obliged to answer. "Well, yes."

"And does she love you?"

"Yes, but—"

"So what's the problem?"

The Texan tossed another log onto the fire, dashing Gregory's hope that his companions would retire to the nearby tents soon and leave him alone in his misery.

"Miss Princeton is . . ." He searched for a way to describe her. "Reckless."

"Reckless?" The word escaped all four men in perfect harmony.

He sighed. It wasn't like him to talk about personal matters. Drawing attention to himself was not his style. Back home in Phoenix people expected their ministers to be dignified and sedate. At age thirty, he'd served his church well. He could only imagine what his congregation would say if they knew how their esteemed leader bared his soul to a group of near strangers.

"Maybe that's not the right word but . . ." He couldn't think of another. "She taught our church ladies to play rounders." Women wielding sticks was shocking enough, but irate husbands insisted the games also interfered with the women's household chores.

The eye behind the monocle never wavered from its examination of him. "Far as I know, rounders isn't a sin. Why are you all riled up?"

Gregory blinked. Did he have to spell it out? "I'm a very conservative man. I run a conservative church. The most daring thing our deacons ever did was lock spiritual horns with the Methodists next door." Denominational rivalry ran rampant in the West where only the best-attended churches could survive. "What's more, Miss Princeton sided with the Methodists."

"No!" the preacher from Wyoming exclaimed with a hint of amusement.

"She also discussed politics in the churchyard."

"Shocking," exclaimed the reverend from Colorado with mock gravity.

Gregory studied the others; were they not taking him seriously? "And she made the children laugh during Bible class. Can you imagine? Laughing in church? And when I disapproved of a young couple holding hands during the Doxology, she called me a stuffed shirt."

One of the preachers leaned forward. Gregory tried to recall his name. Albert? Alden? That was it: Reverend Alden. "The other day in leaders' class you said that until recently your church experienced low attendance."

"Yes, but—"

"Would it be accurate to say that your lady friend has had a positive influence in that regard?"

Gregory sat back aghast. "Are you suggesting that Miss Princeton's rounders tournaments had something to do with the recent rise in church membership?"

The older man shrugged. "Times have changed. We have the railroad and telegraph to thank for that. If the church doesn't change accordingly, I fear we'll all be in trouble."

The man from Wyoming pulled out his watch. "Perhaps God sent Miss Princeton to save your church and you at the same time."

"That's crazy," Gregory said. Why would anyone think *he* needed saving?

Alden arched a dark brow. "Is it?"

"Of course it is. Marriage is out of the question. It's highly unlikely that God means for her to be a preacher's wife." Such a woman would have to be modest, reserved, and obedient— all the things Elizabeth Princeton was not.

"As unlikely as Sarai and Abram having a child in their old age?" Alden asked.

"Or Moses, a man slow of speech, becoming a leader and great orator?" added the preacher with the watch.

The Texan gave a nod. "Or a lowly shepherd boy takin' down Goliath without benefit of a firearm?"

Soon a friendly game was in progress with the four older preachers vying to name God's most unlikely servants.

The man from Wyoming summed it up. "The one thing I've learned in all my years of ministry is that God sometimes brings unlikely people together for a purpose. *His* purpose."

Reverend Alden poked at the fire with a stick. "Reminds me of a couple I once knew." He chuckled at the memory. "You never saw two more mismatched people in your life."

The other ministers were all anxious to share stories of their own.

Alden tossed the stick into the fire and sat back. "I'll go first, then you can each take turns." The matter settled, he continued, "My story involves a couple named Maizy MacGregor and Rylan Carstens who are living proof that God has a sense of humor. Let me tell you . . ."

Spitfire Sweetheart

Mary Connealy

CHAPTER ONE

Saurita, New Mexico, 1879

MAIZY MACGREGOR LEANED HER HEAD BACK AGAINST the rocks, accidentally knocking her Stetson off. She grabbed it as it fell, then tossed it aside in disgust. She had on men's clothes—the hat, britches, shirt, boots, even a six-gun she wore on her hip. It had never bothered her before Rylan Carstens.

She wiped her eyes. It was sure enough bothering her now.

The water roared beside her, cascading down in a rush. She came here when she needed to be alone. And she really needed that now.

Tossing aside her buckskin gloves, she pulled her red handkerchief out of her hip pocket—no lace kerchief tucked up her sleeve for Maizy—and wiped her eyes again, then blew her nose in a completely unladylike way.

How had she let herself get this upset? And over a man, of all things.

Over the neighbor whom she'd long ago accepted would never see her as anything but a child, and an unattractive, annoying child at that.

She was used to it, and she ignored it mostly, but today it stung. He'd found her walking among his Angus cattle.

Maizy looked to her left and watched the sleek black herd spread out along the downhill slope. Usually she didn't go near them. Instead, she'd just slip into this spot. She'd been using it for a getaway since childhood. But this morning, not for the first time, she'd walked among his herd. They were gentle cattle, not a horn on a single one of them. They weren't tame enough to touch—they gave way if she got too close. But they didn't run for the hills one day, then attack the next like longhorns tended to do.

She'd heard they were gentle, even the bulls. And she was savvy about cattle. She knew how to judge their tempers and stay clear of them when necessary. Her eyes rested on one especially young calf that might have been born just today, long after cows usually threw their calves.

Maizy knew better than to go near a new mama, no matter how easygoing she'd been before her calf was born.

She'd told Rylan all that and tried to make him see she was in no danger. He'd thrown her off his land anyway and even followed her home to complain to Pa, like she was a misbehaving child. He'd forbidden her to trespass ever again.

But the minute she could get away, she came here, to her

special place. The river was the border between his property and her pa's, and it was true she was, right this minute, on the trespassing side. She barely had a toe over the line, and she was completely safe from his placid, fat cattle, so surely he wouldn't complain about that.

She took a little pleasure in defying him. And it was a harmless defiance, especially if he didn't know she was here.

Her horse was tied well across the river, on MacGregor land, cropping grass. She couldn't see the brown-and-white pinto from here and neither could her neighbor.

Hoping to get control of her hurt, she let herself soak in the peace of stone and water and air, loving the way this rocky ledge cut off the world. She couldn't hear anything other than the rushing water. Her spot was curved into the rocks, and she could only see straight ahead and to the left. Water cascaded down from the mountain peaks on the right. Her almost-cave hid her from behind and overhead.

She was in her own world, alone with her thoughts.

Then a gunshot cut through the air, and she sat up straight and banged her head.

Looking for the source of that gun, she turned and saw *him*.

Rylan Carstens.

And he was coming straight for her, galloping on his big chestnut stallion. Even at this distance she could tell he was looking right at her. How had he known she was in here?

Another gunshot echoed from his Winchester.

Rylan bent low over his horse, coming as fast as he could

on the rocky ground that rose to this bluff along the river. Was he trying to kill her? If so, he was doing a poor job of it. The bullets were missing, going way over her head. But even on her worst day, she'd never done anything to make the man killing mad.

And Maizy knew, even though Rylan seemed like a mighty cranky man, that he wasn't the type to shoot a young woman, especially not for just being annoying.

He fired again and again, working the levered handle on his Winchester, and she finally realized he was firing warning shots. But warning who—about what?

She scrambled out of the little overhang and took a few running steps to make sure he saw her and wouldn't fire in her direction.

That's when she heard the growl . . . and the bellow.

Spinning around, she looked up. On the ledge that formed the roof of her little cave, standing on its hind legs, was the biggest grizzly she'd ever seen.

Movement to her side forced her to look, though it was madness to turn away. The huge Angus bull that lorded over this part of Carstens's herd pawed the ground, and like all bulls, guarded his herd fiercely. There were only two things between that huge bear and that angry bull.

The shining black calf, born out of season, still wobbly.

And Maizy.

The bull might be threatening the bear, but the bear only had eyes for Maizy. The rest of the cow herd, save the frantic mama, turned and stampeded away.

The bull charged.

The bear dropped to all fours and crouched to attack.

Pound for pound there was no meaner animal on the face of the earth than a grizzly. Maizy had a Colt in her holster, but a bullet wasn't enough to bring one of these huge beasts down. Maybe a perfect shot right into the heart or brain would do it . . . but mostly . . . getting shot just made 'em mad.

The bear's beady, bloodshot eyes were riveted on Maizy.

The bull bellowed and turned the grizzly's attention.

Maizy saw her chance and ran.

A shout and another blast of gunfire sent Maizy running straight down the grassy slope for Rylan. Her eyes locked with his and she saw horror. She thought he'd seen her, but she could tell he'd been out here riding herd and seen the grizzly.

A thud from behind told her the bear was off the ledge. Another growl seemed to blow hot breath on the back of Maizy's neck. Or maybe that was just the hair on the back of her neck standing up in pure terror.

The bull charged, putting itself between the bear and the calf, then stopped to paw the earth with its front feet.

Rylan fired again and again.

Sprinting to get out of the middle, Maizy heard the thundering hooves ahead, the scratching claws of the grizzly right behind, and the deep-throated threats from the bull.

The calf bawled piteously. The anxious mama cow rushed to her baby and began leading it away as fast as its unsteady legs would carry it.

Judging from the growling behind her, Maizy knew the grizzly was more interested in her than a belligerent Angus.

Running, hoping the bear would give up, she raced straight for Rylan.

She saw his eyes take in the danger, then go to his bull, then come back to her. He kept firing and racing forward.

Sprinting flat out, her boots thumped out a desperate beat.

He jammed his rifle back into its scabbard on the saddle and drew his six-gun. He couldn't shoot the bear—Maizy was right in the way—but he kept up the gunfire, probably hoping he'd scare the grizzly into breaking off the attack.

It wasn't working worth a hoot.

"Maizy," Rylan shouted as they closed the gap, "grab my hand."

He kicked his foot out of one stirrup to give Maizy a place to land. He holstered his pistol and took a firm hold of his pommel. Their eyes locked. He nodded at her. She tightened her jaw in grim determination and nodded back.

His hand extended. She slapped her hand into his and he caught her. The grip slid. He clamped onto her wrist with the other hand, leaving the horse without a hand on the reins. He swung her up and she aimed to end up behind him. In the rush, she didn't get a good swing, and Rylan made a desperate heave to keep her from falling to the ground. She landed facedown in front of him, her belly right on the pommel of his saddle. She was glad to be wearing britches.

Rylan pulled hard to bring his horse to a stop, and he unloaded his gun on the bear. The horse tried to rear and tossed its head in fear. The iron bit jingled as the horse fought Rylan's control.

Maizy turned to her left to watch the bear wheel to face the bull. The bull must've thought better of fighting now that his herd was out of the way. He turned and ran.

The bullets were little more than stinging wasps to the bear and only served to turn its attention back to Rylan.

The powerful red horse pivoted, and on its first stride leapt into a full gallop.

Grizzly bears, huge as they were, were mighty fast. Maizy knew that from growing up in the mountains of New Mexico and meeting up with a few, though never this close. But their speed was short-lived—or so she'd heard.

She sure as shootin' hoped that proved to be true. If the horse could outrun the monster for a few yards, they'd make it.

Maizy, head down, clung to Rylan's right leg. The pommel cut into her gut, and her own legs dangled off the other side. She wanted to search for that empty stirrup but was mindful not to jar Rylan or distract him from getting the most out of his thoroughbred.

Those thundering front hooves kicked up nearly to Maizy's face. She lifted her head enough to peek around Rylan's boot and saw the bear gaining on them. Its jaws gaped open. It closed in on the horse even with the stallion going at full speed.

"Hang on." Rylan kicked his horse and the valiant chestnut, already wild with fear, dug deep and found more speed. The bear lunged forward and a huge paw, claws bared, took a swipe and snagged the horse's tail. That swipe broke the bear's charge.

Finally they were stretching out the distance between them as the bear slowed. It dropped to a trot, then a walk, then stood up on two legs, front paws extended in the air, and sent them on their way with an ugly chain of growling threats.

Maizy's belly was being stabbed good and hard. She hadn't paid it much mind until now. The horse was safely away, and Maizy saw the grizzly turn and jog back the way it'd come. "It's stopped," Maizy shouted.

"Hang on!" Rylan's ordered shout brought Maizy's head around, and she saw that the ground was broken ahead. This was Rylan's land, but Maizy had lived here all her life. She knew this was a bad stretch, littered with boulders and cut by water running off the mountain to the river.

The horse was running away, terrorized. Rylan was easing the horse up, but they weren't going slow enough to navigate the dangerous patch. No horse racing full speed could hope to get through it unharmed.

The horse tossed its head and fought the reins, but finally began to respond. Maizy recognized the expert handling of the reins as Rylan tried to gain control of the panicked horse.

They reached the first line of scattered rocks.

Rylan picked his moment and yelled, "Whoa!"

He pulled back hard and the horse skidded until it nearly sat down on its haunches. As they came to a stop, the horse neighed and reared, straight up, higher and higher. Maizy felt the stallion going over backward.

Rylan shoved her so she fell off feetfirst and he dove to the other side. Maizy rolled over and over, afraid of where the horse might land, until she came up hard against a massive stone. She whirled to see Rylan being dragged, one foot stuck in the stirrup. Leaping to her feet, Maizy drew her gun to shoot the horse that had saved their lives, just as Rylan fell free and rolled hard against a boulder.

Maizy heard the crack as Rylan's head struck stone.

She raced on shaking legs to where he lay flat on his back. Out cold. His face white as ash.

Maizy crawled to his side, terrified that he was dead. His chest rose and fell steadily. He was alive! Looking around, she saw that his horse was nowhere in sight. A lump was already rising on his forehead, and seconds later she saw blood soaking through his tattered pants. Drawing her knife, she slit the leg of his britches. His knee was bleeding and his leg already showed some swelling.

It had to be broken.

Maizy looked around. She was miles from anywhere. His horse was long gone. Rylan was too heavy to lift.

A wild cry far overhead drew her eyes up to a soaring eagle. The isolation of this place tightened like a vise around her throat.

Praying frantically for wisdom, she remembered her pinto on the far side of the river. There was a ford. She could get the mare here . . . if the grizzly hadn't scared her into breaking her reins and racing for home.

Maizy would have to go for the horse. Besides that grizzly,

there were rattlesnakes. Buzzards might scent blood, with Rylan unconscious—Maizy shuddered to think of that. There were even wolves and cougars in the area. To get the mare, Maizy would have to leave Rylan utterly defenseless.

She looked at his handsome face. He'd risked his life to save her. He'd abandoned a bull that cost a fortune and used every ounce of his strength to get her to safety.

And now she needed to do as much for him. And to do that, she had to leave him lying here.

No alternative came to her, so she jumped to her feet and ran.

Maizy hurried to her mare in double time. She had worked with her pa plenty, and she knew how to treat a beat-up cowboy, although she'd never seen one quite this beaten before.

When she got back to his side, Rylan lay still as death. His leg was almost certainly broken. Should she cut the boot off? The swelling had gotten so bad she was afraid he had no circulation, yet how much damage might she do removing the boot? Praying for wisdom beyond what she possessed, she decided to leave it, at least for now.

She'd been thinking the whole time she fetched her horse. Now she tethered her horse and rushed toward the nearest slope, covered with quaking aspens.

Feeling the minutes tick by and knowing that boot was strangling Rylan's leg, she hacked down slender saplings with her sturdy, razor-sharp knife and returned to make a travois. Pa had taught her the way of it years before.

She used the lasso on her pommel to weave a triangular net between two trees. Once she was satisfied it would hold, she moved the contraption so the ends of the young trees were on either side of his head. Then, with a remaining stretch of rope, she tied a loop under Rylan's arms, hooked him to her horse, and hoping he stayed unconscious, she pulled Rylan up the length of the travois with aching slowness. He was slim but tall with broad shoulders, made of solid muscle that made him heavy. It took some finagling to get him in place, but finally he lay fully on top of the makeshift travois.

Then she lifted each side of the front ends of the travois and used a pigging string to hitch the ends to her stirrups.

As she lashed the second aspen pole in place, Rylan groaned.

Maizy rushed to his side.

His blue eyes flickered open, but he stared through her, still dazed. She rested one hand on his shoulder.

"Lie very still. I'm taking you home."

"Maizy." Rylan spoke that one word, then passed out again.

Because she was praying so hard when she felt a twist of fear about his leg, she decided it was God putting the notion in her head. She'd get the boot off while Rylan was unconscious.

She slit the tough leather to the ankle until it was loose enough to be safe. She left it on to act as a splint. She swung astride her pinto and clucked to the well-trained horse. They set out slowly, crossing the boulder-strewn ground, trying to avoid bumps. Maizy turned on her saddle and watched Rylan nearly every second, only glancing ahead to check the terrain.

He never stirred.

Rylan had come to Pa's house several times in the year since he moved in. There were no other ranches for miles and even their places were far apart. He'd never been friendly—to her. Though she had caught him looking at her a few times when he'd come by.

Except for those occasional looks, she'd always had the impression he was avoiding her. And the fact that he was so attractive pinched hard.

She'd done her best to ignore him, but she'd taken a liking to his herd of shining black Angus cattle. In fact she liked them a whole lot more than him.

When he'd followed her home earlier that day and told her pa the bulls were dangerous, Rylan had looked at her in the eyes for the first time, forbidding Maizy from riding on his land. He'd also said a few words about a woman dressing in britches and running around the country alone. Said it was dangerous. But Maizy had worked hard alongside her pa on the ranch since she could sit a saddle. She could take care of herself.

She was tough, but the handsome cowboy made her doubt herself. She liked not wearing dresses and fussing with her hair. She could cook well enough and she did chores in the house. But they rarely went to town since they lived over an hour away. When they did, she wore a dress, but she grumbled the whole time.

And now, because she'd defied Rylan and had gone on his

land again, he was lying here, unconscious. Most likely hurt
badly enough to be laid up for a long time.

How could she make this right?

Time passed as she inched along. The sun dropped low
in the sky. October had brought an end to the worst of the
heat and turned the aspens golden and the waving grass to
brittle yellow. As soon as she was within earshot of Rylan's
place, she pulled her six-gun, took a firm grip on her pinto
so the mare wouldn't startle, then shot into the air three
times.

Once the echoing gunfire was passed, Maizy shot three
more rounds. She started on again. Only a few minutes had
passed when Rawhide Engler came thundering toward her.

"Run for the doctor," Maizy hollered. "Your boss is hurt."

"On my way, Miss." Rawhide turned and kicked his horse
for town.

Maizy rode slowly on toward the RC Ranch. Finally his
place came into sight. He'd moved in to a log cabin built by
the previous owners. There was a sturdy barn, a bunkhouse,
and a corral. She reached the front door of the cabin and
stopped. She knew Rylan ran a lean operation, but she didn't
know it was this lean. There were no more cowhands.

Maizy swung a leg over her horse's rump and dropped to
the ground. She lashed the horse to the hitching post outside
Rylan's cabin and rushed back to check her patient. He lay,
unmoving, on that stretcher.

She looked at the cabin and had no idea how she'd get
him in there. The horse was too big to drag him all the way

in, even though the cabin was a nice size. She wasn't strong enough to do it herself.

It would be close to an hour on a galloping horse to get the doctor back here. The sun had finally dipped behind the nearest mountain and the night grew cool.

High overhead, an owl swooped out of the nearby trees with a low cry, then vanished back into the forest.

The pinto shifted its weight, and Maizy had a sudden vision of the horse bolting and dragging Rylan with him. The image felt so real, she decided to unhook the travois. First she guided the horse and dragged Rylan as close to the door as she could. Then she untied and eased the aspen poles from her stirrups to the ground, then led her horse back to the hitching post.

Returning to Rylan's side, she felt his left hand. It was cool. Maizy dashed into the cabin, almost stumbled when she saw what a jumbled mess it was, then shook her head and ducked into a back bedroom and grabbed a blanket. She returned to his side and wrapped it around him, then knelt there and said more than a few prayers for Rylan's healing and for forgiveness.

CHAPTER TWO

"CARSTENS TOLD ME HE'S IN A MIGHTY BAD FIX."

Maizy's stomach swooped. She'd been waiting for this. As they rode home together, she knew her time was up.

"He's conscious?"

"Yep, finally."

Maizy braced herself for what Rylan had said about her. Pa had gone with her for the last three days to help work Rylan's property. And Pa had been too busy, and Maizy too evasive, to get at the whole truth of Maizy's part in Rylan's injuries.

She'd peeked in at Rylan every day but let Pa and the doctor see to his care. He'd come around a few times, but he was groggy and not making any sense. It was like a sword hanging over her head. The time had finally come when she'd have to face what she'd done.

That they rode on in silence told Maizy it was bad.

"I'll put the horses up. You go on in the house. We need to have a serious talk."

Maizy waited, her dread growing as Pa took far too long to come back.

When he came in, he swallowed hard before he said, "He told me what caused the accident."

Pa's shoulders slumped, and for the first time Maizy realized how old he was. Pa wasn't going to live forever. She'd been born in her parents' old age. Ma had been near fifty, and she'd died when Maizy had just turned five years old. Pa was a bit older than Ma. They didn't pay much attention to birthdays at the MacGregor Ranch, but Maizy was eighteen years old. That made Pa around seventy. He'd always seemed ageless. Until Maizy's recklessness had nearly killed a man.

"You didn't exactly give me the whole of what happened, did you, girl?"

Maizy was unable to look up from the toes of her battered boots. "I told you he saved me. I told you a bull and bear fight nearly caught me in the middle. Rylan got hurt protecting me."

"But you didn't tell me you'd been on his land." Pa's mouth tightened in anger, and Maizy knew she shouldn't defend herself. Pa had the right of it. "Just hours after he said you weren't to come back."

"I had no intent to keep it from you. I just reckoned the time to talk about it was after we were sure he was going to be all right."

Pa said, "Carstens is hurting with every breath. He's seeing double from that knock on the head."

Swallowing hard, Maizy waited for her pa to start yelling. She deserved this.

"The doc won't let him out of bed for weeks. It's near to impossible for him to do for himself, and busted up bones don't always heal straight. Rawhide's been caring for him with me and Doc helping out, but, Maizy, I've got to get back to working our place. And Rawhide is needed outside at the RC. Carstens has those Angus calves he's been aiming to sell, and the sale is coming up. Everyone knows he stretched his money mighty thin to buy those black cattle. If he don't get 'em sold this fall he might lose his spread. Your tomfoolery has done real harm this time."

"I'm so sorry, Pa." Scuffing her boot on the wooden kitchen floor, she added, "I want to make it right."

She peeked up, hoping he understood how truly repentant she was.

Frowning as if he'd never smile again, Pa said, "I've heard that from you too many times, girl. I reckon I can't believe you, no matter how much I want to."

Pa wasn't angry, he was sad. Ashamed of her. He sounded like a man who had given up.

"What does that mean?"

"It means"—Pa dragged his battered Stetson off his head and looked at the floor as if he couldn't face her—"I've been a bad influence on you, Maizy girl. I've been a bad pa, and it's time I admitted it."

Gasping, Maizy flew to him and wrapped her arms around him. Pa stumbled back when she hit him. His hat went flying and he awkwardly returned the hug. They'd never done a lot of hugging.

"You've been the best pa a girl could ever have. Don't blame yourself. You've told me to settle down often enough. Well, now I'm going to."

He patted her on the back. "I've scolded you often enough, but I 'spect we both knew I didn't really mean it."

Maizy had known. In fact, she'd counted on it.

"I liked having you tag along with me on the ranch when you were just a sprout. I was hurtin' bad from missing your ma, and I wanted you with me." Then Pa took her by the shoulders and held her away from him. "And ever since you was half-grown, you did your share and part of mine. I've needed you. Truth be told, I doubt I could've made a go of this ranch without you. I've been a selfish old man who decided I didn't have to live by any rules but my own, and that's my sin."

"Pa!" Maizy stepped back, shocked. "You didn't do a thing wrong. I wanted to help you. It's no sin for a girl to work a ranch."

Shaking his head, Pa didn't answer. "I think I know a way to fix things, for now. I ain't sure Carstens'll go along with it, but we're gonna try."

"Try what, Pa?"

"We're gonna try having you act like a lady."

The notion almost sent Maizy stumbling backward. "How do I do that?"

Pa looked straight at her. "I don't rightly know, Maizy girl. But I've listened to Carstens over the last year. He comes from a fine family back in Texas. So we're gonna let him tell us."

"What?"

"First thing in the morning, you're gonna go over to his house, apologize for trespassing and causing him all this trouble. And you'll do it in proper female clothes and behave in the way a lady should." There was a little smile on Pa's face like he thought this was a great idea, an inspired idea. But there was something more. Something devious in Pa's expression. Maizy was a little bit afraid of what it might be because Pa had gotten a few wild ideas in his day.

She didn't ask though because a whisper inside of her told her it was time to grow up. Time to put aside childish ways. And she did owe Rylan for saving her life. She'd brought this trouble on her own head.

The thought twisted her gut, but she'd do it. She'd leave off her britches and wear a dress and try to remember some manners. And she'd apologize, though she had no knack for it.

"I'll do it, Pa. I'll go over to Carstens's ranch and apologize to him and do it proper." She swallowed hard and went on, "Like a proper lady. I'll let him have his say, yell at me all he wants, because I owe him that."

Pa studied her. "I know better than to believe you can change, Maizy, but I think asking for forgiveness is the exact right thing to do. And you might as well start tonight, by taking the time to clean up good for once. Take a bath and wash your hair. Tomorrow you'll put it up like a grown woman."

He gave a pointed look to the two braids she always wore. "I'll do the chores by myself." He clamped his hat on, turned, and left the house.

Maizy realized that Pa had more idea of how a woman should conduct herself than he'd ever let on.

And a whole lot better idea than she had.

CHAPTER THREE

RYLAN'S LEG WAS IN HEAVY PLASTER. HIS HEAD THROBBED until it made him want to empty the contents of his belly.

He'd been brought low at a time he needed to work with every ounce of his strength. Thanks to Maizy MacGregor, he had a very good chance of losing his ranch.

Someone knocked on his front door, someone brave because Rylan knew he'd not been fit company for anyone.

"Come in!" Whoever was knocking had better be Rawhide, his hired man, telling him there was progress made getting ready for the bull sale.

Lying there, unable to do anything to make that sale go well, was driving him out of his mind.

The door swung open. Rawhide and the doc had shoved some of the jumble aside and dragged his bed into this room so Rylan could look out the window and see his barn and corral. It gave him a nice view while he fretted.

A pretty blonde woman stepped in the door. Her cheeks were flushed pink, and she had eyes the color of the Texas bluebonnets that had bloomed by his childhood home. She clutched her hands together in front of her. He studied the neat calico dress—it was faded blue and scattered with white flowers. She wore a straw bonnet and looked demure and ladylike to the bone. The doctor had talked of finding someone to come out and take care of him, but surely they hadn't sent this innocent miss.

And then Auggie MacGregor came in behind her.

Rylan's eyes widened as he realized who this proper little woman was. That little spitfire cleaned up good. Knowing just how good almost tumbled him off the bed. Yet he knew who she was under the calico.

"You!" Rylan surged forward and the pain knocked him flat. Forcing his eyes open, even though every flicker of his lashes hurt, Rylan saw her rush toward him.

"Rylan, I'm so sorry."

He was so busy fighting to hold the moans inside that he didn't speak. He needed control of his mouth. He'd been ruined by this girl . . . no . . . not a girl. He saw the way that dress fit. She was a woman. He'd known that, of course. Known it all too well. It was one of the reasons he'd kept his distance for the last year. A man flirting with bankruptcy had no business thinking of a woman. Which of course hadn't stopped him. And it was all the worse because, strange as it was to see her dressed up in manly clothes, there was no denying that the woman made a pair of britches look mighty fetching.

He'd stayed away from her, and when he couldn't, he'd hid his interest in cool words. But he couldn't help the occasional long look when she wasn't paying attention.

Mostly, it'd been no hardship to keep his distance, considering he'd been doing the work of five men for the last year.

Auggie stepped in front of Maizy as if he needed to protect her.

"Maizy came to apologize. She ain't pretending that this isn't every bit her fault. She was trespassing and you ended up hurt. If you're too upset to listen we'll go, but my girl knows she done wrong. She's rude, she's reckless, she's stubborn. She's got a bad temper, and there ain't much backup in her. It's all because I raised her to have no notion of how to walk and talk and think and act like a decent lady."

Rylan looked past his neighbor to see Maizy's shoulders slump lower with each word. She didn't speak up, didn't sass her pa or say a word of protest.

She tugged on the sleeves of her dress as if they were too tight, then ran a finger along the high collar as if it strangled her, but she seemed to accept the discomfort. Her expression said that whatever insults her pa hurled at her, she deserved.

Rylan felt a twinge of sympathy. Auggie MacGregor was not a bad man, just a man with no idea how to raise up a girl child.

"I know this ain't the first problem she's caused you, but it'll be the last." Auggie said it in such a grim way that Rylan forgot his anger at the girl . . . woman.

He snapped his attention back to the old man. "What does that mean?"

"I have laid down the law, and Maizy is making some changes, aren't you, girl?" Auggie glared over his shoulder at Maizy.

"Yes, Pa."

Rylan could see that being polite really didn't suit her.

"She's gonna give up her hoydenish ways and be a proper lady. Iffen she don't change now, she will go on shaming me forever and never find a man that'd have her for a wife."

A protest rose to Rylan's lips at the harsh words. He glanced past Auggie's stooped shoulders and saw one tear trickle down Maizy's cheek. She swiped it away with the cuff of her pretty dress. Her eyes had been fastened on the floor as she was heaped with criticism, but she glanced up and saw him watching. Her cheeks flushed pink with embarrassment, and for just a second, her eyes looked as if she was begging. As if she didn't want him to mention the crying. Was that because her pa hated tears? Or that she did? Didn't she want to gain one ounce of sympathy?

She tugged on her sleeves again. He could tell the dress was bothering her something fierce. Well, he could understand that. He'd've been mighty uncomfortable in a dress himself, and she was probably no more used to a dress than he was.

"Pa, can I say something, please?" Her voice was quiet and ladylike. A tone he'd never heard from the sassy little thing before.

"Only if Carstens is willing. Do you want to talk to her?"

Auggie asked. "Say the word and I'll take her away and keep her out of your sight."

Maizy wrung her hands.

"Yes, I'll hear what she has to say."

Auggie stepped aside and gestured Maizy up to the bedside. "Speak your piece, Maizy. But don't expect much. What you've done is near unforgivable."

A flash of anger at Auggie made Rylan remember a few pranks he'd pulled in his life. To say something was unforgivable was a terrible thing. How much had they all been forgiven by God? Sure, the little pest had been on his land. Sure, she'd defied him the first moment she'd gotten a chance, when all he'd wanted was to keep her safe. Sure, he was lying here flat on his back, wondering how it would feel when the bank came to reclaim his land.

But that didn't mean what she'd done was unforgivable. He forgave her on the spot without her asking. And now that he had, he really wished she and her pretty blue dress would get out of his house. A man in his position had no business showing interest in a woman, and Rylan wasn't sure how long he could keep his hidden.

CHAPTER FOUR

RYLAN WAS BATTERED ALMOST TO A PULP.

Maizy studied the wounds that showed and wondered about the ones that didn't. He had a goose egg on the right side of his forehead. The bruising started there and covered that side of his face down to his cheekbone, including an ugly black eye. He had a wary look, like he wished she wasn't there. Or like maybe he was afraid that she'd break something else on him.

His right leg was in a white cast up to his knee. He wore a nightshirt that was open enough that she could see the tight bandages wound around his chest.

"Maizy here has a way to make this all up to you, Carstens," Pa said.

Maizy jerked her head up, surprised. All she could think to do was apologize, promise to never trespass again, and endure whatever anger Rylan planned to aim at her. What did Pa mean, make it up to him?

"I'd do anything to make this right." As she made that heartfelt offer, it occurred to Maizy that she might be going a bit too far. *I'd do anything?* She clamped her teeth together to keep from taking that back.

"There's no need to make anything up to me. It was a bad situation. Now, if you don't mind, I need rest. Thank you for stopping in." Rylan wasn't up to throwing them out of his house bodily, but he sure enough wanted them gone.

"You need help." Pa wasn't taking the hint. "And Maizy here caused you trouble."

"She shouldn't have been trespassing"—Rylan gave her a quick, annoyed glance—"but who could guess a bear—"

Pa cut him off. "She's going to stay and feed you and clean this house. She'll come early and stay late, and she'll keep doing that until you're well."

Maizy's eyes locked on Pa, then shifted to Rylan.

"Oh no. There's no need for that." Rylan *definitely* wanted them gone.

Which was starting to irritate Maizy. The man just didn't like her. It reminded her of how she'd sat by the river, crying like a little baby, her feelings hurt. His not liking her had led to this trouble to begin with.

But beyond his desire to have them gone, she saw pure pain. Pain that was a result of his saving her life. No matter what her feelings were, Maizy owed Rylan more than she could repay. She did some growing up in that moment, or she sure hoped so. Whether Rylan wanted her here or not, he needed her.

"I'll do it."

"No, you won't," Rylan insisted.

"I'll cook for you and see to meals for Rawhide too. I'll tend your wounds and clean your cabin." She'd do the right thing, and if his dislike hurt, she was enough of an adult to do the right thing anyway.

She glanced at the unholy mess and almost lost her determination, but she soldiered on. "And I'll do anything else you'd like. I'll be your feet until you're able to care for yourself. And I will do it with a good spirit too."

The go-home look in Rylan's eyes faded just a bit. Maizy suspected he was thinking of how badly he needed help. So badly he might even bring himself to put up with her.

"And she will do all of this," Pa added, "as a lady."

"What?" Maizy's eyes flew to Pa, horrified to think she'd need to keep this strangling dress on.

"I reckon I've ruined her by letting her be a female cowpoke. But if it's not too late, maybe we can fix her."

"But, Pa, I can't tend a house in this dress! The floors needed scrubbing. I need to see to the garden, haul water, wash clothes, and do the—"

"Women do those things in dresses all the time, Maizy girl."

"Well, yes, of course they do, but they're all fools."

A strange choking sound drew her attention to Rylan. She narrowed her eyes. Was he laughing at her?

"Well, we can try it," Rylan said with a straight face.

Pa nodded, then turned to Maizy. "You do all the caring for him as a well-behaved young lady. I want your word on that, Margaret Catherine." Pa never used her full name.

Maizy swallowed hard, a motion that almost strangled her in this blasted dress, and she nodded. "You go on, Pa. I'll get to work right now. I can walk home in time to get you a meal tonight and—"

"Absolutely not!"

Maizy turned to Rylan. "Why not?"

"You're trying to be a proper lady. A lady doesn't walk the countryside alone." Rylan said to Pa, "You come for her just before sunset. And you bring her back at sunrise."

"Pa doesn't have time to—"

"It's dangerous," Rylan insisted.

"I do it all the time."

"A grizzly bear almost ate you last time you did it."

Drat, the man had a point.

"I'll be here to see her home," Pa said with a single jerk of his chin, "and she won't go about unescorted. Not now and not ever again. You're right, Carstens."

Pa clamped his Stetson on his head and patted Maizy awkwardly on the shoulder, then wheeled toward the door and left.

Maizy watched him go. Then slowly, because she was afraid of what she'd see, she turned back to Rylan. They looked at each other in dismay, and she knew just what he was thinking.

He wanted her gone, but he needed her.

She wanted to help, but she wanted to do it wearing britches.

Neither of them had a hope of getting what they wanted.

CHAPTER FIVE

RYLAN WAS TRAPPED IN THE CABIN WITH THE WOMAN WHO had destroyed his future.

And she was so pretty he couldn't think straight when she was anywhere near him. "Your cheeks are a little flushed." Maizy touched his forehead with a hand hard with calluses, but it was a gentle touch nonetheless. He had to get her away from him.

"I don't think it's a fever. Let me get a cool cloth." She ran one fingertip over the bump on his forehead and down his cheek. Her face held a frown of such sweet regret Rylan's heart ached.

He told himself she was just trying to doctor him, but it felt like more than that. It felt caring . . . intimate.

"You must have a terrible headache."

Rylan had never seen her like this. All womanly and gentle. Every other time he'd seen her, she'd worn a six-gun strapped to her hip, for heaven's sake. Who knew she could be so . . . so . . . so female?

"Even without a fever, a cool cloth might reduce the pain." Maizy left off touching him, thank heavens, and rushed to the basin of cool water by his dry sink, clomping across the floor like a field hand.

There was the tomboy. Rylan felt a bit more in control by the time she hurried back to his side.

Folding the wet cloth neatly, she laid it on his forehead. He winced at even that bit of touch, but the cool cloth really was soothing.

She was a terror, but she worked hard. Since he'd moved in, Rylan had talked with Auggie many times, and he knew Maizy probably worked harder than her pa. That ranch wouldn't survive without Maizy's help unless that old skin-flint Auggie hired some men. Which was what he should have done years ago. It wasn't a big spread, so that outlay of cash for cowpokes might make a tight budget snap. Rylan knew that for a fact.

"Does it hurt terribly?" Maizy's voice surprised him. It was so kind, so concerned. Her blonde hair was in a neat bun, just a few wisps escaping to curl over her ears and touch her neck. Her blue eyes shone with concern and kindness, not the thoughtless recklessness she'd displayed before.

He closed his eyes so he couldn't see her. But, like a man who had stared at the sun too long, she was burned into his brain. Her dress was too tight and worn so thin it hardly had any color anymore. It had been blue about one hundred washings ago.

"The worst is my chest, the broken ribs. Seems like a man can't move anywhere without causing his ribs to ache."

"I really am so sincerely sorry you got hurt. I haven't even said thank you yet. You saved my life." Her voice wobbled.

Rylan's eyes shot open to meet her blue ones and he saw them brimming.

She blinked quickly and dashed away the tears with a swipe of her wrist. "Now, can you tell me what you'd like for an evening meal? If you've got beef or venison, I might need to get it on to roast right away. I'll make plenty for Rawhide too. Then I can turn my attention to cleaning. It's a fine cabin but . . . but . . ." She looked a bit lost as she studied all the clutter stacked through the cabin. "I need to knock a f-few cobwebs down."

Rylan saw about a hundred cobwebs without turning his head.

"And the floor needs to be swept and scrubbed."

She had to find the floor first.

"And you've got things stowed here and there. I can tidy those stacks up."

That was putting it nicely. The cabin was jammed with junk left by the previous owners, whoever they'd been. He'd barely even noticed it until Maizy started her fussing.

"The house was here when I bought the ranch, and this clutter came with it. I've added my own things to the mess, and I haven't spent a lick of time tending it. I reckon that's pretty easy to see."

"I'll tidy it up in my spare time. First, after I get a meal on, I'll do the washing. I'll get some water on to heat for that. It takes awhile. It's a cool enough day that a fire in here will be welcome, thank heavens. Doing the washing in the heat of the summer gets tiresome."

"Maizy," Rylan began, his spirits rising at the thought of getting so much help, "I don't expect you to clean up a mess I've spent a year ignoring. I just need someone to cook and wash up the dishes and help me out of bed a few times a day."

"I'll do everything you need, and what spare time I have, I'll use to clean. I'm not a girl to sit idle."

She tugged at the neck of her dress. "Let me cool this cloth off again." She lifted it from his aching head, went back to the basin, wrung it out, then returned.

"That really does feel better. Maizy, is—" He broke off, then asked, "why do you go by Maizy? Your pa called you Margaret."

"I was named Margaret after my mother. Pa got to calling me Crazy Maizy when I was a young'un. I guess I was running wild even back then. Maizy stuck."

"It's hard to think of you as a Margaret. Maizy suits you."

"I doubt I'd answer to anything else." Maizy smiled as she adjusted the cloth.

"That really does feel good." Rylan hadn't slept much since his head had cleared yesterday. Everything hurt too much to fully relax and sleep. He realized, with that cloth soothing the worst pains, he was exhausted.

"I think the cloth will stay on." Maizy's voice seemed to come from far away. It was as soothing as the cloth with none of her usual irritating sass. "I'm going to get some work done. But I'm just a step away."

Rylan wanted her to stay close. He tried to open his mouth and tell her not to go, but his eyelids were heavy and the cloth was staying put. It was too much effort to speak.

CHAPTER SIX

MAIZY WONDERED IF RYLAN EVEN HAD THE GUMPTION to chew, let alone handle a knife and fork.

He stirred from a long afternoon of sleep and she quickly scooped mashed potatoes onto a tin plate. She slid on an elk steak she'd simmered to tenderness, then diced into bite-size pieces.

This meal was going to be as easy on Rylan as she could make it.

She reached Rylan's side just as his eyes flickered open. His sleep-dazed, handsome blue eyes made her think of the river, the one beside her hidey-hole. It reflected a perfect New Mexico sky, the same color she saw in his eyes.

He focused on her and seemed confused for just a bit, then he shifted his weight as if to sit up, and everything was driven out of his expression except pain.

A gasp tore from his throat. "I forgot." The words were barely above a whisper as he instantly lay still.

Pain she'd caused.

"I've got a meal for you, Rylan." Except she was afraid to touch him, let alone have him sit up. Could a man eat flat on his back?

Rylan's eyes closed, and he breathed as if each breath had to be taken carefully. Finally he opened his eyes. "If you slide an arm behind my shoulders and slip a rolled-up blanket behind me, I can sit up enough to eat."

Each word echoed with pain as if he knew it was going to hurt. Then he added, "It smells good, Maizy. Thank you. Rawhide ain't much of a cook."

A compliment and thanks. For some reason that touched Maizy's heart in a way nothing ever had. Rylan was a brave, kind man. And here he was, battered and broken because he'd risked his life to save her. That only made the words mean more.

Maizy got the blanket rolled up just right and laid it beside Rylan, then slid her left arm under him, just as he'd said. He didn't make a sound, but she saw the way he clenched his jaw.

An inch at a time, Maizy lifted. His head and wide shoulders were pressed against her. His soft dark hair rubbed against her neck. She was closer to him than she'd ever been to a man, not counting Pa—and she didn't get overly close to him most times. It took all her strength to lift Rylan. She never could have done it on her own, but he helped. As soon as she could, she tucked the blanket behind him and eased him back. He took quick shallow breaths as he adjusted to the new position.

Finally, through a weak smile, he said, "You're a lot more

careful of me than Rawhide."

Maizy quickly sat beside him on the bed. She was on his left side and his injured leg was on the right, so she didn't have to contend with it.

"I can manage." He grasped the fork, but his hand trembled as he tried to stab a piece of elk.

"Let me." Without asking permission, she plucked the fork away and offered him a bite of meat. He opened his mouth, most likely to say he could do it himself. Before he could fuss, she stuck the food in. He chewed, then his mutinous expression changed.

"This is delicious."

Maizy smiled. "I made plenty for your cowpoke too. When he comes in, there'll be a hot meal ready."

"He'll be late. He's working all the hours God made trying to keep up with a job that was too much for the two of us to begin with."

Because of Maizy.

Rylan didn't say it, but Maizy knew.

She had a tin cup of milk and she gave him sips now and then. She'd baked biscuits and fed him those too. When the plate was clean, Rylan sighed in contentment.

Maizy picked up the bowl of peaches. She'd found a can, sugared some of her biscuits, then poured the peaches over them and added a bit of sweetened cream.

By the time they'd finished, Rylan was eating with enthusiasm, and he'd even adjusted the position of his broken leg a couple of times with minimal groans of pain.

There was little time for talk between bites, and Maizy discovered she enjoyed this quiet caring for a man. Meals were no-nonsense back at home.

She set the bowl aside.

"Thank you. I haven't been able to eat much. Rawhide's meals lean toward tough, mostly burned meat. Maybe a good meal will help me regain some strength and knit these bones a bit faster."

"I hope so." Maizy reached for the dishes.

She took them away, then wrung out a cool cloth and brought it back to rest on his brow. "Do you want to stay sitting up?"

"Yes, awhile longer."

Maizy went to work. Knowing Rylan was watching her made her conscious of every move. She tried to stand in a more ladylike way, though heaven only knew exactly what that was. Her dress choked her a bit less when she stood straight, so she tried to think of being ladylike as a way not to strangle. It wasn't surprising the dress was tight, since it was a fifteen-year-old hand-me-down from Ma. Pa said she'd been close in size to Maizy, but it was likely Ma was a wee bit smaller.

Lighting the lanterns as dusk came, Maizy had the dishes clean. Rylan cleared his throat and drew her attention.

He was looking at her in a markedly uncomfortable way.

"What is it?"

"I, um . . . think you're going to have to . . . to . . . help me stand."

The very thought made her stomach swoop. She'd hurt him badly just sitting him up. "Why?"

"I need the"—he cleared his throat—"the privy." A tinge of pink showed on his cheeks, and Maizy knew that he would have preferred to have waited because Rawhide and Pa were due soon.

Determined to be very matter-of-fact, she said, "We'll get it done."

He was dressed in some sort of a nightshirt. He wore britches that'd been slit up past his knee on his right leg so the white plaster showed.

"My ribs are the worst. The leg hurts but the cast keeps that from being so bad."

"How can I help?"

"First, help me sit all the way up, then help me lift my broken leg and swing it off the bed."

"Let's go slowly." Maizy took up her spot on his side, arm under him, just like before. Only one gasp of pain escaped as he straightened.

"All right." His voice was hoarse as if he controlled the need to shout in pain. "Get my leg."

Maizy lifted as Rylan inched around.

She lowered the cast to the floor. "Let me get on your left side."

Nodding, Rylan said, "My left leg can take my weight. And I can stand on my broken leg for a few seconds while I step forward. If you get under my left arm to help me balance, we can do this. It's only a few steps outside the back door."

He made it sound easy. Maizy soon knew it was anything but. He had his left arm around her neck, and when he put weight on his broken leg, he so tensed from the pain he liked to choke her. Beads of sweat popped out on his forehead and his jaw was a grim, tight line.

She had her arm around his waist. As they stepped out the back door, which had two steps to contend with, she gripped his waist tighter, wringing a gasp out of him.

"Your ribs," she whispered as she realized what she'd just done. A wash of tears surprised her. She fought them back, but hurting him tore at her heart.

"I've had busted ribs once before. They'll start shaping up in another week or two. A bone takes six weeks to heal, the doc said. But ribs quit the worst of their hurting long before that . . . mostly."

Maizy was afraid he'd fall as he hopped down the steps on his left leg. The hopping jostled his ribs. He groaned every time he landed and had to gather himself for the next step.

At last they made it. He closed the outhouse door, and she retreated to the back stoop and nearly collapsed on it. Her knees trembled more from worry than effort.

Maizy sat on that step, her knees primly together, her back straight. While she waited, she prayed.

For Rylan to heal straight and strong.

That he wouldn't lose his ranch over her foolishness.

That God would forgive her.

She wanted Rylan's forgiveness, too, and he'd given it. But how could he mean it when she couldn't forgive herself?

She'd do whatever Rylan asked. And if her collar strangled her, or if it was awkward scrubbing floors in a dress, then she'd remember Jesus on the cross and how He'd suffered. Then she'd compare her own meager pain and endure it quietly.

A trace of peace crept through her as she prayed and thought on sacrifice, and when Rylan swung the door open, her knees were steady and her shoulders bore his weight as they limped back to the bed.

As slowly as he'd risen, Rylan lay down. She could see that his face had gone gray from the effort of moving.

Once he was back in bed, she rushed for a cool cloth and laid it on his forehead. Flickering his eyes open, he whispered, "Thank you."

Then his eyes fell shut.

She stayed close and watched the tension ease from his face, hoping that meant the pain was going too.

At last his breathing deepened and became steady. A tiny, soft snore told her he'd fallen asleep. She sat by his side for an hour before she heard hoofbeats outside. Quickly, quietly, she rushed out to see Rawhide Engler riding up. She hurried to him and waited as he reined his horse.

The man looked exhausted and none too happy. He glared at her in a way that said he clearly knew his long hours were her fault.

"Rylan is asleep. I'll bring you out a meal so we don't wake him." She didn't wait for a response. She was pretty certain she didn't want to hear what he had to say.

Rawhide would take care of his boss until Maizy came

back in the morning—though from Rylan's enjoyment of her food and other things she'd done, Maizy could see Rawhide's help was uncertain at best.

As she headed back toward the house and Rawhide reined his horse toward the barn, Maizy saw Pa driving up. She told Pa to please wait outside.

Then she got Rawhide his meal, checked sleeping Rylan one more time, and climbed aboard the buckboard, already wishing she was back with Rylan. He needed her.

CHAPTER SEVEN

RYLAN WATCHED MAIZY SET TO WORK TRANSFORMING his cluttered cabin into a tidy home. She'd been at it for two weeks now, and she'd worked hard every day, and still there was more to do. With a back entry room that was cluttered with junk and two bedrooms—one stacked with abandoned boxes Rylan had never even looked through—Maizy might be able to clean for months.

Now that she was here working on it, he was ashamed of himself for neglecting his home to this extent.

He'd have allowed himself to enjoy watching her work if each passing moment didn't bring him closer to the day he was going to lose his ranch.

Every time he thought of it, he veered his mind away. He tried prayer, knowing God said not to worry.

Consider the lilies of the field.

Rylan pictured his big black cattle grazing on lilies when

they should be grazing on lush grass. Rylan hoped Rawhide was saving the good grass close to the ranch house for the last week.

Cast your cares upon the Lord.

When Rylan thought of the word *cast,* he only thought of the one on his leg.

Let not your heart be troubled.

Oh, he was in big trouble. No doubt about it. That loan would be called in the day after his sale, and if there wasn't money to pay it, the ranch was lost.

Take therefore no thought for the morrow: for the morrow shall take thought for the things of itself.

Rawhide needed to move the big beeves tomorrow. Rylan was sure they'd discussed that, but Rawhide wasn't a hard-working man—at least not as hardworking as Rylan needed him to be.

I will lift mine eyes unto the hills, from whence cometh my help.

Rylan's ranch had some grassy hills. He couldn't remember if he'd told Rawhide about all the highland pastures or not.

Praying should help, remembering Bible verses should help. Rylan figured he must be doing it wrong because it was only making him worry more.

So he forced his thoughts from those worries and found himself watching every move Maizy made. That was another kind of madness.

Truth was, the little woman worked mighty hard and

got him everything he needed, often before he realized he wanted it.

He watched Maizy, kneeling, sorting through a stack of who-knew-what, knowing he'd be better off going back to worrying than entertaining wild thoughts about the very pretty Miss MacGregor. They'd taken to talking as she worked. It occupied Rylan's mind.

She was full of stories of growing up like a cowhand. He talked about the upcoming sale, and sometimes that would lead him to talk of his childhood in Texas and how badly he wanted to make a go of ranching to make his father proud. Rylan tried not to share so many of his worries. She was so sympathetic it made him want to succeed all the more, and that made his fear of failing cut so deep he couldn't stand it.

Then the sound of a wagon distracted him, like a gift straight from a merciful God.

And then he saw Parson Alden drive up in his buggy. God had sent a parson. Rylan must be more desperate than even he realized.

Maizy jumped to her feet to look out. "We're not ready for company."

It hit a chord deep in his chest to hear her say *we*. He shook off the strange feeling as he slowly eased himself to a sitting position. In the last few days his ribs had stopped the worst of their aching, but everything still hurt plenty.

Maizy looked around frantically as if she wished she could hide the clutter in the cabin. It looked so much better than the parson had ever seen it that Rylan nearly laughed. Yes, there was still junk in the corners and plenty of stuff to clear out in the two small bedrooms. But she'd scrubbed every inch of floor as she uncovered it, and she'd gotten rid of all the cobwebs. It was a whole lot better than when she'd begun.

With a helpless shrug, she muttered, "He'll just have to take us as we are." Rolling the sleeves of her dress down, she buttoned them at her wrists as she went to the door and swung it open.

"Parson Alden." None of her upset sounded in the friendly greeting.

"Maizy," Rylan could hear the older man say, "the doctor said you'd stepped in to care for Rylan. I thought I'd come out for a visit."

Rylan wasn't good at church attendance. He was a believer, but he found Sundays to be as demanding on a ranch as every other day, and he'd let his worship time slip. He resolved to change that when he got well, if he didn't lose his ranch and have to leave the area. Even if he did, he was sure he could find a church somewhere to spend time with other believers.

"It's kind of you to come so far out to see us." Maizy stepped back and waved him in. "Come out of the cold. The place is a mess. But I've baked cookies and I have coffee on."

The stout parson's eyes lit up at the mention of cookies. Smiling, he stepped in, drawing his flat-topped black parson's hat off of his mostly bald head.

Maizy closed the door, then bustled about making the parson comfortable.

Rylan slowly swung his legs around to sit on the edge of

the bed. "Parson Alden, thanks for riding all this way out. I think I'm feeling up to joining you at the table."

Maizy frowned. "If you're sure you're up to it."

"I'm mighty tired of that bed."

"I imagine you are." Her sympathy was genuine. Rylan felt it all the way to his bones.

Maizy helped him to the table and eased him into a chair. Then she got them both coffee and a plate of sugar cookies.

"Maizy is a godsend, isn't she, Rylan?"

"That she is, Parson Alden. And she's doing her best to turn this neglected bachelor cabin into a tidy home. Caring for me slows her down, of course."

"But that's my main job." Maizy smiled.

Rylan liked how it felt sitting there, talking to the parson, Maizy so generously pouring their coffee and serving the cookies she'd baked. It felt like a real home. It felt like a family.

He pictured Maizy here, permanently. His. He liked the idea so much it shocked him. And then he pictured her at his side when they got thrown off the land.

She'd stick by his side and he'd have to drag her off somewhere to find a new living, start all over again. Away from her pa. Possibly fail again. He felt himself frown. To get his mind off that disaster, he asked, "How are things in town?"

Thankfully, the parson was a talker. He entertained them with the outrageous goings-on in the rugged frontier town of Saurita. It wasn't a friendly place for a man of God, but the parson had found a place for himself preaching among heathens.

By the time Parson Alden left, stuffed with cookies and

coffee, Rylan was visiting with Maizy so comfortably he stayed at the table. They went on talking while she worked. It was a pleasant afternoon and when she was leaving, she looked over her shoulder and smiled at him.

"I'll see you tomorrow."

Her pa was coming up to the door as he did every night to help get Rylan settled into bed. Maizy always waited outside with the horses. Each morning her pa came in and helped Rylan get dressed, and Maizy patiently waited. Rylan was exhausted after his first afternoon of sitting up, but he decided that tomorrow he might be able to dress himself, if Auggie would leave his clothes within reaching distance.

It was all part of Rylan starting to heal and get back to work. And when he did, she'd leave.

Rylan hated to see her go. But he knew if he talked her into staying permanently, he'd end up dragging her down with him when he failed. And that would hurt worse than broken ribs any day.

CHAPTER EIGHT

"Why do you tug at your collar like that?" Rylan asked.

His accident had happened a month ago. He wasn't in a lot of pain anymore, if he didn't move. It was the first of November and his sale was at the end of the month. The doc had been out yesterday and unwrapped his ribs. They hurt more but the doc said it was just a matter of time. Rylan had another two weeks with the cast on his leg, which would leave him only two weeks before the cattle sale.

"It's just a little tight." She hooked a finger under the collar again.

"Why don't you wear one that fits?"

"It's the only one I've got." Maizy rose to her feet from where she knelt scrubbing the floor of his now-clean cabin. She did it so easily Rylan was swamped with envy. She really was a spry little thing.

"Just one? Why don't you make yourself another? Your pa's ranch is doing okay, isn't it?"

Maizy waved a dismissive hand. "I haven't had much use for dresses. And no time for sewing."

"You could make yourself a dress here at my place . . ."

"I'm here to take care of you."

"You've got things so tidied, you could spend some time sewing for yourself and still tend to me."

She placed her hands on her hips and surveyed the place. "It's true I'm done sorting the clutter, but now I've started fall cleaning. I can keep busy for the next two weeks with no problem."

"Fall cleaning? There's different cleaning for the fall than other times of the year?"

She looked at him quizzically. He really didn't know much about housekeeping, that was sure. "I didn't expect you to do all this work, Maizy. You probably don't even need to come over every day."

And that made him feel so sorry for himself. What would he do without her company? *Get back to work,* the answer came. Most of his ranching was done from horseback. He might manage riding with a busted leg.

Maizy furrowed her brow and studied him, then went to her basin of water by the kitchen sink and wrung out a cloth. She brought it to his bedside and sat in a chair she'd stationed beside him. Sitting straight and proper, she rested the cool rag on his head.

"You're worried about the sale, aren't you?"

He was pretty sure he felt himself relaxing just because she was close. That worried him since nothing could come of it, but he couldn't help enjoying the undivided attention. "My ribs are well enough and my leg barely hurts anymore. I might be able to sit a horse if I could figure out a way to mount up."

Her mouth gaped open. "With your leg still in a cast? You most certainly will not! Why, Rylan Carstens, that is the most—"

"Ladies don't yell." He said it with such smug pleasure it was all he could do not to smile.

Maizy's mouth clamped shut so hard her teeth clicked. She narrowed her eyes at him as if plotting revenge.

His smile almost escaped but he fought it. The truth was, he was feeling much better, but he was still a prisoner in this bed. Teasing Maizy, who was doing a fine job of being a lady, was the only thing that kept him from losing his mind.

Finally Maizy composed herself in what Rylan thought was her attempt to be polite and genteel. She looked like she wanted to strangle him. "So, tell me about this calf sale coming up?"

"Surely by now you've heard it all a dozen times."

"I like hearing about your dream though. It's nice. Tell me again."

He liked to talk about his cattle—if he could keep from talking about all the work he had to do to make it happen. "The herd I drove in late last summer had two hundred Angus cows, all bred to an Angus bull. After they dropped their calves I had near two hundred of those shining black babies.

I've advertised far and wide, and gotten a lot of letters from ranchers saying they're coming to the sale. I have land enough to grow my herd so I'll keep about fifty of the heifer calves, but I have a hundred bull calves and fifty heifers I don't need. If the sale goes well, I could get a lot of money for each calf. If it goes poorly—if no crowd shows up to bid against each other—I'll lose my shirt, because I paid a hefty price for these Angus cows and the adult bulls."

"Your black cattle are a big change from the longhorns my pa runs."

"The longhorns are a tougher breed, but Angus do all right, especially around here with the good water and grass. They are bigger all around and they gain faster. And they're a nicer animal. Longhorns are rattlesnake mean."

"Unless they decide they need to protect one of their calves from a grizzly."

Nodding, Rylan said, "Maizy, I know you've always had a lot of freedom growing up with no ma and working beside your pa, but it's not safe out alone for a woman."

Even now he remembered the day he'd been riding herd and come across Maizy, on foot, her horse tied to a shrub at the edge of the herd. Just as he'd come up, she'd walked right past a bull. The old boy had pawed the earth and lowered its head. Maizy had backed away quickly—she was savvy about cattle. She gave them all plenty of room. But Rylan knew she easily could've been crushed under that old bull's hooves. Thinking of her hurt made him furious. He'd followed her home, fussing at her and complaining like an old hen.

"I'm as tough as any man in these parts, Rylan. I can shoot and ride. I know the land and have a good sense of how to avoid trouble."

Rylan arched a brow at her, and he could see from her sheepish shrug that she got his message about bulls and bears and being ready for the unexpected.

The truth was he'd overreacted that day because he didn't like running into her. Sure, there was danger from wild bulls and grizzlies in the area—though Rylan hadn't foreseen the two tangling. But the real reason it upset him to find her was she wasn't exactly safe from *him*. Oh, he'd never physically harm her, but he might end up spending time with her and talking and learning all about her.

Sort of like they'd done this last month, alone, together, in this small house.

"Tell that to the grizzly who almost had you for supper."

Maizy gave him a side smile. "And that's how you ended up hurt. And here you are, laid up, unable to get ready for your sale."

"Yes. I had wanted to drive them all to the best grass. Make sure they kept their bellies full and gained weight. That takes moving them constantly from one pasture to the next and feeding them hay when I need to. Then I've saved the best meadows close to the house to drive them in right before the auction. I've told Rawhide exactly what I want, but he's an old longhorn man, and he thinks the whole idea of fattening the cattle for a sale is stupid."

"You've got a month until the sale," Maizy said. "You've

got two more weeks to heal, then the last two weeks to get things ready."

"If the doc agrees to cut this cast off the first possible day. But he said I have to promise to be careful. How'm I supposed to be careful while pitching hay and riding a horse?"

"You'll have Rawhide to do the heavy work."

"He's worn clean out, and his attitude gets worse by the hour." If Rylan had a red cent to spare, he'd've fired the old codger and hired someone who didn't complain over every chore.

"Can you push back the date of the sale?"

"It's too late. I've sent posters out all over the state. I've got no way to stop the folks coming on that date, or if I could stop them, then what if a few still showed up? Wouldn't I have to hold the sale? If the sale isn't on the advertised date, no matter how hard I tried to get the word out, I might get the reputation of a man who broke his word. Then I'd be finished all across the West. No, the sale date is set. No changing it."

Maizy's eyes sharpened and she opened her mouth, then snapped it closed.

"What are you thinking?"

Shaking her head, she said, "Nothing. So the doctor said you need to spend more time sitting up. Do you want—"

"Maizy," Rylan interrupted, "what were you going to say?"

Her mouth curled down to a rebellious frown, but Rylan glared at her, and she finally gave a little huff of annoyance. "I was going to offer to help."

Silence stretched between the two of them.

Finally he said, "You mean help Rawhide? Help get ready for the sale?"

"I can't do it and keep my promise to behave in a lady-like way."

Rylan's gaze locked on hers.

"I really am good at ranching, Rylan. I've had to work beside Pa all these years. And I think—" Her voice broke. Suddenly her eyes looked all watery like they were going to overflow.

Rylan couldn't stand to see her cry, so he did the only thing he knew to make it stop: he said something to make her mad. "Well, crying is mighty ladylike. I reckon you've turned right into a soft little filly at last."

That put a determined frown on her face. "We live a long way out. Riding a horse wearing a dress is flat-out dangerous. And sitting in the house being all proper when we had cattle to tend was a stupid waste of a strong back and a good mind. You can see I know how to tend a house. But I'm a top hand on horseback. I could help you." She crossed her arms in front of herself.

Rylan reached out and touched her hand. She quit talking. He studied her close and finally smiled. "I've seen you rope and ride. I know why your pa lets you help. He said himself he'd never've kept the ranch without you."

Maizy closed her fingers over his.

"You're tempting me, you know," he went on. "I could really use the help."

Maizy shrugged one shoulder.

Rylan laughed. "You're tempting me in more ways than one."

Maybe it was his restless need to do something. Maybe it was just Maizy's own hardworking, cowgirl self. Rylan didn't know what prompted him to tug on her hand and pull her toward him. He fixed his gaze on her pretty blue eyes, and she let herself be reeled in.

When their lips touched, Rylan forgot every ache and pain in his body.

The kiss caught fire.

CHAPTER NINE

MAIZY WAS AWASH IN THE PLEASURE OF KISSING A MAN. She'd never done such a thing before, and she'd never dreamed it would be so nice.

Rylan gently eased her away from him. His hand slid out of her hair and rested on her cheek. Her blonde curls drooped past her face. It had been in a tidy bun just a few moments ago.

"I like having you around." Rylan gave her another quick kiss. "You're so pretty and sweet."

Maizy's head, fogged by the kiss, cleared with his words. So he liked her, did he? She remembered very clearly that before she'd put on her dress, he hadn't liked her at all.

"You like having me around?"

"Very much." His good hand slipped from her face and slid over her shoulder and down her arm.

"You think I'm pretty and sweet?" The hurt in her heart cleared her head further.

Rylan nodded, studying her face, but some of his contented pleasure seemed to fade at her tone. "You're a beautiful woman, Maizy."

"As I am now?" Her voice was flat.

"Yes, you're wonderful." There was uncertainty in his voice. He seemed to be waking from the spell of the kiss. Well, good, because she was waking up too.

"Now I'm wonderful."

"What's the matter?" His hand slid up her arm, and his touch sent her heart to thumping hard.

"You've decided you like me, but you were awful to me before."

"But you've changed. I can see the real you since you started dressing and acting as a lady ought."

But you've changed. Those words hurt all the worse because she knew he didn't mean them to hurt her.

"If you think that's a compliment, you're wrong." She had no business kissing a man who didn't like the real her.

Rylan's expression was wary now. "But I thought we agreed you needed to be more ladylike, and you've proven you can be."

"So, as long as I behave to suit you, you like me. Of all the miserable tricks . . . When I think back on it . . ." The bite in her voice could have left tooth marks on his hide. "You were hostile to me from the beginning."

"I only wanted you to behave. I didn't like seeing you in danger."

Behave. That sounded like something an adult wanted a child to do. He'd always treated her like a nuisance child.

"Remember the first time you rode over, right soon after you'd moved into the area? I was saddling a horse in the corral while you talked to Pa. You didn't notice me until I swung up on the horse and rode over to where you stood leaning on the fence. I thought I'd welcome you to the neighborhood. You looked up at me and saw that I was a woman and frowned."

"I remember like it was yesterday. You took me by surprise." Regret flashed in Rylan's eyes.

"The first words out of your mouth were, 'You let your daughter wear britches?' You said that to Pa and you looked at me as if I smelled bad. As if I disgusted you."

"No, I was never disgusted," Rylan said.

"Then you said, 'Women don't flaunt themselves like this back where I come from.' You said that right to me. If it wasn't disgust, then you pick a word, but you meant it as an insult and don't try to pretend you didn't."

"I was just surprised was all."

"Surprised into speaking your true thoughts." Maizy couldn't stop the angry words boiling to get out. "I was working. I wasn't hurting your Angus cattle, nor had I said a single unladylike word. I hadn't done one speck of harm to you. You like to blame all the trouble between us on me, but you started it. Now, when I'm being a false version of myself, you kiss me and flatter me. The real me, the cowhand Maizy, you disliked on sight."

"That wasn't the real you. This is the real you."

"So if I dress as you want and act as you want, you'll approve of me." Her voice got louder, rising in anger. "All I have to do is just be exactly who you want me to be, and I'll be lucky enough to share a kiss with you. *Isn't that right?*" She was shouting by the time she was done.

"Maizy, no, I didn't mean it like that. I just thought—"

The door banged open.

Maizy jumped, startled.

Rawhide stomped in. His eyes shifted between the two of them, and he seemed to realize he was interrupting something. A sneer twisted the scowl on his face. "I got a message from my sister in Santa Fe. Her husband was arrested. That good-for-nothing robbed a stage. She needs my help, and I'm sick of workin' like a slave on foolishness like black cattle. I'm done." Rawhide tugged on the brim of his hat and wheeled around.

"No, wait!" Rylan shouted, but the door slammed shut.

Maizy knew the man had just drawn his wages two days ago. He didn't even mention that he had two days of money coming.

"Engler," Rylan roared, "you get back here!"

Pounding hooves drew her attention to the window. The old codger galloped down the lane toward the road with more energy than he'd ever given his chores.

Maizy's eyes went to Rylan's. He looked shocked. Worse yet, he looked frantic. She knew he was about ten seconds from trying to get out of bed.

"You stay right there." She nearly jabbed her finger into his nose. There was none of the ladylike murmuring she'd made for weeks. None of the agreeable, submissive servant and nurse. She found every inch of her inner cowboy and aimed it right at Rylan.

"I'll do Rawhide's job." Despite their argument she didn't easily forget that kiss. It'd suit her better to stay farther away from this mangy coyote. Yet she'd vowed to make up for the injury she'd caused. Here was a way. "Two weeks from now you'll get that cast off. I'll stay and help through the sale so you won't overdo it. Then I'm leaving."

"No, Maizy. I won't ask that of you."

"You ain't asking. And I ain't interested in gettin' your go-ahead." She felt her western drawl return, and she liked it. "As long as you're flat on your back in that bed, there ain't much you can do to stop me."

The rattle of a buckboard sounded and Pa pulled up.

"Pa's here. The two of you can yell and scold all you want. But I'll save this ranch, and that's as it should be. But I won't have you kissing me and saying I'm wonderful . . . only not the way I really am. Once you're on your feet, I'm leaving and you won't have to suffer my mannish ways ever again."

"Maizy, wait!"

"I'm not waiting for you or any other man to tell me anything ever again." She took one second to enjoy watching his mouth gape open, then she stormed out of the house to meet her pa, slamming the door before she could hear another hurtful word.

CHAPTER TEN

It felt good to wear britches again.

Maizy rode her own horse to Rylan's the next morning. She'd told Pa that Rylan was up to dressing himself now, though his ribs more than anything still made him move mighty slow.

It gave Maizy far too much pleasure to poke her head in the cabin door. "Get yourself dressed. I'll be in to make breakfast in a half hour or so."

She headed for the barn to see what chores she'd tackle first.

One step inside and her stomach twisted. Rawhide hadn't hung up a piece of leather or forked old straw out of the horse stalls in what looked like weeks. He probably hadn't done it since Rylan had been hurt. She'd have her work cut out for her tending all this while also herding and sorting cattle and choosing the best pasture, but it wouldn't do for ranchers to ride in for a sale and see a poorly run outfit. They'd wonder if the black cattle had been tended well. And Maizy was beginning to doubt they had been, at least not on Rawhide's watch.

Rylan had talked about his ranch a lot, so Maizy had a fair idea of what needed doing, though she couldn't be sure of much until she rode out and saw how the grass was holding up.

As she forked dirty straw out of the milk cow's stall, the familiar mindless work settled her. She finally prayed for the first time since she'd been kissed. If she did this for Rylan, she could forgive herself and leave his ranch.

She worked through half the barn then went striding toward the house. She could feel how different she was in britches. She hadn't minded wearing the dress really, not once she got used to it. She might even take to wearing one regularly when she got away from here, at least after work. Maybe she'd make herself a dress that felt less like a noose.

Bracing herself for what was sure to be trouble, she swung the door open and faced Rylan. He was dressed. He had his Stetson on and was on his feet. He looked like a man heading for work . . . with a broken leg.

"Get back to bed."

It was humiliating how easily a man could be pushed around when he had a broken leg.

Rylan found himself tucked back in bed and Maizy was

making breakfast before he really knew what had happened. It didn't help that he was dizzy.

He wasn't sure if that was from his injuries, or did a man who'd laid around for a month have to get back to standing upright a bit at a time?

"I want you to fetch the doctor out. My leg isn't hurting. I'm going to get this cast off and tend my ranch myself."

Maizy peeled a potato so fast he could barely follow her hands. She attended to her cooking as if he hadn't spoken.

With her usual impressive efficiency, she cooked up a storm, and she did it so quickly he wasn't sure what all the woman was doing. She had a big pot simmering on the stove, and she fried up some eggs and scooped them onto his plate, dropped a couple of biscuits on the tin plate, added a side of pork, and brought the food to Rylan's bedside table. She slapped it down with a loud crash.

"You think you're so ready to work, then sit yourself up and get to eatin'. I'll bring you milk and a cup of coffee." She bustled about as she talked, wearing those blasted britches that drew a man's eye, or at least drew his when it was Maizy wearing them. "You look lively enough to get yourself around and find a meal. I've got a stew simmering, and it should be done for dinner and last for supper. After you eat, slide it to the back of the stove so it won't dry out. Plenty of biscuits too. I won't be back to dish either meal up. I've got work."

She stalked toward the door and as she swung it open, she turned back and said, "You're not even steady on your feet.

You wouldn't last two minutes on the back of a horse, and I sure as shootin' ain't riding to town for the doctor. So you can just forget gettin' that cast off today. The doctor wouldn't agree to that fool notion anyway."

She slammed out of the cabin, going out to run his ranch. And whether he thought it was proper or not, she'd probably do a good job of it. The girl was a mighty fine cowpoke.

He didn't see her again until the next morning when she came in and cooked for the whole day.

Maizy no longer let her pa escort her, which left Rylan with little choice but to figure out how to dress and undress himself. He had plenty of time for it because Maizy left him almost completely on his own.

Maizy rode over and back on her own schedule. A woman shouldn't ride the countryside alone, but this corner of New Mexico had gotten downright peaceable and he knew she was probably fine. If she did run into trouble, she wore a gun on her hip and could protect herself as well as any man.

At the end of the first week of her having little to do with him, she came in one evening long after Rylan had finished his supper.

"We need to settle a few things before tomorrow." She was filthy. It wasn't a hot day but she was soaked in sweat. She had a milk bucket in one hand and a basket of eggs in the other, and she sat them with a thump on the kitchen floor.

"We sure do." Rylan suspected they wanted to talk about different things.

"I brought the smallest herd up to the canyon pasture.

That's nice grass, but not a whole lot of it. There's good grass along the spring, and you said you wanted the biggest herd there, so I moved them. There are two more herds of cattle—"

She sketched out what she'd done with his herds as she strained the milk and washed up the eggs. Then she cleaned up the rest of his house.

Rylan felt himself flush, and he was glad she had her back to him. He could have cleaned up after himself and not left that for her. He'd declared he was going back to work, but he hadn't thought of working in here. He could ease her load, but it'd be tricky. Heating and pouring water while standing on one leg was a nuisance. But it was time to prove he could handle a small job before he tackled a big one. He didn't run her off though. He kept quiet and let the little spitfire tidy up one more time. He'd start taking care of himself tomorrow, right after she fixed him breakfast and left him a dinner and supper. He was no hand to cooking even on his best day.

"Maizy, I've got one more week. That'll be a full six weeks in this cast."

Maizy kept scrubbing, working on a big pot that Rylan realized he'd left to sit until the food had dried on. If he could have reached it, he'd have kicked his own backside.

"Maizy!" He swung his legs out of bed. He'd been practicing. When he was alone, he got up and hobbled around, trying to get past the dizziness whenever he stood.

He lurched toward her.

Rinsing the pot as if he hadn't yelled, Maizy set it upside down to drain, then turned to him. "What is it?"

He'd yelled and it hadn't even fazed her, not one little bit. It struck Rylan hard that this was a woman who could tolerate his short temper and the long hours of ranching. And she was a woman to work hard alongside a man, pull her own weight and a whole lot more.

A perfect wife for a rancher. She was going to save his ranch. He had hope for the future for the first time since he'd signed that bank loan.

And no amount of trousers and sweat-soaked shirts could change the fact that she was about the prettiest thing he'd ever seen.

Now that he had her attention, he wasn't sure exactly what he wanted to say. All he could think of was that kiss he'd stolen, how she'd seemed to respond, and how she'd never gotten near him again.

Probably because she was afraid she'd respond again.

A smile teased at his lips, but he fought it. "Can you come over here and sit down please? I'd like to ask you a few questions." He made his way to the table and sat.

Her eyes were mighty wary, but she clomped right over to him in her boots. She pulled the chair a nice, safe distance away from him, then flipped the chair around and straddled it, deliberately behaving in the least ladylike way she could manage.

"All right. Let's talk."

Talking wasn't what Rylan wanted to do at all. He had to

get her to scoot that chair closer. He knew one place he could start. "Thank you, Maizy."

She blinked and sat straighter. Well, he'd surprised her at least. "Uh . . . um . . . you . . . you're welcome."

"You've done so much for me and what's more, I've had time to think. You're right. I did cause most of the trouble between us. I tore into you right from the first for no better reason than I'm a stubborn, bullheaded man. Where I come from, the women stayed to the house and the menfolk went out to work." He'd also noticed just how well her britches fit, and it had affected him in a way he didn't want anyone to know.

"But out here things are different. A man is just as likely to end up cooking his own food and washing his own clothes, so why shouldn't a woman work at what I was fool enough to think of as a man's job? I'm sorry."

Maizy's mouth opened and closed. For a time words seemed to be beyond her. Rylan decided to make his move. With what he hoped was a reasonable lack of awkwardness, he stood. That put Maizy well within reach. He lifted her straight off that backward chair and pulled her into his arms.

She squeaked once before his lips silenced her.

CHAPTER ELEVEN

WHEN RYLAN SET MAIZY DOWN, HE TURNED HER CHAIR around. It was a good thing he did, because if that chair hadn't been right behind her, she'd have slumped all the way to the floor.

"Now, Maizy MacGregor, I want to tell you one more thing." Rylan smiled at her in a way that made her feel things that honestly shocked her. He stood there, his leg encased in plaster. He'd been laid almost as low as a man could be—by her. And yet he looked strong and in control.

"Um, all right." She swallowed hard and saw his eyes flicker to her throat, then her lips.

"I may have saved your life, but you've saved this ranch. Your hard work has"—Rylan's voice broke and he cleared his throat, then cleared it again—"has saved me. And being forced to spend time with you has opened my eyes. Maizy, I want to marry you."

"What?" Maizy almost toppled off the chair. She gripped the seat beneath her to stay upright.

"I have depended on you more than anyone I've ever known. What's more, I need you. And not just to save the ranch but for the rest of my life. I need your strength, your determination, your kindness."

He needed her just as she was. He cared for the woman she truly was.

"But once I do, I promise I'll let you go back to caring for my house. I'll let you do womanly things and never ask such unladylike behavior of you again."

Maizy's joy plummeted. "Wh-what?"

He sank down so he sat on his chair facing her and reached across to hold both her hands. His pain was mostly gone. He was well and he'd soon be fit and whole again.

"I'm saying you can stop wearing the britches for good after I'm well. You won't have to shame yourself with manly ways ever again." He smiled as if he were offering her a bunch of posies instead of his usual judgmental arrogance. So he needed her and he'd use her, even though he considered it shameful.

To her way of thinking that made him a low-down sidewinder. She remembered now exactly why she'd gone to war with him when they'd first met. He'd seen her in her britches and before he'd opened his mouth, she'd been riveted on his handsome face and masculine form. The woman in her, which had been sleeping all her life, woke up and wanted him.

Every soft and feminine part of her heart was exposed and vulnerable . . . and he'd sneered.

The female side of her had lived just long enough to be terribly hurt. Maizy had dug deep to keep that hurt from showing and found anger.

The same thing was happening now, and she reacted in the same way.

It took all her courage because the earlier hurt had been about her pride. But this time her feelings were involved. She'd learned he was a good man and she'd respected him, and with the kiss just now and his proposal, she knew she loved him.

But how could she love someone who was ashamed of her?

In the sweetest voice she could manage, considering she was on the verge of strangling him, she said, "So you never have to be shamed by me if I give up my cowboy ways, is that right?"

He nodded, smiling. "You can make yourself dresses that fit and leave off the wrangling. You're a beautiful woman, Maizy, and a fine housekeeper and cook. You can do all those things while I work the ranch."

The lunkhead looked so happy with his generous offer she knew he expected her to thank him.

"I can think of another way that will keep you from ever having to be ashamed of me." Maizy kept her voice calm and chipper. She'd clenched a fist though, in the hand Rylan wasn't holding. But she wasn't going to punch him.

"We don't need another way. Marrying me will solve everything." The man wasn't even scared, which proved Maizy had good control of herself.

Surprising what a woman could do at the same time her

heart was breaking. "I've learned something really important in this month we've spent together, Rylan."

"Good. I'm glad." He reached forward as if to press a hand to her cheek. She couldn't bear for him to touch her so she stood, paced away, then turned back, her hands shoved in the back pocket of her britches.

"I've learned that there's nothing to be ashamed of in the way I am."

The smile shrank off Rylan's face, replaced by confusion.

"And I've learned that no man who considers me shameful is worthy of being my husband."

"Wait—" Rylan struggled to his feet, but Maizy had no doubt she could outrun him.

"I reckon I'm going to spend the rest of my life alone, because I will never . . ." Her voice rose but she couldn't stop it. She'd meant to be very calm, but she wasn't going to be able to do that. "I will *never* be with a man who doesn't love who I am. Exactly who I am. I have served you well this last month, Rylan, and by way of thanks you tell me I have to change to be someone you approve of. You propose marriage with the same breath you tell me you're ashamed of me."

"Maizy, I didn't mean—"

A harsh, furious laugh tore out of her throat. "I'll stay to get through the sale. I said I would and I'm a woman of my word. But after the sale, I'm leaving. I'm sure I will find many people who will sneer at me, but at least they won't be people I care about. Here, with you and Pa, it hurts."

She sweetened her voice to molasses. "So no, thank you. I won't marry you. And I'd say you're well enough to tend your own house and feed yourself, even though that's *women's* work." She whirled and stormed out, slamming the back door so hard it shook the house.

She was halfway to the barn when the door behind her banged.

Rylan roared, "Maizy!"

A shout of fear and a dull thud whirled her around. He lay on the ground, struggling, pushing to sit up and try to stand, but he was helpless.

"Maizy, come back. Please." He was facedown, as if prostrate with grief.

Disgusted but helpless to stay away, she walked back and crouched beside him. "Lie still before you re-break your bones. How am I going to get you back inside?"

He managed to roll over so he could look her in the eyes. "Maizy, I'm sorry."

Shrugging to cover up how much she hurt, she studied him, all but his eyes. "Just be quiet while I figure out how to get you up."

Rylan sat up, grabbed her arm, and dragged her forward until she landed on her knees and nearly fell on top of him. "I won't be still, not when I've hurt you so badly."

Their eyes met.

Maizy ripped herself loose and fell backward onto her seat, then rolled onto her knees and crawled until she could be sure of avoiding his strong hand.

But she'd made the mistake of catching his eyes, and he held her that way. "When that door banged, it was like my life was slamming shut on me. Maizy, don't go. Don't leave me. I don't want you to be anyone but yourself."

It was a plea she heard all the way to her heart. "You said that before. Or at least I thought you did. When you needed me. But I won't tie myself to a man who is ashamed of me. Even if you say now that you accept me as I am, how can I trust you to mean it?"

"I do mean it."

"Right now, I reckon you mean it. But deep inside I suspect you really are ashamed of me."

"No, I think you're wonderful. I was trying to make you happy. Your pa has always worked you like a cowhand. I thought giving that up would make you happy. I thought you liked it in the house."

"Which just means you think I'm wrong to live like I do. And maybe I *am* a shameful woman."

"You're not. I'm sorry."

Maizy ignored him. "I was raised to work hard, to love the land and cattle, and to know how to handle them. I don't want to change. Truth is, I doubt I can. And I'm not going to. Not for anyone."

Silence fell between them. Maizy saw Rylan sitting there, helpless. She wanted to help him in every possible way. Help him get into the house. Help him run his cattle. Help any way he needed. A helpmate. She could be that for him, but she'd do it as she was, and if Rylan didn't accept her, the real her, then when she was done helping him and he was back on his feet, they were done.

"You're wonderful, Maizy. You can help me outside all you want. But I'm going to give you a choice. Once I get the Angus sold, I'll be able to afford to pay some cowpokes good wages. It seemed to me like your pa never gave you much choice. There's no denying you're as strong and able as any hired hand, but you won't have to be. I am not ashamed of you. Just the opposite. I'm so proud of you I could burst."

Maizy had never heard such sweet talk before and, oh, how she wanted to believe it.

"It like to broke my heart when you walked out. And that pain is a hundred times worse than a broken leg. If you won't forgive me, then I'll be left broken inside and out."

Breathing deep, Maizy knelt there, and as long as she was on her knees, she prayed. Not daring to believe him but wanting to so badly.

Finally, because the indecision was ripping her up, she set it aside. "Let's try and get you up."

Rylan got a stubborn mule look, like he was going to demand she accept his apology and his proposal before he agreed to move. Then he looked around and said, "I think I can get up on my own. I'll boost myself up on the back steps, then I should be able to stand from there."

Maizy stayed back. "Give it a try. You may not need my help."

"I will always need you, Maizy, and not just because I need your hard work." They were looking right at each other. Her kneeling, him sitting. Then he smiled. "Don't wander off."

He was the best-looking man Maizy had ever imagined.

With decent agility he scooted on his backside up the stairs. Then, using his left leg, he did a fair job of getting to his feet.

Once he was standing, he reached out one hand. After a long hesitation, she took it, not at all sure that was wise.

"Maizy . . ." Rylan rubbed the back of his neck with his free hand and frowned at the toes of his boots as if he thought the words he wanted to speak might be written on them.

She waited. It was a fine thing to respect her and want her in his life as she was . . . *if* he did. But he still hadn't said the one thing that would make her risk everything. And Maizy suspected he never would.

Finally he raised his head, and his eyes blazed with a fire she didn't understand. "You want to know why I said those things to you the first time I saw you wearing britches?"

She wasn't sure she did.

"I'd been in the country two weeks. I'd just spent every penny I had and borrowed a bunch I shouldn't have to make a go of raising Angus cattle. I knew I had years of hard work to prove myself to my pa. One look at you and I wanted to forget all of that."

"What?" Whatever she'd expected him to say, it hadn't been this.

"One look at you in those blasted britches and I wanted you more than I wanted my ranch and my cattle and my pa's respect. And I've been trying to stay away from you ever since. I kept thinking when things were good and I knew I'd made it, then I could think on things like a wife. But then, after I got hurt and it looked like I'd lose everything . . ." He shook his head. "I've been trying to get you to go away so when I disgrace myself and lose my ranch, I won't drag you down with me."

"Rylan, you're not going to lose the ranch. We'll get the cattle ready on time."

"You mean *you* will. You're saving me, Maizy." Rylan reached out and took her other hand. "Maybe not being able to do it on my own should pinch my pride—the good Lord knows I've got too much of that. But right now all I can think is, I've been a fool not to accept the gift God put right in front of me. And I've shown myself to be a fool in about every way a man can."

Maizy probably should have protested, but there was too much truth in what he was saying. For all his words, though, he still hadn't said what she needed to hear.

"I should have grabbed you the first time I saw you riding in your pa's corral, pretty Maizy. I should have known that minute that I'd just met the love of my life."

And there, he'd just said it.

"That's what I realized when you slammed that door. Up until then I was acting out of pride and fear and anger, all made worse by pain from my injuries. But when I realized you might be leaving me for good, well, I knew I didn't want you to stay for dressing a certain way or working a certain way. I want you to stay because I love you. I love the woman who has worked tirelessly, inside and out, to save my ranch for me, to care for me. But more than that, I want you to stay because I believe you're the woman God prepared for me, from the moment of my birth. And from this moment on, I'm going to try and be a man who is worthy of you. I'm so sorry for the way I've acted, and I think if I stop trying to push you away, a lot of the trouble . . . my . . . behavior . . . my . . ."

"Insulting, rude, obnoxious, low-down—"

Rylan put one hand gently over her mouth. "Yes, all that and more. That's all because I was trying not to do this." He pulled her into his arms and kissed the living daylights out of her.

When he finally let her go, Maizy shook her head. She didn't want to believe it because if she did, she'd have to admit she loved him back. And she'd have to trust that he'd remember his words when she was not behaving as a woman ought.

He tugged her into his arms and kissed her again.

She turned her head aside and Rylan kissed her cheek, her neck, her hair. "Say you'll marry me. Please say yes."

What was a woman to do? She wound her arms around his neck and said, "I love you too, Rylan. A man I didn't care about could never hurt me so badly."

He silenced her with a kiss. And when he had well and truly driven every thought out of her head, he said, "I'll try my best to never hurt you again, but I suspect you'll find me a trial on many occasions."

"As you will me."

"I hope, if we can just remember this moment when we

declared our love, we can get through the rough places in our lives. Marry me, Maizy."

"I'll marry you. I love you with all my heart."

※

The next day when the doc came to see Rylan, he brought Parson Alden, who had known Maizy only from her occasional appearances at Sunday services and the one visit to Rylan's house. And she'd always worn a dress.

"You're wearing trousers?"

"Well, Parson, I've got chores to do, and Rylan sure as certain can't do them." It seemed foolish to bring a change of clothes for an hour-long wedding.

Scowling, the parson said, "I find that mighty disrespectful, Miss MacGregor. Shameful, even."

Rylan stepped between Parson Alden and Maizy. "She saved this ranch and she will continue to do so until I'm well. She's given selflessly in the finest kind of Christian service, and she's done it wearing those britches. I won't stand by while someone calls that kind of love and generosity shameful. You'd best apologize to her and get on with speaking those vows."

Feeling her cheeks heat up with pleasure at Rylan's defense of her, Maizy looked past his shoulder to the parson.

Parson Alden, confused but kind, looked at her, then shook his head. "No, you're right. I suspect you getting married in britches is exactly the right way to start off your lives together. If it's all right with you"—he looked nervously between Maizy and Rylan and cleared his throat—"could you please at least wear a skirt to church? There's no sense in bringing unneeded judgment on yourself from others."

Maizy relaxed. Rylan chuckled. "I reckon we can go along with that, Parson."

A smile broke on the parson's face and he said, "I've got some preacher friends who will enjoy hearing about the little spitfire who got married wearing trousers. Let's get on with the ceremony."

Five days after the wedding, the doc cut the cast off Rylan's leg and gave both of the newlyweds a scolding so Rylan wouldn't overdo it with work.

When he left, Maizy said, "My ears are still ringing from all his terrible predictions if you don't take care."

Rylan pulled her close. "I'll be careful. I promise. But did you notice all his talk was about work?"

"Well, of course. What else would he talk about?"

Rylan pulled his wife close. He kissed her soundly. As she was clinging to him, he raised his head just enough to say, "The doc didn't say a word about overdoing a honeymoon."

Maizy's eyes grew round. "Why, no, he didn't."

They both laughed and began their married life finally, fully, and passionately.

CHAPTER TWELVE

RYLAN'S BLACK ANGUS STOOD BELLY-DEEP IN LUSH grass, fat and contented. Every one of them sold to ranchers who were willing to pay well for the privilege.

For the sale, Maizy wore a dress she'd made for herself. She was a hand at sewing. She'd made clothes for herself and Pa all her life.

After the sale, money wasn't so tight for Rylan. With a bunkhouse full of hired men, Maizy didn't have to ride the range except for pleasure, and for a while she and Rylan did a lot of riding. She discovered such a thing as a split skirt so she could ride her horse astride and still not put on britches.

She tapered off after it was clear that a baby was on the way. A second child followed, then another and yet another. The little ones slowed down her ranching something fierce.

Maizy, with Rylan's full support, raised her children, boys

and girls alike, to take pride in themselves and to demand respect. The boys were headed to being ranchers themselves, and the girls were well on their way to being little Texas spitfire sweethearts.

A Love Letter to the Editor

Robin Lee Hatcher

Dear Editor:

Do you think there are men in this world who can value a well-educated woman with a mind of her own and the courage to speak it? Is it possible for a man and a woman to have an equal partnership in marriage, seeing each other as God intended them to be? After thirty-five years on this earth, I have begun to doubt it.

Sincerely,
Wishful in Wyoming

CHAPTER ONE

Killdeer, Wyoming, August 1879

MOLLY EVERTON FLUNG OPEN THE DOOR TO HER FATHER'S office in the *Killdeer Sentinel*, not caring that it hit the wall with a loud crack. "Is it true, Father?"

Roland Everton looked up from the papers on his desk. "Is what true?"

"You know good and well what I mean. Have you hired someone else as editor of the paper?"

Her father removed his glasses and pinched the bridge of his nose. A familiar delaying tactic. She'd seen it many times in her thirty-five years.

Molly closed the door and then stepped closer to his desk, trying to check her temper. "It isn't fair. You know it isn't fair."

"My dear, you should know by now that many things in life are not fair. Far from it."

"Why did you send me to college if you didn't want me to put the knowledge I gained to good use? I have all of the qualifications needed to serve as the paper's editor. I have worked beside you. I know what needs to be done."

Her father released a sigh. "Oh, Molly. Speaking your mind freely has its consequences. We must do business with the merchants here in town. We can't afford to offend them or their wives. I need someone in charge of the paper who understands the delicate balance required."

Molly's anger evaporated, leaving behind a desire to weep.

"Sit down, Molly."

She obeyed.

"I was wrong not to tell you sooner," her father said, his voice gentle. "I suppose it was this precise scene I was hoping to avoid. It seems all I did was delay it a little."

Molly stared at her hands, clasped tightly in her lap. "What is his name?"

"The new editor? Jack Ludgrove."

"Where is he from?"

"Iowa."

"And when does he arrive?"

Her father didn't answer at once.

Molly lifted her gaze to meet his.

"This afternoon. I expect him on today's stagecoach."

She sat a little straighter. "He'll be here today?"

"Yes."

There was no hope, then. No hope of changing her father's mind. No hope of helping him see that this was her turn, her right.

"Molly—"

"No. Don't say anything more, Father. Not now." She rose to her feet. "You have made your decision." She moved to the door and opened it, slowly this time. "I will see you at supper." She left her father's office and moved toward the front door of the newspaper, holding her head high.

She stopped on the boardwalk and looked to her right, down Main Street toward the Wells, Fargo office. The stagecoach from Green River usually came through Killdeer at about four o'clock in the afternoon. That was a good two hours from now.

Molly turned in the opposite direction and walked toward home. She nodded to a couple of women she passed on the boardwalk outside of the mercantile. She waved at Reverend Lynch, standing at the top of the church steps on the corner of Main and Elm.

Offend the advertisers, her father had said. Who had she offended? It wasn't fair of Father to say that without giving her any specifics.

Fair. There was that word again. And her father was right about life not being fair. Especially for a woman. Especially for a woman who valued independence and learning above men and marriage.

Not that she had any objection to the institution of marriage itself. There were numerous examples of good marriages right here in her own town. Her parents, for one. But few men seemed to want a wife with the courage to speak her mind openly. At least, no men she'd met. Even her father preferred that she keep most of her opinions to herself.

When she turned thirty-five earlier this year, she'd accepted that she was—and would remain—an old maid. Being unmarried wasn't the worst fate in the world. But she did want to be useful. She would like to feel as if the work she did was valued by others.

What would she do when her father sold the newspaper? Something he'd begun to talk about more and more often. Would a new owner employ a woman reporter? Or a female editor? Her father wouldn't even make her the editor. Why would someone else?

But if she was already the editor when her father chose to sell the *Sentinel*, that might make a difference to the new owner. If she could prove herself capable. More than capable, invaluable. If she could do that, then she might be able to stay on.

Only Mr. Ludgrove stood in her way.

She stopped walking. Mr. Ludgrove might not like living in Killdeer. He might not stay. And if he didn't . . .

I'll make him want to leave. A smile played across her lips. *It can't be that hard to make him want to go back to where he came from.*

"True hope is swift, and flies with swallow's wings," she whispered, quoting Shakespeare. "Kings it makes gods, and meaner creatures kings."

Feeling a great deal better than she had moments before, Molly hurried on toward home.

Jack Ludgrove stepped down from the coach. After moving aside for two other passengers to disembark, he stopped and looked down the main street of Killdeer, Wyoming.

By George! Wyoming Territory! He was here at last.

Ever since he was a boy, Jack had longed for adventures in the West. Stories of fur trappers. Tales of the Oregon Trail. Accounts of the California gold rush. They'd all fueled his childhood imagination.

He might have come west right out of college, if not for four bloody years of civil war. He'd joined the Union army at the age of twenty-one, soon after the hostilities began. He fought for his country and survived unscathed to the bitter end. But those years exacted a heavy toll on his family. His two brothers died in the conflict. Then his father seemed to give out from the grief. Jack was needed to stay in Iowa to care for him, so that was what he did. But his heart had never stopped yearning for the West of his dreams, and with his father's passing had come his freedom.

Jack Ludgrove, managing editor of the *Killdeer Sentinel*, in Killdeer, Wyoming. Sounded good to him.

He took up his bags that had been removed from the rear of the coach, then started walking.

Killdeer was laid out in a square on the high desert land. Beyond it to the north rose the rugged Rocky Mountains. As soon as he owned a horse and had the time, he meant to ride up closer to those mountains and do some exploring.

Roland Everton, the owner and publisher of the *Sentinel*, had written in his letter that their offices were in the center of town on Main Street. It couldn't be hard to find. Killdeer was not exactly a thriving metropolis. However, it looked exactly as Jack had hoped it would. Whitewashed buildings. False storefronts. At least one church. Large livery stables. Wide, dusty streets. Horses hitched to posts. Cowboys in wide-brimmed hats standing in the shade.

He could smell the adventure.

At his age, he supposed he shouldn't find it all as exciting as he did. By thirty-nine, most men were settled. Job. Home. Wife. Children. Most men knew what their futures looked like: the same as their pasts.

Jack saw the newspaper then. *Killdeer Sentinel* was painted across the large plate glass window. The name was also on a sign up high on the storefront. He crossed the street and opened the front door. Newspaper smells greeted him.

A man appeared from the back of the building. He had a bad leg and leaned heavily on the cane in his left hand as he approached. "Mr. Ludgrove?"

Jack nodded. "Yes, sir."

"Welcome to Killdeer. I'm Mr. Everton."

"Pleased to meet you, sir."

They shook hands.

Roland Everton motioned toward a door to the right. "Let's go into my office." He moved in that direction. "I apologize for not meeting the stage, but as you can see, walking is a bit difficult for me. Especially the constant on and off of the boardwalks."

"Don't give it a thought. I liked getting a look at the town."

The publisher's office was small—and made smaller by the books and stacks of paper and newsprint on every available surface. Roland Everton went around to sit in his own chair. Jack took the one opposite him.

"Mr. Ludgrove, I have arranged for a room for you at Mrs. Simpson's boardinghouse. It's clean and reasonably priced, and I'm told she is a very fine cook."

"Sounds good. I imagine I'll spend much of my time at the newspaper, so I don't need anything fancy."

"I thought you should have a few days to get your bearings. You can begin work here on Monday."

"That's very generous of you, sir, but I am willing to begin at once if I am needed."

Roland waved away the comment. "Not necessary, Mr. Ludgrove. Monday will be soon enough."

Jack nodded.

"As I'm sure I told you in my letters, the running of the *Sentinel* has been mostly a family affair these past ten years. My daughter, Molly, writes a regular column, and she usually chooses what letters to the editor are published, depending upon topic and what space is available. She's a capable reporter as well."

Oh great. Jack hadn't known about the daughter. That was the last thing he needed to deal with. Nepotism in the newspaper business seldom served the best interests of the readership. That must be as true for a small town's weekly as it was for a city's daily.

"And, of course," Roland continued, "I have served as

the managing editor from the beginning. Hank Morrison is our typesetter. He's fast and efficient. You will see that for yourself."

Jack nodded, thinking it best not to say much about the staff until he'd met them. He would judge their qualifications by his own standards.

Roland got to his feet. "If you'll come with me, I will take you to the boardinghouse. Though my wife is expecting you to be our guest for supper your first night in Killdeer."

"I wouldn't want to put her out, Mr. Everton." Jack stood.

"Nonsense. She would never forgive me if we didn't show you the proper hospitality. First impressions are important, and we want your impression of Killdeer to be a positive one. Now come along."

CHAPTER TWO

"MOLLY, DO GO ALONG AND CHANGE INTO ONE OF YOUR nice dresses. We are expecting a guest for supper."

At her mother's words, Molly felt herself go hot and cold and hot again, in quick succession. A guest for supper. The new editor. It had to be. And her parents had kept everything about him a secret from her. Oh, how could they?

Then again, perhaps it was just as well she got a look at him here at home rather than in the office. She would have the advantage seated at the Everton dining room table.

She excused herself and went upstairs to her bedroom. One of her nice dresses. What her mother meant was something more fashionable. Molly favored dark skirts and simple white blouses. Clothing that was practical and allowed her to move and breathe. Ruth Everton wanted her daughter in handsome suits with gathered flounces and lots of fringe, and a corset that laced her into the perfect *S* shape that fashion demanded. Forget breathing altogether.

A frown creased her brow. How she wished she'd asked Father more about this Jack Ludgrove instead of storming out in a huff. How old was he? How long had he been an editor? Was he a married man? A father? A grandfather? What papers had he worked for?

She sighed as she reached for a mauve-colored gown. Her mother had bought it for her on a trip they'd made to San Francisco two years ago. She'd worn it twice. It was too frilly for her taste, although she did like the color. It went well with her complexion, bringing out the rose in her cheeks.

Molly moved to the mirror and gazed at her reflection. Should she be congenial and welcoming at this first meeting? She had no experience with subterfuge and underhanded schemes, but that did seem as if it would be the best way to achieve her desired end. Could she fool Mr. Ludgrove into believing she was glad he had come to Wyoming?

"I must," she whispered. "There's no other way."

She would put on this fancy gown, sweep up her hair on her head, and act the perfect and proper lady for the evening, all the while looking for where this man from Iowa might be most vulnerable, most easily driven back to whence he came.

Reverend Lynch would not approve.

She tamped down the voice of her conscience. This wasn't a time to be missish. This was a kind of war, and in war, one must have a battle plan at the ready.

God would not approve.

She groaned and made an even greater attempt to silence her conscience.

A tap at the door announced her mother. "I thought you might need help with your corset," she said as she looked into the room.

"Yes, I will need help. Thank you, Mother."

"Oh, good. You're going to wear the gown we brought back from San Francisco. It is lovely, and it's not much out of fashion."

"It's certainly good enough for Killdeer."

Her mother moved to stand beside her. "If we want our town to become more civilized, we must act as if it is civilized already."

Molly looked over her shoulder. "Mother, Killdeer will never be a large city. We aren't a gold rush town. We aren't a port city. Even when they bring the railroad spur through here as promised, we cannot expect things to change all that much. Killdeer is here to serve the ranchers and farmers. I like it the way it is."

"Do you?" Her mother gave the corset laces a good pull. "What about all of your progressive ideas? What about women's suffrage?"

"What has that to do with liking Killdeer the way it is?"

"Heavens, I don't know. You always do this to me, Margaret Ruth. I get so confused." Another good pull on the laces. "But from what I've seen, the cowboys and farmers around here don't appreciate your ideas. If you want to get married before it's too late, you'd better learn to either hold your tongue or pray for God to send a man to Killdeer who thinks like you do."

A man who thought like Molly did. "Think you there was or might be such a man / As this I dreamt of?" she quoted to herself.

"What was that, dear?"

"Nothing, Mother."

"Please try not to talk to yourself when Mr. Ludgrove is here. It's a very bad habit."

Molly swallowed a sigh. "I'll try, Mother. I promise."

The Everton home was a short distance to the north of town. It was two stories tall with a wraparound porch. Its yard, surrounded by a white picket fence, sported green grass, colorful flower gardens, and trees all around.

Roland Everton drove the buggy to the front of the house and reined in the horse. It took some maneuvering for him to get down from the buggy, his right leg not seeming to bend in the normal fashion. Jack had to resist the urge to try to help the man.

"Come along, Mr. Ludgrove," Roland said once both feet were solidly on the ground. "Mrs. Everton is eager to meet you." He opened the picket gate and motioned Jack through.

"How long have you lived here, Mr. Everton?"

"Better than ten years now. When we built this house, we thought the town would grow right up to us in no time. Hasn't happened as fast as we expected."

"The grounds are beautiful."

"My wife excels at growing things."

And the Evertons had a well that didn't run dry. The emerald color of their lawn made that plain to Jack's eyes.

Roland opened the front door and again waved Jack to go before him. He stepped into a small entryway. To his right was a parlor. To his left the dining room. The rooms were tastefully decorated. Nothing ostentatious. The Evertons were well-to-do, but they didn't flaunt it.

"Ruth?"

A moment or two later, a woman appeared from the back of the house. "Roland, I didn't hear you come in." She smiled at Jack as she approached.

"My dear, this is Jack Ludgrove. Mr. Ludgrove, my wife, Ruth Everton."

"A pleasure to meet you, Mrs. Everton."

"Likewise, Mr. Ludgrove. And welcome to Wyoming."

"Thank you. It's good to be here."

Roland asked, "Where is Molly?"

"Upstairs. She'll be down shortly." Ruth Everton turned and moved into the parlor, and the two men followed.

She was an attractive woman, perhaps in her early- to midfifties. Jack guessed her to be at least ten years younger than Roland. Her light brown hair was sprinkled with gray, but she had the face and form of a woman who could be Roland's daughter rather than his wife.

"Please sit down, Mr. Ludgrove," Ruth invited.

He was about to do so when the rustle of skirts drew his gaze toward the parlor entrance. Molly Everton, no doubt.

She wasn't what he'd expected, though he didn't know

for certain what that had been. She wasn't what he would call beautiful, but there was something appealing about her refined features. Tall for a woman. Slender and not too curvy where women were supposed to be curvy. Sharp angles to her face. Honey-brown hair piled high on her head. Wide, almond-shaped eyes of blue. She carried herself erect, and he sensed the strength in her spine had nothing to do with the corset beneath that fancy gown. No, hers was an inner strength.

"Mr. Ludgrove," Roland said, "our daughter, Molly Everton. Molly, this is Jack Ludgrove."

"Miss Everton."

"Mr. Ludgrove."

"Your father tells me you write a column for the newspaper."

"Yes."

"I look forward to reading it."

There was a coolness in her gaze as she inclined her head.

He had the feeling she didn't like him. Not a familiar feeling either. Most women were fond of him. He'd never lacked female companions, although none had ever tempted him to wed.

Ruth invited them all to be seated, then began asking Jack polite questions about his home in Des Moines, his family, his journey to Killdeer. He answered them and interspersed a few questions of his own. And then it was time for the family to go in to dinner.

The host and hostess sat at opposite ends of a modest-sized

table. Jack and Molly were seated on the sides, facing each other. A maid—a girl of about twenty—served the meal.

Jack wondered how many household servants the Evertons employed. And then there was the manicured lawn. Ruth Everton might be an excellent gardener, but he didn't envision her pushing a cylinder mower around the yard. How much could a weekly newspaper earn for its owner? Doubtful it was enough to make a man rich. Which left Jack to assume Roland or Ruth Everton or both came from money.

Interesting. And if true, why had they moved to a place like Killdeer? Jack had come west for the adventure. What had brought the Evertons?

"You seem deep in thought, Mr. Ludgrove."

He raised his eyes to look at the woman opposite him. "Woolgathering, I'm afraid."

A small smile curved the corners of her mouth. "You don't strike me as the type to let his thoughts wander."

"Don't I?" She was right, of course.

"No. I believe nothing escapes your notice."

She was right again. "A danger of my profession, I suppose."

Her eyes narrowed and the smile disappeared. "And of mine."

Ah, she was sensitive about being a columnist. Why was that? Maybe she'd been told her column wasn't good. Maybe she knew she only had the job because her father owned the newspaper. Maybe—

"What made you apply for the editorial position at the

Sentinel?" she asked. "I can't imagine you ever heard anything about our little town before."

"No, Miss Everton. I hadn't heard of the *Sentinel* or of Killdeer until I saw the notice about the position. I applied because I have wanted to see the West since I was a boy. This was my opportunity to do exactly that. I'm hoping to have an adventure or two. The kind I read about when I was younger."

"If you're looking for adventure, then I don't suppose you plan to stay long in Killdeer. There are many more exciting locations than this."

Jack had to swallow a laugh. That she would like to see him gone was as plain as the aristocratic nose on her face.

I'll stay in Killdeer and at the newspaper just as long as I wish, Miss Everton. Don't think I won't.

CHAPTER THREE

Molly and her mother arrived at the church early on Sunday morning, carrying fresh flowers in their arms. From the first blooms of spring until the first hard freeze in the fall, the Everton gardens provided lovely floral arrangements for the sanctuary and narthex.

Molly wasn't passionate about gardening. That was her mother's favorite pastime. But she didn't mind helping with the flowers on Sunday mornings. There was something restful about being in the building, just the two of them. Sometimes they talked. Most times they worked in silence, the perfume of the flowers teasing their noses.

Molly was arranging roses in a large vase in the narthex when she heard footsteps behind her. Assuming it was the minister, she said, "Are we late, Reverend Lynch?"

"I'm not the reverend, but I don't think you're late."

Her stomach thudded as she turned toward Jack Ludgrove.

"I believe I'm early," he added as he removed his hat.

Good gracious, he *was* a ruggedly handsome man. That had been her first thought when they met on Friday evening—much to her chagrin—and it disturbed her to have it be so this morning as well. Tall. Broad shoulders. Dark hair. Dark eyes. Square jaw. She was aware of it all. "Like a rich jewel in an Ethiope's ear; / Beauty too rich for use, for earth too dear!"

Jack frowned. "Come again?"

Oh dear. Had she said that aloud? "Nothing. Good morning."

He grinned. "Thank you. It's good to see you again, Miss Everton."

She smiled briefly but did not return the sentiment. She hadn't yet decided how best to deal with Jack Ludgrove. Before she could make up her mind, Reverend Lynch arrived. Jack introduced himself. The reverend was effusive in his welcome as the two men shook hands.

Molly used that moment as her excuse to slip away. She didn't want to continue her conversation with Jack Ludgrove until she was better prepared for it. She would have liked it better if he were the sort of man to frequent one of the saloons rather than church. It would give her one more reason to dislike him.

As if she needed another.

Outside, she rounded the church and sat on a wooden bench in the shade. She liked it here. It was private and quiet. People on their way to church couldn't see it because of a swell in the land between the church and the roads that approached it. The reverend's wife, Emeline Lynch, had told Molly this was where her husband practiced most of his sermons, weather permitting.

Molly drew a deep breath and let it out slowly. *Now think. What am I to do about Mr. Ludgrove?*

A frown furrowed her forehead. Her father would not tolerate rudeness, so she couldn't be obvious about her true feelings for the newly hired editor. That would make things harder, she supposed, but not impossible.

I need to get to know him. Find his weak spot.

He'd come west for the adventure. She should help him experience one. Maybe he could run into a grizzly bear up in Yellowstone. Now that would be an adventure he wouldn't forget. Assuming he survived to tell about it.

Oh, that was a wicked thought. She didn't wish him harm. She simply wanted Jack Ludgrove to go elsewhere. Was that such a terrible thing to wish for?

She set her jaw and rose from the bench, refusing to ask that particular question of God. She didn't want to know the answer. It would have something to do with loving her enemy and turning the other cheek and doing good to those who spitefully used her. Not that Mr. Ludgrove was her enemy. He hadn't spitefully used her. All the same, she wanted him gone from the newspaper and gone from Killdeer. The sooner, the better.

With a *harrumph* for good measure, she drew herself up straight and headed for the front of the church for the second time that morning.

Other members of the congregation had begun to

arrive. She exchanged hellos with people she'd known for years. Many of them had moved here soon after the founding of Killdeer, just like the Everton family. There was Mr. Whitaker, blacksmith and owner of the livery stables. There were Mr. and Mrs. Cook, owners of the mercantile. There were the Holbrooks, who had a farm about five or six miles out of town. Mr. and Mrs. Holbrook were a good ten years younger than Molly, and already they had five children.

As soon as Molly stepped from the brightness of morning into the dim light of the narthex, she was met by her mother. "Where have you been?" Ruth Everton whispered, taking Molly by the arm.

"Enjoying the cool of the morning."

"Your father is introducing Mr. Ludgrove to everyone."

Molly followed her mother's gaze. Her father and Jack were talking to the Shoemaker sisters, Jane and Ada. Both of the young women were looking at Jack as if they would like to devour him. Had they no shame?

"Come along, Molly." Her mother propelled her across the narthex. "Good morning, Miss Shoemaker. Miss Shoemaker." Her mother nodded toward each sister. "Isn't it a lovely summer morning? But it shall be hot by the time we have our Sunday dinner." She turned her eyes on Jack. "We would be honored to have you join us in our pew, Mr. Ludgrove."

Good heavens! Her mother couldn't possibly be attempting a bit of matchmaking. Hadn't she learned her lesson after years of countless disasters?

"I would be honored, Mrs. Everton. Thank you."

And then, of all things, Jack Ludgrove offered his arm to Molly. If only the floor would open up and swallow her whole. What could she do but accept? She slipped her fingers into the crook of his arm, at the same time feeling heat rising in her cheeks, and they followed her parents into the sanctuary.

CHAPTER FOUR

Early Monday morning, Jack left the boarding-house and walked toward the newspaper office in the center of town. Killdeer was quiet at this hour. He suspected Killdeer was quiet at most hours in comparison to Des Moines.

He drew in a deep breath. Even the air smelled different out west. Maybe it was the altitude—over six thousand feet above sea level where he walked right now. Or maybe it was the mountains to the north and west. The photographs he'd seen hadn't done them justice—couldn't in black–and–white. Those mountains beckoned to him to come and explore. He would too. Soon.

At church yesterday, Jack had learned that George Whitaker, the blacksmith, had a number of saddle horses for sale. Reasonably priced, according to the blacksmith. Jack meant to see if that was true later today.

Arriving at the *Sentinel* office, he opened the door—

already unlocked by someone—and went in. He grinned. The air didn't smell different in here. It was the same as every other newspaper office he'd ever known. Sounds from the back room confirmed that he wasn't alone in the building. He moved in that direction.

Hank Morrison was seated on a high stool, his back toward the front office, setting type for the next edition of the paper. Jack had met the typesetter on Friday, but they hadn't had an opportunity to say more than a few words to each other.

"Good morning, Mr. Morrison."

Hank didn't look up, though he did raise his hand and give a brief wave. Typesetting took concentration. A man had to be able to read backward. Not an easy task, especially for the small type used in articles. Jack decided not to disturb him further.

The door in the rear of the building opened. Jack expected to see Roland Everton, but it was Molly who came through the doorway. She looked very different from the young woman he'd sat across from on Friday night and the one he'd joined in the pew at church yesterday. This Molly wore a plain, dark blue dress. No fancy flounces or bustles. And though he was no expert on such things, no tight corset beneath either. Her hair was pulled back from her face and captured in a bun at the nape. Simple. Practical. No-nonsense.

She didn't smile when she saw him. "Good morning, Mr. Ludgrove." There wasn't any warmth in her tone either.

Indifference at best, but he suspected her feelings were stronger than that. Why did she dislike him?

"Father will be along shortly," she said as she reached for an apron and tied it around her waist.

Jack walked toward her, skirting the Washington handpress. "Perhaps we could use this time for you to tell me about your column, Miss Everton."

"It might be easier for you to just read some of my older ones."

"Oh, I will do that. But I'd like to know what made you want to write for the newspaper."

There was a challenging light in her eyes. "Do you think such employment is unsuitable for a woman?"

"Not at all." *Well, maybe a little.*

"The world is changing, Mr. Ludgrove, as is a woman's place in it. The suffrage amendment introduced by Senator Sargent in January of last year may have been defeated, as it was again this year, but one day it—or an amendment like it—will pass. One day women will have the right to vote. We will have the right to control our own properties and our own destinies as well. We will no longer be subject to the whims of our fathers, our brothers, or our husbands, no matter our age."

"Believe it or not, Miss Everton, I agree with you."

Her eyes widened. "You do?"

"Yes." He was in earnest and hoped she knew it.

"Not many men agree."

"Perhaps not."

Molly drew herself up, her back stiff as a rail, her surprise obviously forgotten. "No perhaps about it. Most men believe women haven't the intelligence to do anything other than cook, clean house, and raise children." The light in her eyes had become a passionate fire. "But I assure you, give us the same opportunities for education and we can do most anything a man can do. We have just as much value in God's eyes. We are weaker vessels only in our physical bodies."

"Different but equal." He smiled. He couldn't help it. Molly Everton amused him.

The sentiment was not returned. She made a funny little sound in her throat as she whirled away and marched toward the front office.

Jack might have followed, but the door in the back of the building opened a second time, admitting his employer.

Roland grinned. "Good morning, Mr. Ludgrove."

"Good morning, sir."

"I trust you are ready to begin." He hung his hat on a peg on the wall.

"I am, indeed."

"Then come with me. I'm afraid all three of the offices up front are cramped, but they do afford us some privacy and quiet when we need it." Like his daughter before him, Roland headed for the front of the building.

Jack followed, a sense of excitement thrumming in his chest.

Molly seethed as she sat at her desk, trying to decide what to write for her next column. She couldn't think of anything except Jack Ludgrove's smile. And the more she thought about his smile, the madder she got. Was it any wonder? He'd tried to placate her with words while at the same time laughing at her. Oh, he hadn't laughed out loud, but he'd been laughing at her all the same.

"*Believe it or not, Miss Everton, I agree with you.*"

She didn't believe him. How could she? Even her father thought she was too outspoken for her own good. He wanted her to keep her ideas to herself. Father and Mother said she put men off with her progressive ideas.

But was she really different from most other women? Didn't they all want to be heard? To be valued for who they were? To be able to speak freely, at least with the people most important to them? But even when a young woman obtained a higher education, she usually found herself back in her parents' home again, expected to sit and wait for a young man to come along, propose, and make her life mean something. It ought not to be that way.

Molly believed life should be lived to the fullest, and that included engaging her mind. Marrying and having children shouldn't preclude intelligent thought. A husband and wife should inspire and encourage each other, like iron sharpening iron.

If only . . .

She gave her head a determined shake. Those two words never improved a situation. Never. And besides, she had a column to write.

She took the pencil in her right hand, suddenly remembering what she wanted to write about. The matter of fire safety had been uppermost in her thoughts for quite some time. She'd read a survey that stated fire hazards in US theaters caused one in every four such establishments to burn down within four years of erection. The average life of a playhouse in the country was a mere twelve years. Gas lighting, flammable scenery, and too few exits combined to make theatergoing risky entertainment. On a visit to a concert hall in Cheyenne this past spring, Molly had confirmed the dangers with a little poking around prior to the start of the play. It had left her nervous throughout the entire production.

She scrawled a few words across the top of the paper on her desk, paused and worried her lower lip, then began to write in earnest, letting the words come as they would in this first draft. On the second time through, she would pay more attention to grammar and structure, but now her goal was simply to get the words on paper. When she was still a child, her father had told her many times that words in her head couldn't be fixed. "Get it down, Molly. Write first. Edit later."

Finally, the article written, the words in her head spent, she set down the pencil and leaned back in her chair with a sigh. Her eyes lifted to the open door of the tiny room she called an office. On the opposite side of the building, she saw her father seated at his desk and Jack Ludgrove standing near him. Both of them were looking at papers on the desktop.

It wasn't fair. She deserved to be the new editor of the *Sentinel*. She'd earned the right to it. True, this was a man's business. There were a number of women columnists employed at newspapers around the country, usually of the housekeeping variety. Only a few became reporters of real news. Even fewer advanced to a position like managing editor.

But I should have been one of them.

She swiveled her chair to the side and rose. A glance at the clock on the bookcase told her close to two hours had passed. No wonder she felt stiff. When she was writing, she often forgot to get up, move around, stretch—and she paid for it later.

Jack Ludgrove came out of her father's office at the same moment she stepped through her doorway. With a nod, he walked toward her. "Your father tells me you are at work on your column."

Oooh. Hearing him say that made her teeth ache. "Yes. My columns are due on Tuesdays. Unless, of course, you decide to change the schedule."

"I don't intend to change the schedule or anything else about the paper. At least not anytime soon."

"You should get to know the town and our readers."

"Excellent idea, Miss Everton. Perhaps you would be good enough to take me on a brief tour of Killdeer. I met quite a number of folks in church yesterday, but there is more to see and there are more people to meet."

"I really should finish my column."

"But you've been at it for a long while. A bit of fresh air would do you good. It would do us both good. Exercise clears the mind." He motioned with one hand toward the front door. "Please."

What could she do but agree to his request? He was, after all, her new boss.

Jack was about to offer his arm to Molly, but she moved toward the door before he could. He had no choice but to follow. She didn't wait for him to open it either. He had to quicken his steps to catch up with her on the boardwalk.

Molly looked one way up Main Street and down the other. "As you can see, Killdeer is laid out in a nice square. No winding roads for our town planners." She turned right and started walking. "Killdeer was nothing but a trading post for many years. The wagon trains that followed the Oregon Trail went south of here thirty years ago, but folks who wanted to head northwest into Idaho Territory could take this cutoff. Some chose to settle in these valleys. And now the railroad plans to bring a spur through this way too. Father says it will take a good five years for the entire length of it to be completed, but it will happen. And when it reaches us, Killdeer will grow. It's doubtful our town will ever become a real city, but we will be large enough to prosper."

Jack enjoyed watching her as she spoke. Her love for this place was obvious in her expression as well as in the tone of her voice.

"The nation's first national park, as I'm sure you know, is to the north. Not quite two hundred miles from us. Some Yellowstone visitors come through Killdeer on their way to see Old Faithful. And there is Bear Lake over the mountains to the west of here."

All very interesting, but Jack wanted to know more about

Molly and her family. "And what brought the Evertons to Killdeer?"

She stopped walking and looked at him, eyes narrowing, as if trying to decide whether to answer his question. She must have decided in his favor.

"Our lives were very different after the war." She gave a slight shrug. "The town we lived in was hit hard. So many young men of our acquaintance died, my cousin among them."

"I lost two brothers in battle."

She was silent for a moment, then said, "I'm sorry, Mr. Ludgrove. I know the pain of loss."

He acknowledged her words with a nod.

"Then you understand why it became so difficult for us to stay where we were. Father wanted to move away from the heartache. He longed for a fresh start where we wouldn't have reminders of the war, so he looked for a town out west in need of a newspaper, and this is where we came."

Jack wondered if Molly had also lost a young man in the war, someone she might have married if he hadn't died. If Jack had guessed her age right, she would have been around sixteen or seventeen at the start of the Civil War. But he couldn't ask what he wondered, so instead he cleared his throat and asked her to tell him about the businesses that lined Main Street.

As she answered, they walked again, the pace leisurely. When they met someone on the street—man or woman—Molly and Jack stopped and she introduced him. She always added something kind about the other person in her introduction. Mrs. Perkins made the best pies. Mr. Ingram was an expert watchmaker.

Jack wondered what townsfolk would say to him about Molly Everton if given the chance. And what was wrong with the men of Killdeer, Wyoming, that one of them hadn't snagged her for his bride in the decade she'd lived here? Weren't women in short supply out west? That was what he'd heard.

Eventually, their circuitous route about town brought them to the livery.

"Do you know anything about horses, Miss Everton?" Jack asked, not waiting for an answer before he said, "Would you mind looking at some with me?"

"If you like."

They moved into the cooler interior of the barn.

"Mr. Whitaker?" Jack called.

"Be right with you," came a reply from the darker recesses. The blacksmith was true to his word. He appeared less than a minute later, wiping hands on his leather apron. "Ah, Mr. Ludgrove. You came." He grinned at Molly. "Howdy, Miss Everton. You must be showing your new boss about town. Is that it?"

Despite the distance between them, Jack felt Molly stiffen.

"Saw you together at church yesterday." George Whitaker's grin broadened.

Jack hadn't known Molly more than a few days, but he knew the blacksmith's comment would not sit well with her.

Almost too softly for Jack to hear, she whispered, "His wit's as thick as Tewksbury mustard."

What was she talking about? He wanted to ask her to repeat it, but he was convinced her words had been meant for herself alone.

George Whitaker said, "I reckon you want to see the horses I got for sale. Follow me. They're out back."

Jack waited until Molly started forward, then he brought up the rear. When she stepped outside again, the light formed a kind of halo around her.

Halo? Why was that the first word to come to his mind? Miss Everton didn't strike him as the angelic type. Pleasant. Attractive. But definitely not angelic. He cleared his throat, as if doing so would clear his thoughts as well. Then he quickened his stride, hurrying to catch up with the blacksmith.

He was here to buy a horse, after all. Not gaze at his employer's daughter.

CHAPTER FIVE

THE FIRST EDITION OF THE *KILLDEER SENTINEL* WITH JACK Ludgrove as its managing editor came out that Friday. The *Sentinel* wasn't a large paper—just one sheet folded in half to make four printed pages. While almost half of the space was taken up with advertising, there was a good deal of local, national, and world news included.

Molly Everton's column, "Killdeer Corner," was on the second page.

Jack had been pleasantly surprised when he read her article for the first time. Her prose wasn't florid or vapid as was true of some female writers. And the column wasn't a place for gossip or the sharing of banal personal thoughts, as he'd feared it might be. It was solid and interesting. Almost good enough to be a front-page news item.

Molly knew the who, what, when, where, and why of modern-day news gathering. She had her supporting information, key quotes, and background information. Jack was so impressed that he decided the next time he attended a theater, he would make certain he got a seat close to an exit.

Roland Everton appeared in the doorway to Jack's office. "Time to call it a day. We close early on Fridays."

"I guess you told me that. I forgot." He folded the newspaper and placed it on his desk. As he rose from his chair, he said, "You won't have to remind me again."

"Mrs. Everton wondered if you might come for Sunday dinner."

"That's very kind. But I was a guest only a week ago." He rounded his desk, heading toward the door. "Wouldn't want to wear out my welcome."

Roland clapped him on the shoulder. "Nonsense. We wouldn't have asked if we didn't want you."

"Well then. I suppose it would be rude to refuse."

"That it would. Besides, you won't be the only guest. My wife likes to have folks over regular for Sunday dinner."

The two men left the building through the back door, Roland locking it behind them. Jack waited until his employer was in his buggy, then he waved and started toward the boardinghouse. But after only a few steps, he stopped and turned in a different direction. Toward the livery where he boarded the horse he'd purchased from the blacksmith the previous Monday.

George Whitaker was busy at the forge and no one else was around, so Jack was able to saddle and bridle the black gelding without interruption. When he was done, he removed his suit coat and draped it over the stall door. After rolling up his shirtsleeves, he stepped into the saddle and rode out of the barn.

He followed the road north, first at a slow trot, then a canter. The horse had an easy gait and Jack felt free to look around, noting the passing countryside. There were a number of smaller farms closer to town. Eventually it became more difficult to tell how much land belonged to one owner. There were fewer crops and more cattle. Occasionally a house was easy to see from the road. Other houses, he supposed, were far from the main road or hidden by trees and rolling landscape. And some of the land had to be open range, belonging to no one.

The afternoon was hot and Jack took pity on his horse, reining him to a walk. To the east he saw evidence of a water source—a copse of trees peeking up from a gully. He turned the gelding in that direction. When they came over the rise, they were greeted with the sight of a creek, the water as clear as glass. Horse and rider went down the incline and into the welcome shade of the poplars growing along the banks of the stream. After getting a drink, Jack splashed some cool water onto his face and the back of his neck, then he stood back and breathed deeply.

Pleasure washed over him. A sense of rightness. He belonged here. He felt it in his bones. He'd waited several years to see his dreams of the West realized, and he was grateful not to have been disappointed by reality.

Molly Everton's voice played in his memory: *"Then I don't suppose you plan to stay long in Killdeer."*

He chuckled. Something he hadn't been able to do the night she'd said those words to him. Maybe, when it was time for him to move on, he would tell her father she should be named editor. From what he'd observed thus far, she was qualified, and it hadn't been difficult for him to come to understand she wanted that title.

But he wouldn't be leaving anytime soon. Molly Everton would have to wait for her heart's desire, just as he'd had to wait.

Molly added some canned peaches to her shopping basket, the last of the items on her mother's list. She turned from the shelves on the wall at the same moment the bell above the mercantile door announced the arrival of more customers. She glanced to see who it was.

Jane and Ada Shoemaker. They smiled and giggled, then hurried toward Molly.

Jane said, "Good afternoon, Miss Everton."

"Jane. Ada." She could not bring herself to call them by their surnames. She'd looked after them more than once when she was in her midtwenties and they were little girls in braids. In her mind, they were little girls still.

"We were so excited to read the newspaper when Papa was finished with it this morning. Weren't we, Ada? Mr. Ludgrove's editorial was wonderful."

Wonderful? All Jack Ludgrove had done was introduce himself to the community and to the subscribers of the newspaper. Nothing wonderful about it. Informative and competent at most.

Ada said, "I didn't expect him to be so handsome. You'd never guess he's as old as he is."

Old? They must think the same of Molly.

"Mother says he would do quite nicely as a husband for one of us," Jane preened. "I wouldn't object."

Molly felt a desperate need to escape. She gestured with her basket. "I really must pay for these and return home. Please excuse me."

The sisters didn't take the hint. They followed her to the counter where the proprietor, Ethan Cook, waited near the cash register.

"What is it like to work with him, Miss Everton?" Ada asked.

Molly felt her jaw tighten. "The same as with any editor." She sent a pointed look in Mr. Cook's direction.

"Is this everything?" he asked.

She nodded. *And please hurry!*

Jane leaned in close to Molly. "He'll come to the barn dance, won't he?"

"I haven't any idea. Maybe no one has told him about it."

"Then we'll tell him. Won't we, Ada? Let's go to the *Sentinel* right now." The sisters turned in unison and hurried away.

Molly let them go, though she could have saved them the effort. The newspaper office would be closed by now.

Intruding on her thoughts, Mr. Cook gave her the total for her grocery purchases. She paid him, then bid him a good day and started for home. She didn't hurry. Nothing in the basket was required for supper. Besides, it was too hot. She kept to the shade as much as possible, but as she left the heart of Killdeer, there was an absence of trees and buildings. It wasn't long before trickles of sweat were meandering down her spine. Her forehead grew damp as well, although her straw bonnet protected her face from the sun.

She was thinking about a cool glass of lemonade when she glanced up and saw Jack Ludgrove riding toward her. He waved and she came to a standstill. Not that she wanted to speak to him. Her feet seemed to stop of their own accord.

"Good day, Miss Everton," he said as he reined in his horse.

"Good day."

"I wanted to tell you again what a fine column that was on theater fire safety."

"Thank you," Molly replied, though she tried not to let him see how much his words pleased her.

"I didn't see you in the office this morning."

"Didn't Father tell you? I don't come to the paper on Friday mornings."

"Hmm. Maybe he did tell me." Unexpectedly, he dismounted. "Allow me to carry that basket for you, Miss Everton."

"It's not necessary. It isn't all that heavy, and I haven't far to go now."

He smiled as he took hold of the handle. "Perhaps not, but we wouldn't want you to get overheated. The sun is quite relentless today."

Molly tightened her grip for a few moments, then let go. He was right. It was hot. Too hot to argue with him. Easier to let go and get home as soon as possible.

Carrying the basket in his left hand and leading the horse with his right, Jack fell into step beside her, matching his stride to hers. His nearness made Molly uncomfortable. Perhaps that was why she said the first thing that popped into her head.

"Are you planning to go to the barn dance at the Holbrook farm?"

"Barn dance?" His brows drew together in a thoughtful frown. "Oh, yes. I read something about it in an earlier edition of the paper. Next week, isn't it? I guess I hadn't thought about it. I suppose most folks from around here will be there."

"Most, yes."

"Then I really ought to go too." The slightest of smiles curved the corners of his mouth as he looked at her. "You'll be there, of course. Wouldn't want to go and not get to dance with you, Miss Everton."

A strange sensation coiled in her belly. "I'll be there," she answered softly. Then she quickened her pace, afraid the heat was affecting her ability to make sense of things.

Again, Jack adjusted his pace to hers, but he didn't try to continue the conversation. He seemed satisfied with the silence. When they reached the front gate to the Everton home, he opened it before her, then offered her the shopping basket.

She took it with a "Thank you, Mr. Ludgrove."

"Delighted, Miss Everton." He tipped his hat. "I look forward to Sunday."

Sunday. She'd forgotten. Her mother had invited Jack Ludgrove to Sunday dinner. And Jack must have accepted.

After a quick nod, she walked up the stone walk to the front porch, trying not to appear as if she was fleeing his presence—although she feared that might be exactly what she was doing.

CHAPTER SIX

ALTHOUGH BERTHA SIMPSON'S MEALS AT THE BOARDING-house were more than adequate, Jack decided to eat breakfast the next morning at Florence's Restaurant. It made sense, as editor of the paper, for him to become better acquainted with the business owners in Killdeer. They would be his advertisers from here on out. Without them, the paper would fail.

He'd heard several times from different sources that Florence Perkins made the best pies west of the Mississippi, but he would have to discover the truth of it for himself another time. Pie was not on the breakfast menu. When the waitress came, he ordered coffee, bacon, and a stack of flap-jacks. Then he leaned back in his chair and looked around the room. Two men sat at the table nearest the window. A young woman and school-age boy sat near the far wall.

The front door opened and a man about Jack's age entered the restaurant. A man he hadn't met over the course of the past week. His suit proclaimed him a businessman. The wire-rimmed glasses perched on his nose made him look studious. Doctor? Teacher? Lawyer? Most likely one of those professions.

The man in question saw Jack looking at him. He removed his hat and approached Jack's table. "You must be Mr. Ludgrove, the new editor of the paper." He offered his hand. "I'm Stedman Jones. Attorney-at-law."

Ah, a lawyer, as suspected. "How do you do?" Jack shook the proffered hand.

"I was out of town on business when you arrived. Just got back on yesterday's stage. Would you mind if I joined you?"

Jack motioned to the other chair at his table. "Not at all. Please."

"Thank you. Most kind of you." Stedman hung his hat on a spindle on the back of the chair, then sat. "How have you found our fair town? Must be quite different from Des Moines."

"I like it here. People are friendly. And the mountains are spectacular."

Stedman leaned forward and lowered his voice a little. "And how are you getting along with Miss Everton?" One corner of his mouth curved upward. He looked pleased with himself.

The question and smirk irritated Jack.

"I ask because Molly Everton isn't one to keep her opinions to herself. Don't suppose that makes it easy to be her boss."

"I like people who speak their minds. Men or women."

Stedman chuckled as he leaned back. "Then you should

get along with Miss Everton quite well." His gaze shifted to the waitress who was walking to the table with Jack's cup of coffee.

The conversation paused while the lawyer gave his breakfast order to the waitress. The lull allowed Jack to wonder about the annoyance he'd felt when Stedman Jones asked about Molly, even before he'd made the comment about her opinions.

"And hurry with that coffee, please," Stedman said as the waitress walked away. Then he looked at Jack again. "Have you eaten here before?"

"Today's my first time."

"You're staying at the boardinghouse, I heard."

"Yes."

"Well, you won't starve to death. I know. I lived there myself when I first came to Killdeer. Mrs. Simpson serves generous portions at every meal. But Mrs. Perkins is by far the better cook. Eat at this restaurant when you can." Stedman grinned. "'Course, now that I'm married, I don't come often."

So why are you here now? Trouble with the wife?

The lawyer chuckled, as if Jack had asked his questions aloud. "The missus and I were in Denver. I had business with other attorneys, and my wife and I were staying with family. Violet—that's my wife's name—stayed on with her parents for a few more weeks. We'll have you over for supper when she gets back."

"Very kind of you, Mr. Jones."

"Not at all. I remember what it was like to be new in town, without any friends or family."

Jack wondered how much work a lawyer could find in a small town like Killdeer, but he decided not to ask.

The waitress arrived with a tray and set a plate of food before each of them. After she left, Jack closed his eyes and said a silent blessing. When he opened his eyes again, Stedman was about to take his first bite of scrambled eggs. Silence ruled the table for a short while. But Stedman Jones—Jack had already learned—was not someone who let conversation die for long.

"Roland runs an excellent paper. Lots of news to help his readers stay informed." Stedman took a sip of coffee. "Good man. I respect him a lot."

Jack nodded.

"I called on his daughter for a while a few years back."

"Molly?"

Stedman grinned again. "Only daughter he's got."

Jack wondered what had happened to the courtship.

"I quickly learned she and I weren't destined for each other." He shook his head. "Not at all. I'm now convinced higher education isn't a good thing for women. It fills their heads with too many ideas. Ideas that make them forget their proper place."

Jack's annoyance returned. He was beginning to dislike this friendly, too talkative lawyer.

"You know what I mean?" the other man added.

"Yes, I know what you mean." *And I think you're dead wrong.*

Jack hurried to finish his breakfast, wanting to be on his

way. After the last bite, he bid Stedman Jones good-bye, paid for his breakfast, and left the restaurant. Out on the boardwalk, he paused a moment and drew in a deep breath. The flapjacks felt like lead in his belly, but not because there'd been anything wrong with them. No, it was the company who had turned his stomach sour.

Jack and Stedman were not destined to become the best of friends.

Molly held the timepiece in the palm of her left hand. "It's exactly what I wanted, Mr. Ingram. Thank you." She glanced up at the watchmaker. "You will keep it a secret. I want Father to be surprised on his birthday."

"Won't breathe a word of it, Miss Everton."

The shop door opened behind Molly, but she didn't turn around. Her gaze had returned to the pocket watch in her hand. The front of the gold watch was engraved with a locomotive. On the inside, the white dial had large black Roman numerals, and the time was marked by black minute and second hands. It would be easy for her father to read, perhaps even without his spectacles.

"Good morning, Miss Everton."

Her heart jumped at the sound of Jack speaking her name. She closed her hand around the watch as she turned to look at him. "Mr. Ludgrove."

"An unexpected pleasure."

Heavens! Was she blushing? Her cheeks felt unusually

warm as she turned back to William Ingram. "If you'll put it in a box, I'll take it with me."

"Of course." The watchmaker took the pocket watch from her and went into the back room.

"For your father?" Jack asked.

He'd seen the watch. He couldn't help but see it, she supposed. "Yes. For his birthday. Please don't say anything to him. I want him to be surprised."

"Your secret is safe with me, Miss Everton." He smiled.

Something about that smile made the moment feel special, intimate. Not wise. Not what she wanted. He wasn't her friend. He was her boss. A boss she hoped would leave Killdeer, sooner rather than later. She needed to make him want to go.

"I had breakfast this morning at the restaurant. On my way out, I remembered what you said about Mr. Ingram." Jack pulled a watch from his pocket. "Mine's been losing time. A little each day. Thought I'd see if Mr. Ingram could repair it."

"I'm sure he can."

"I met Mr. Jones at breakfast. Rather loquacious, isn't he?"

Molly felt the expression freeze on her face. Stedman Jones. One of her failures. The most recent and the last. When their brief courtship had ended, she'd sworn never to go through such an experience again.

But Jack was right. Stedman was loquacious. A less polite term would be *gossip*. Stedman kept quiet about his clients and their legal concerns, but he was plenty free with words about anything or anyone else. Undoubtedly he had said something to Jack about her. Something less than complimentary.

And Molly hated being gossiped about more than anything. Thinking about it made her eyes smart.

"Here you are, Miss Everton." Mr. Ingram returned to the counter and handed her the small box.

She opened her reticule and withdrew the money to pay for the watch.

"Miss Everton?" Jack said.

She looked at him.

"May I ask, when is your father's birthday?"

"Tomorrow."

"Ah. Then it is fortuitous that I ran into you. I wouldn't want to be the only one to come without a gift."

Gracious! She'd forgotten again. He was coming to Sunday dinner. And Father, who'd issued Mother's invitation, hadn't told Jack that they would be celebrating his birthday. Father would have left out that part on purpose, no doubt.

"You needn't feel obliged to bring a gift. Father wouldn't want you to."

"I know. But I'd like to bring something all the same."

It wasn't fair. She wanted to dislike Jack Ludgrove. She wanted to dislike him a lot. But he was so naturally likable.

It simply wasn't fair.

CHAPTER SEVEN

JACK WOULD HAVE BEEN THE ONLY DINNER GUEST ON Sunday who came without a gift for the host. He thanked God he'd learned of the occasion in time to bring something. Roland Everton seemed extremely pleased with the book Jack gave him—a history of the Roman Empire.

Molly, who was seated on Jack's left, leaned close and whispered, "How did you know?"

"Know what?"

"Father's interest in the Roman Empire. Did he tell you?"

Jack turned to look at her. "No. I bought the book before coming to Wyoming."

She drew back from him, chin held high.

"It's still new. Haven't had time to read or leaf through it even. I just thought it would make a nice gift, and since I only found out yesterday about your father's birthday, I—"

"You're interested in the same thing Father is?" Her

gaze and voice were filled with skepticism. "About the Roman Empire?"

"Among other things, yes. History has been a passion of mine since I was a boy. Any history, really, but I have a special fascination for ancient Rome and Egypt."

"Hmm."

Perhaps he should have been insulted by her disbelief. It was almost the same as calling him a liar. But he wasn't insulted. He was amused. Molly Everton had that affect on him more often than not.

Her eyes narrowed. Her mouth thinned. Then a slow smile curved her lips. "Tell me, Mr. Ludgrove. According to Gaius Suetonius Tranquillus, who were the twelve Caesars?" She might as well have slapped him with a glove and challenged him to a duel. Subtle she was not.

Jack couldn't help it. He laughed aloud.

Everyone at the table turned to look at him. Or rather, at the two of them.

"Does that mean you cannot name the twelve Caesars?" Molly asked, triumph in her voice.

Still grinning, he answered, "It does not. I suppose you want them in order. The first, of course, was Julius Caesar. The rest were the eleven emperors who followed after him." He touched the index finger of his left hand and began to count them off. "Augustus, Tiberius, Caligula. Next came Claudius and Nero. Then Galba and . . . and . . . oh yes, Otho. Then Vitellius, Vespasian, Titus, and finally Domitian. I believe I got them all right."

From the head of the table, Roland said, "You did, indeed, Mr. Ludgrove. Well done." Then he applauded and the others followed suit.

Everyone except Molly.

Jack considered asking if she could name all the female rulers of the British Empire from the time of the Norman conquest, but he decided to do so would be less than gracious. It would be tweaking her nose for sport, and he didn't want to be unkind. He liked Molly Everton, perhaps more than he should.

Ruth Everton must have sensed they were wading in dangerous waters, for she chose that moment to rise from her chair at the end of the table. "Please, everyone. Let's go into the front parlor. Reverend Lynch, did you bring your violin?"

"Yes, I did."

"Then you and Molly can play for us." Ruth looked at Jack. "Molly is an accomplished pianist."

"Indeed? I look forward to listening." Jack stood and stepped behind Molly's chair to pull it out from the table. Though he couldn't see her face, the back of her neck told him she was blushing.

After she rose, she faced him and in a low voice said, "Mother exaggerates. It's something she does whenever—" She broke off abruptly, then hurried out of the dining room.

Whenever what? Jack would have paid good money for the answer.

He moved with the rest of the party into the parlor. While others found places to sit, Jack chose to stand to one side of the doorway, leaning a shoulder against the wall. A good place from which to observe the assemblage—especially Molly.

The lilac-colored gown she wore was pretty and looked to be of the latest fashion, although he wasn't the sort of man who kept up with such things. He was used to seeing her in simpler attire—a dark skirt and a tailored white blouse. Sometimes she added a vest. No one had to tell him Molly was more comfortable in her usual day wear.

She sat on the piano bench, waiting while the reverend readied his violin. Then, after a brief exchange of words too soft for Jack to hear from where he stood, they began to play.

As with women's dresses, Jack was no expert on music, but he'd heard Tchaikovsky's Piano Concerto No. 1 performed in concert in Chicago last year and recognized it. While it wasn't as impressive with only a piano and a single violin, not to mention a room without the proper acoustics, compared to a full orchestra and a concert hall, there was a beauty in the music—and in Molly's playing—that caused Jack to stand straight and let it sweep over his soul.

Her mother hadn't exaggerated. Not in the least.

He was . . . enchanted.

When the last note drifted through the parlor, the small party of guests applauded, and the abrupt sound broke the spell that had held Jack captive throughout the concerto. He cleared his throat and looked around, hoping no one watched him. No one did. Their eyes were all on Molly at the piano and Reverend Lynch with his violin.

Jack followed their gazes. Molly chanced to look toward

him a heartbeat later. He smiled at her. She didn't return the smile. If he didn't know better, he'd have said she looked frightened. *Frightened? Of him?* That seemed unlikely. She was the bravest woman he'd ever met.

She lowered her gaze to the piano keys.

"Please, my dear," her father said, "play another one."

Although he didn't give into it, Jack felt a sudden need to leave, to put some distance between himself and whatever melody Molly might play next.

Maybe he was the one who needed to be afraid.

CHAPTER EIGHT

MOLLY STARED AT HER REFLECTION IN THE MIRROR.

I'm failing. I'm not trying hard enough.

Where was her resolve to make Jack Ludgrove as miserable as possible? To make him want to leave Killdeer and go have his western adventures elsewhere? Oh, she'd made some half-baked attempts, but he'd seemed to enjoy those efforts, not be offended by them.

She closed her eyes, remembering that moment yesterday when their gazes met and he'd smiled at her. It had frightened her, that smile. In that moment, she'd understood this man could break her heart.

Molly had been courted by several nice men after her family moved to Wyoming. Each time she'd hoped to fall in love—but she hadn't. And when the courtships fizzled, she hadn't been as disappointed as she thought she should have been.

But Jack Ludgrove . . . He was different.

She shook her head slowly, then looked into the mirror again.

"It's not as if he's come courting," she whispered. "He's your editor. He's your boss. You don't even like him."

She could taste the lie of those final words on her tongue. Maybe she didn't *want* to like him. Maybe she was trying her best *not* to like him. But her best wasn't good enough. Not this time.

"How could I let myself like him? He came west for adventure, not for love. And he took my job in the bargain."

Her reflection didn't answer her. With a sigh, she left her bedroom and went downstairs.

"Molly," her mother called from the dining room, "I thought you were never coming down. Come and eat your breakfast."

She wasn't hungry, but she obeyed.

"Where's Father?" she asked as she filled her plate from the dishes on the sideboard.

"He already left for the office."

"Am I that late?"

"No, dear. He was up early. But he took that book Mr. Ludgrove gave him for his birthday, so I doubt he'll get much work done today. Mark my words. He'll be reading it still when you get there."

Molly made a soft sound to let her mother know she listened.

"Amazing, that young man and your father both have such a passion for ancient history. I never understood the interest myself. But it is nice that Roland will have someone with whom he can talk about it to his heart's content."

"Mmm." Molly sat at the table and put the cloth napkin in her lap.

"Do you fancy him, Molly?"

Her first bite of scrambled egg got stuck halfway down her throat. She had to swallow several times to get it moving again.

"Because you seem different somehow." Her mother studied her. "Not quite sure what it is."

"I don't fancy Jack Ludgrove, Mother. He's a nice enough man, I suppose, but he won't settle long in Killdeer."

"How do you know?"

"He said so himself. He wants to explore the West. He is looking for an adventure. Not a lot of that to be found in our little town."

"I don't know about that, my darling daughter. Love can be quite an adventure."

Molly could tell that her mother thought of her father as she spoke. There was a certain look in her eyes, a certain smile on her lips, and it warmed Molly's heart. It also made her wish for something she didn't believe she could have.

After a few more quick bites, she patted her mouth with her napkin and rose from the chair. "I must get to the office. I have a column to write."

"What is it to be this week?"

"President Hayes's veto of the Chinese immigration bill

and what it means to California and other states and territories on the Pacific coast. And the unfair wages paid to the Chinese immigrants, especially by the railroads."

"Oh dear."

She stepped toward her mother, leaned down, and kissed her on the forehead. "I love you." Then she hurried out of the dining room.

Outside, it was another beautiful August morning, the temperature quite pleasant. Molly walked briskly toward town, trying to focus her thoughts on the column she intended to write. But instead she recalled her mother's question: *"Do you fancy him?"*

Molly might have given up on men and marriage, but her mother had not.

"Love can be quite an adventure."

Her heart fluttered, and a strange light-headedness caused her to stop and draw a few deep breaths to steady herself. Then she continued on but at a more sedate pace. The odd feeling was still with her when she entered through the *Sentinel*'s front door a short while later. As she passed the doors to their individual offices, her father and Jack looked up and greeted her. She nodded to acknowledge them, then went into her own small office and closed the door.

She sank onto the chair and only then realized how weak her legs felt. Was she ill? Did she need to see the doctor?

No. Of course not. She was rarely ill. Whatever the cause, it would go away if she ignored it. She would write her column and by the time it was finished, she would be herself again.

Jack leaned back in his desk chair and rubbed his eyelids with the pads of his fingers. He hadn't slept well last night and his body was bone tired. When he opened his eyes again, he looked toward Molly's office. The door remained closed, two hours since she'd come in. He wondered how her new column was progressing.

Wondering about Molly was the main reason he was so tired. It had kept him up most of the night.

Maybe he needed another horseback ride. A longer excursion next time. He'd like to take a trip up to Yellowstone, but he would need more than a week for such a journey. He couldn't very well ask Roland Everton for time off when he was still new to the job. Exploring the national park would have to wait until next summer.

He drew a deep breath as he rose from his chair. Then he walked from his office into the back room. Hank was at his desk, setting type for the upcoming issue of the paper. Most reporters and editors started out doing this job, but few had real talent for it. Not like Hank Morrison. The best typesetters could reach into the many drawers of typecase, withdrawing letters of the right size with surprising speed, as Hank was doing now. And as this was a Monday, Hank would be setting advertisements—the lifeblood of newspapers, large and small.

Jack considered walking closer to observe the typesetter's work but decided against it. Hank Morrison wasn't one for idle chatter, nor did he need supervision. Best to leave him be. Instead, Jack returned to the front office and went outside onto the boardwalk. The day was warm and growing sultry, dark clouds approaching from the west. Rain was on its way. The wind had picked up and dust twirled down Main Street. Businessmen, cowboys, and womenfolk held on to their hats as they made their way to chosen destinations. It surprised Jack when he realized he could have greeted many of them by name. Almost as if he'd always been a citizen of Killdeer.

Molly's voice taunted him from his memory: *"Then I don't suppose you plan to stay long in Killdeer."*

No, he didn't plan to stay long, and feeling at home in Killdeer wasn't going to change that.

"Good morning, Mr. Ludgrove."

He looked to his right to see the Shoemaker sisters standing on the boardwalk. He nodded in their direction. "Good morning."

"Looks like we're going to get some rain," Ada said.

"Perhaps it will cool things off," Jane added. "It would be nice if the weather was cooler for the barn dance on Saturday."

"You are coming to the dance, aren't you?" Ada asked.

They were pretty girls, both of them, but young. Easily half his age. And he didn't have to talk to them more than a time or two to know they had little in their heads besides finding themselves husbands. He could have told them they were wasting their time flirting with him. He wasn't looking for a wife. Especially not a silly one. And besides, he liked intelligent women who weren't afraid to show it.

Like Molly.

"Mr. Ludgrove?"

He gave his head a shake to rid it of that last thought, then nodded. "Yes, I will be there."

The sisters looked at each other and giggled.

The sound annoyed him. "Please excuse me, ladies. I had best get back to work." He offered a slight bow, then turned on his heel and went inside the *Sentinel.*

Molly's office door was open. He walked toward it. She wasn't there.

"Jack," Roland said.

He turned toward his employer's office.

"Molly went out back for a bit of fresh air."

Jack nodded, knowing he should return to his desk even as his feet carried him toward the rear of the building. When he opened the door, he saw Molly pacing back and forth, hands clasped behind her back, eyes locked on the ground a few steps before her. For a writer, it was the look of someone not pleased with what she'd written.

He moved toward her, unnoticed until he announced his presence by clearing his throat.

She stopped and looked up, her surprise evident.

"Not going well?" he asked, thinking Molly Everton had the most beautiful eyes he'd ever seen.

Those selfsame eyes widened, as if she'd heard his thoughts.

He resisted the urge to clear his throat again. "I could look at it if you like."

"It isn't ready to be seen by anyone but me. Not yet."

"Are you sure? Sometimes it helps to mull it over with someone else."

"I'm sure."

He shrugged. "Suit yourself."

Molly stood a little straighter, head held high. "Have you ever written a weekly column, Mr. Ludgrove?"

"Your father has started calling me Jack. Do you suppose you might do the same?"

"A weekly column, Mr. Ludgrove. Have you ever written one?"

She was a little like tinder. Just waiting for a spark to set her aflame.

He answered, "I did. The year after I came back from the war."

"You were a soldier too?" There was a softening in her expression. Her right hand rose to press against her collarbone, a gesture of empathy. "Like your brothers who died?"

He nodded.

"You didn't mention that before."

"Not something I care to talk about." He drew a deep breath. "Long time ago now. Better forgotten."

"Can it be forgotten for those who lived through it?"

A fierce need swept over him. A desire to take Molly in his arms and hold her close. He looked away, staring off into the distance in an effort to distract himself.

Softly, she said, "Give sorrow words: the grief that does not speak / Whispers the o'er-fraught heart and bids it break."

Shakespeare. She was quoting Shakespeare. He'd heard

her do it before on several occasions but he hadn't been sure of what she was saying. Now he was sure. Shakespeare. And he had the distinct impression it was a habit she was scarcely aware of. For some reason, it made him want to hold her all the more. Only with tenderness.

"Mr. Ludgrove, perhaps it would be helpful to have you read what I have written after all."

Good. Back to the newspaper business. To columns and writing. A much safer place to focus his thoughts.

"I'll bring it to your office," she added before walking toward the back door of the *Sentinel.*

CHAPTER NINE

KENDALL DOBSON STORMED INTO THE *SENTINEL* OFFICES late on Friday morning, his face red as a beet. When he saw Molly coming through the doorway from the back room, he glared at her, then shouted for her father. "Mr. Everton. I'd like a word with you!"

Molly came to a standstill.

Kendall Dobson. He owned the largest cattle operation in the southwest corner of Wyoming Territory. He'd come courting Molly less than a year after his wife died in childbirth. But Molly had known quite soon that the two of them wouldn't suit, and she had told him so. As kindly as possible but leaving no doubt that he couldn't change her mind. Besides, he'd needed a nursemaid for his infant son, not a wife for himself. He'd wanted someone to do his bidding without question. That definitely wasn't Molly.

Leaning heavily on his cane, her father came out of his office. "Mr. Dobson. What is the matter?"

"This!" Kendall slammed a folded newspaper onto the front counter. "What on earth were you thinking, printing this claptrap? How do you think it makes me look?" He glanced toward Molly again and pointed at her. "She needs to be fired."

Jack was out of his office by this time and went to stand near her father. "Excuse me, sir. I am Jack Ludgrove, the managing editor of the newspaper. I decide what goes into each edition. Perhaps you would like to come into my office so we can discuss your concerns."

"I would not like to go into your office. I can stand right here and tell you. I serve on the board of directors of the railroad that's bringing a line through Killdeer and on up into Idaho Territory." He jabbed a finger at the paper. "Have you no idea of the sentiment toward Chinese immigrants these days?"

"I am aware of it, Mr. . . . ?"

"Dobson. Kendall Dobson."

"Mr. Dobson, I am aware of the opposition. Especially in California. But the president vetoed the bill restricting immigration as it violated the Burlingame Treaty of 1868 between the United States and China."

Kendall sputtered something. Words Molly couldn't make out.

"Sir," Jack continued, "does Miss Everton's column claim as fact anything that is not fact?"

Kendall's irritation was evident even as he answered, "No."

"Then I'm afraid I don't see anything that can be done about it."

"We don't need her making the Orientals who work for

the railroad want more than they get. That's what it'll do. You should fire her for stirring up that kind of trouble."

"That isn't going to happen, Mr. Dobson. Miss Everton did her job, and she did it quite well, I might add."

Kendall swore at Jack.

"This conversation," Jack said, his tone icy, "is at an end. Good day, Mr. Dobson."

With another curse, Kendall swept the newspaper off the counter and marched out of the building, slamming the door behind him.

From behind Molly, Hank Morrison said, "What a windbag. Good for Jack for putting Dobson in his place."

Only then did Molly realize tears had welled in her eyes and her throat had grown too tight to swallow.

The typesetter patted her shoulder. "Don't let it bother you, Molly girl. Nobody cares what he thinks."

She nodded, then made a beeline to her office and closed herself in. After sitting in the chair, she folded her arms on the desk and hid her face against them.

How humiliating. That Jack Ludgrove, her new boss, should have to defend her to a former suitor. *Please don't let Jack know that's what Mr. Dobson is. Let him just think Kendall is an angry customer.*

There was a light rap on her door. She straightened and wiped at her eyes before answering, "Yes?"

The door opened and Jack looked in. "I hope he didn't upset you."

She shook her head. A bald-faced lie.

"It's a good column, Molly. You have nothing to apologize for. Not to anyone."

"Mother thinks I should use the column to share household hints. Maybe she's right. Who could get angry over a recipe for apple cobbler?"

Jack grinned. "I don't believe I would like reading those as much as what you've written in the past. I would miss the passion you feel for your stories."

Mortification drained away, replaced by a pleasant feeling she couldn't identify. Or chose not to.

Every chair at the dining room table in the boardinghouse was occupied that evening. Like Jack, one man and two women were full-time residents of the house. One elderly couple was in town to visit their son, the barber who lived in the back room behind his shop. A room too small to accommodate three adults. Another two men were salesmen, just in town until the next day's stagecoach would take them on to the next place. And finally there was Bertha Simpson, the landlady, and her daughter, Louise Simpson, the schoolteacher.

Dinner began with a minimum of conversation. Mostly what was said was "Thank you" as serving platters and bowls were passed counterclockwise around the table, followed by some idle chitchat that held little interest for Jack. His thoughts soon began to drift.

It was Louise Simpson who pulled him back to the

present. "I hear tell Mr. Dobson didn't take kindly to Miss Everton's column in today's paper."

Jack looked up from his dinner plate and frowned. How had she heard? He couldn't imagine Molly or her father would speak of that morning's display to anyone, and Hank Morrison didn't seem the gossiping sort.

"Apparently he left the newspaper and went straight to the saloon where he told everyone who'd listen that Molly Everton should be fired."

"She isn't going to be fired." Jack set down his fork.

"Of course not," Bertha Simpson replied. "We all know Mr. Dobson's anger had lots more to do with Miss Everton scorning him than about what she wrote in the paper."

Scorning?

Louise nodded. "Mr. Dobson's right full of his own importance, but Miss Everton wasn't impressed when he came calling after his wife died. He's resented her ever since. Mostly 'cause he told folks he meant to marry Molly Everton, and it embarrassed him when she didn't want him. 'Course, he married the next gal he courted fast enough to make your head spin, so it wasn't like he loved Molly. He went down to Green River City to find someone. Nobody here was good enough for him, I reckon. Not after Molly wounded his pride."

Jack remembered wondering, soon after he'd arrived, what was wrong with the men of Killdeer that none of them had married Molly. Now he'd met two men who had thought to do so—and neither one of them, in Jack's opinion, was near good enough for her.

"What about you, Mr. Ludgrove?" Mrs. Simpson asked. "Have you a girl waiting for you back in Iowa?"

"No. There's no one waiting."

"That's a shame. You know, the Bible says it isn't good for a man to be alone." She glanced toward her unmarried daughter and back again, her meaning clear.

He shook his head and picked up his fork, determined to concentrate on the meal. If his landlady was going to try her hand at matchmaking between him and her daughter, she was in for a disappointment.

The conversation veered away from talk of marriage, changing to the next day's barn dance at the Holbrook farm. An annual event for the past six years, it was eagerly anticipated by most folks in the area. Even those who didn't like to dance.

Jack liked to dance, though he'd seldom had opportunity to do so. A week ago he'd told Molly he would want to dance with her. It had been the polite thing to say at the moment. Only now he realized how true it was. He did want to dance with her. The idea of holding Molly Everton in his arms, his right hand on the small of her back as they twirled around the floor, caused an unusual sensation to shiver through his chest.

It troubled him, but he chose not to analyze why.

CHAPTER TEN

"Quit dawdling, Molly," her mother called from the base of the stairs. "We're going to be late."

"I'm coming. Just one minute more."

"Father and I will be in the buggy. If you don't hurry, we shall go without you."

Molly turned one more time before the mirror, hating herself for caring so much about her appearance. Hating it even more because she knew the reason why. Tonight she would dance with Jack Ludgrove.

She groaned as she hurried out of the bedroom, grabbing a shawl as she went.

As promised, her parents were already in the buggy. On her lap, her mother held a basket that contained several fruit pies. Molly lifted her skirt and petticoats and stepped up to the back buggy seat. As soon as she was settled, her father clucked to the horse and they set off to the Holbrook farm, right toward the descending sun.

Up ahead, Molly saw clouds of dust rising from the road. More buggies, wagons, and horses, all on their way to the same destination. The nerves in her stomach intensified. A silly, girlish reaction—and she was no longer a girl. Hadn't been one for many years. She was a woman. An independent woman. And happy to be so.

She stiffened her spine, lifted her chin, and drew in a deep, steadying breath. There. That was better. Foolishness all over. Whatever had come over her today was now set aside.

The new feelings of calm and self-control lasted all of ten minutes. Right up until the moment Jack Ludgrove cantered his horse up to the side of their buggy, then slowed to keep pace with them. When she saw who it was, he bent his hat brim in her direction and smiled. An instant later she was blinded by the light of the setting sun from beyond his left shoulder. A good excuse to shade her eyes and turn away.

When they arrived at the Holbrook farm, her father guided horse and buggy to an open space near a fence. Jack stopped his horse to their left, dismounted, and wrapped the reins around the top rail. Then he stepped to the buggy and offered his hand to Molly's mother to assist her to the ground.

"Thank you, Mr. Ludgrove."

"My pleasure, Mrs. Everton. May I say how very lovely you look this evening?"

"Of course you may. A woman never tires of hearing such things, even when she is old and married."

Jack stepped toward the backseat of the buggy and offered the same assistance to Molly. Drawing another quick breath, she placed her fingers in his open hand. Tingles ran up her arm and straight into her heart.

Merciful heavens!

Lowering his voice, he said, "And may I also say how very lovely you look, Miss Everton?"

She felt her cheeks grow warm. How she despised the ease with which he could make her blush.

Jack offered the crook of his arm. "Allow me to escort you inside."

Good manners gave her no option but to accept. She took hold of him, and they walked slowly toward the barn, her parents following behind.

The light of many lanterns spilled through the wide entrance of the barn. Friends and neighbors milled about, greeting one another, visiting, laughing, while the musicians warmed their instruments. It all created a loud, yet pleasant hubbub.

To the far right of the doorway, tables had been set up, covered with white sheets and tablecloths, and now were laden with refreshments. Molly's mother moved in the direction of the tables with her basket of pies. It was the excuse Molly needed to let go of Jack's arm and walk away from him.

Breathing became easier the more distance she put between herself and Jack Ludgrove. She felt almost normal by the time she reached the tables.

Her mother looked surprised to see her. "You needn't have come with me, dear."

Molly gave a small shrug, then looked at Florence Perkins, standing opposite them. "Good evening, Mrs. Perkins."

"Evenin'." The woman nodded.

"Do you need any help serving?" Molly asked.

"If Mrs. Perkins needs help," her mother interrupted, "then I shall do it. Go join the young folk, Molly. The dancing is about to start."

"But I—"

"Look. Here comes Mr. Ludgrove to ask you to dance. I knew he would."

Like a magnet toward the north pole, Molly was pulled around to see his approach. When their gazes met, he smiled, but there was something reluctant about his expression. Almost as if he came against his will.

He stopped before her. "Is the first dance spoken for, Miss Everton?"

She shook her head.

"Then please allow me."

A refusal formed in her mind, but before she could speak the words, she placed her hand in his for the second time that night. He led her into the center of the barn where other couples, young and not so young, waited for the music to start.

"I was told the first dance would be a waltz," Jack said as he faced her again.

Molly loved the waltz. Both the music and the dance, though she seldom got to do the latter. She was particularly fond of the Strauss waltzes. "The Blue Danube" was her favorite to play on the piano. That was the waltz the musicians—seated in the loft of the barn—began to play.

Her heart skipped a beat as Jack took her hand in his and

placed his other hand on the small of her back while the bard seemed to whisper in her ear, "When you do dance, I wish you / A wave o' the sea, that you might ever do / Nothing but that; move still, still so."

For most of his adult life—after he was free of the army and the chaos of war—Jack Ludgrove had been a man of single-minded purpose. Even during the years he'd been forced by circumstances to stay in Iowa to care for his ailing father, Jack had set goals and worked toward them. No woman had been a part of his plans in the past, and Molly Everton wasn't a part of his plan for the future.

So why did she feel so right in his arms as he turned her around the floor in time to the music? And why was he so reluctant to release her when the waltz ended?

"Thank you, Mr. Ludgrove," she said softly.

The proper thing was to return Molly to the side of the floor and to ask another young woman to dance. He would rather not, but she didn't leave the decision up to him. She turned and walked in the direction of the refreshment tables. Jack hurried to catch up with her.

"Molly, will you allow me another dance?"

"I'm sure there are others who are hoping you will ask them, Mr. Ludgrove."

"Won't you call me Jack?"

She glanced around, answering softly, "Not here, I won't. It isn't proper. And you mustn't call me Molly either."

"All right." He couldn't help the smile that tugged at the corners of his mouth. Since when was Molly afraid to defy convention? She seemed to do it as naturally as she drew breath. "Miss Everton, may I reserve another dance with you? The next waltz?"

She stopped walking.

So did he.

She faced him. "Yes, I will dance the next waltz with you. But for now I'm needed to help Mrs. Perkins serve punch and dessert." And off she went.

His smile widened. There was no point denying it. He liked her. She amused him. She challenged him. She wasn't like any woman he'd ever known before. She was unique, and she made him . . . made him . . . made him what?

"Good evening, Mr. Ludgrove," two female voices said in unison.

Jack didn't need to turn his head to know who he would find nearby—Ada and Jane Shoemaker. They wore bright-colored gingham dresses. Ada's of blue and white. Jane's of red and white. Together they made him think of the nation's flag.

"Are you enjoying the evening?" Ada asked.

"We just arrived," Jane added. "We told Papa we needed to hurry or we would miss the first dance, and we did."

Jack swallowed a groan and did what was expected of him. "Will you allow me the pleasure of the next dance, Miss Shoemaker?" He asked it of Jane, whom he knew to be the older of the two by one year.

Jane giggled before answering, "I'd love to, Mr. Ludgrove."

He turned his gaze to Ada. "And will you hold the one after that for me?"

She giggled too, sounding identical to her sister.

The musicians, seeming to be in league against Jack, stopped playing. The dancers in the center of the barn applauded. Some couples moved toward places to sit. Others went to the tables for punch and something to eat.

Jack offered his hand to Jane, and the pair moved to join the other dancers.

From behind one of the tables, Molly watched as couples formed squares in the center of the barn. The musicians struck a new tune and William Ingram's voice boomed, "Bow to your partner."

Even from where Molly stood, she could hear Jane's laughter. But she didn't feel like laughing in response. Something hurt on the inside. She didn't know why.

"Molly," Mrs. Perkins said, "why aren't you out there enjoying yourself? I can manage here just fine."

"I like to help."

The woman gave her shoulders a little push. "Don't be silly. Nobody's going to ask you to dance when you're standing back here. You go on now. This night's meant for fun."

Short of an argument, Molly had no choice but to move away from the refreshment tables. Her gaze swept the barn, looking for someone she could talk to so she didn't appear so alone—and unwanted—while everyone else appeared to be half of a couple.

The ache intensified. She lowered her gaze and made her way outside where gloaming had turned the world to many shades of gray. She moved away from the doorway and the light, wanting the safety of the shadows. Only when she reached the fence of a corral did she stop. One of the horses came close and thrust its head over the top rail, snorting softly. Molly stroked the animal's muzzle.

What is wrong with me? My thoughts are all jumbled. I don't understand what I feel or why.

Not entirely true.

She closed her eyes and pictured Jack. Pictured his smile. Pictured the two of them swirling in time to the waltz. She might not be able to name her feelings, but Jack Ludgrove most surely was the cause.

"Molly?"

She sucked in a gasp as she spun around.

"Sorry." Jack stood a few feet away from her, the night turning him into a dark shadow. "Didn't mean to scare you."

"I . . . I wasn't scared. Just startled. I thought I was alone."

"I saw you leave the barn and thought I should check on you."

She glanced toward the light that spilled through the doorway. "The dance ended already?"

"No. I had to apologize to Miss Shoemaker for stopping before it was over."

"Jane's feelings must have been hurt."

He took a step closer. "You're right. It was rude of me. I'll need to apologize again. But I wanted to make sure you were all right."

"Why did you think I wouldn't be?"

His voice lowered. "You left so suddenly. When you should be dancing."

"That's what Mrs. Perkins thinks."

"She's right." He raised his hand and cupped the side of her face with it. "Molly Everton, there's something I've been wanting to do all evening."

"What is that, Mr. Ludgrove?" she whispered.

His other hand rose to cup the other side of her face. Then he stepped close and lowered his lips to hers.

Molly had been kissed before—but not like this. Her heart seemed to stop beating. The world seemed to spin faster. The barn and the music and the lights and the sounds of people talking and music playing faded away. There was only Jack. The taste of Jack. The warmth of Jack. But then he pulled back from her, and the night air felt cold as it filled the space he'd put between them.

"I'm not sure I should have done that, Miss Everton," he said, his voice almost gruff. "I think I'd better take you back inside."

And all she could think as they walked together toward the barn was how much she wished he would call her Molly again.

CHAPTER ELEVEN

Jack waited until the entire congregation had left the church, headed for their Sunday dinners, before returning to the sanctuary where Oscar Lynch was gathering his Bible and sermon notes from the lectern.

"Reverend Lynch?"

"Yes?" the reverend said without looking up.

"It's Jack Ludgrove."

Now the other man looked up and smiled. "I remember your name, Mr. Ludgrove. It's only been a week since we dined together at the Everton home."

"Of course." Jack swallowed. "I was wondering if I might talk with you."

Reverend Lynch motioned toward one of the pews. "Have a seat."

"I promise not to keep you long. Your wife must have dinner ready for the family."

"Take as long as you need. Mrs. Lynch doesn't set the table on Sundays until I actually step through the front door."

Jack sat on the wooden pew and raked the fingers of one hand through his hair. "I'm not quite sure where to begin."

"Wherever you feel comfortable. I'm a good listener."

Jack figured Oscar Lynch wasn't many years older than Jack himself, but the reverend had an air of quiet maturity that seemed to add a decade to his true age. After drawing a deep breath, he began telling the other man about his four years in the Union army, the deaths of his brothers, and his father's failing health that kept Jack in Iowa while he longed to be set free to explore the frontier.

"I never resented Father," he added. "I want you to know that. His need was real, and I was the only family he had left. He lingered for more than a decade, finally passing away last year."

"Must have been hard for you, seeing your father suffer."

"It was. There were times he begged God to take him. There were times I prayed the same. Not because I wanted him dead but because I wanted him to be free of the pain. I saw lots of suffering during the war. Saw many young men die or lose limbs and eyes. But none of that prepared me for seeing my father in pain and unable to do for himself. Or for it to last as long as it did."

"Mmm." The reverend nodded, his expression grave.

"We weren't a wealthy family, and there wasn't much money left after I buried my father. I despaired of ever achieving my dream of exploring the West. Then I happened upon the advertisement for an editorial position with the *Killdeer Sentinel*. It seemed like an open door at last. Just the first step in what I hoped would be my great adventure. I thought maybe I could write about it. Like Mark Twain's *Roughing It*."

Oscar Lynch chuckled softly. "Enjoyed that book a great deal."

"Yes." Jack ran his fingers through his hair again, this time using both hands. "But you see, it was never my intention to remain in Killdeer for a long period of time. Perhaps two years."

"I see. Did you tell Mr. Everton that when you accepted the position? Is that what's troubling you?"

"No. I mean, yes. Yes, I did tell him I might not stay beyond two years. That isn't what troubles me."

The reverend cocked an eyebrow. A silent question.

Jack looked down at the scuffed wooden floor. "It's Mr. Everton's daughter who troubles me."

The reverend made a sound that was a combination of cough and croak.

Jack looked up again.

Oscar Lynch rose from the pew, clasped his hands behind his back, and took a few steps away from Jack. After a short while, he turned to face him again, his expression difficult to read.

He'd be good at poker.

"Perhaps you'd care to elaborate, Jack."

That was part of the reason he was here. The difficulty in elaborating. "I . . . I've come to care for Molly. But if I don't intend to stay in Killdeer long, I don't know that I have the right to care for her. What could I offer her?"

"There are many kinds of adventures. Do you believe she has come to care for you too?"

Jack thought of Molly the previous night, the way she'd felt in his arms as they danced, the rightness of his lips upon hers when they'd kissed. She hadn't resisted. She'd welcomed him. So different from when he'd first come to town. "Yes, I think maybe she has."

"Then would it be fair of you to make this decision on your own? It concerns her as well."

Molly had been hurt by men in the past. Jack had met two of her former suitors—neither one worthy to polish her shoes—and he didn't want to be like them in any way. He didn't want to hurt her. If he didn't mean to stay in Killdeer, he had no business encouraging her affections. But could he live in the same town and not want to be with her?

The reverend returned to the pew and sat down. "I believe this might be a good time to pray and ask the good Lord for guidance."

Jack couldn't have agreed more. Divine guidance was what he needed. Human reasoning sure hadn't given him any answers, and all his heart had done was confuse him more and more.

❧

The Everton family and their guests—Isaac and Dinah Holbrook and their children—had barely started eating when

Molly excused herself from the table and unobtrusively left the house through the back door. It would have been pointless to stay. She couldn't have eaten a single bite. Not with her thoughts and stomach churning the way they had all day.

It wasn't until she saw Reverend Lynch closing and locking the church door that she realized how much she wished to speak to him, that if he hadn't been at the church she would have gone to his home. She quickened her footsteps. "Reverend Lynch!"

He turned and when he saw her, he smiled briefly. "Hello, Miss Everton. What brings you back this way?"

"I . . . I was hoping I might talk to you about . . . about something."

There was that hint of a smile again before he turned and placed the key back in the lock. "Come inside." Although the day had grown warm, the shadowed sanctuary felt somewhat cooler. The reverend led the way to the front pew and the two of them sat. He looked at her, his gaze filled with patience. "Now, tell me what's troubling you."

"I'm feeling . . . confused, Reverend Lynch. So many things in my life don't seem to make sense anymore."

"I see."

Did the reverend see? How could he when she didn't understand it herself?

"Go on."

"I was angry with Father when he didn't make me the managing editor. I could have done it. I'm qualified. I went to college, and I've written for the paper almost from the day we arrived in Killdeer. I learned to typeset when I was very young just because I thought it was fun. I know about deadlines and advertising and production costs and good reporting. I couldn't understand why Father hired a man he didn't know over me, and I was determined not to like Mr. Ludgrove." She lowered her gaze to her hands, folded in her lap, embarrassed to confess the rest. "I planned to make Mr. Ludgrove's life so miserable he would leave Killdeer as quickly as he could."

"Well . . . I didn't know that."

"Not very Christian of me, is it? I know I'm to love my enemy and do good to those who misuse me."

"Is Mr. Ludgrove your enemy?"

Tears welled in her eyes. She blinked them away before looking up again, answering in a small voice, "No."

"Has he misused you?"

She shook her head. "No."

"Well, I'm glad to hear that."

"As it turns out, he's a fine editor. So much better than I expected, probably better at it than I would be. His suggestions have made my writing stronger, and he's taken a great load off of Father's shoulders. But he doesn't plan to stay in Killdeer. He wants to explore the West. He wants something that he won't find here." She stopped and drew a breath, letting it out slowly. "Of course, when he goes, Father could make me the editor after all."

The reverend smiled slightly. "And that thought doesn't make you as happy as you thought it would."

"No." The tears welled up again.

"And that's why you feel confused."

Molly nodded, then shook her head, then nodded again. Finally she shrugged and said, "Reverend? Is it possible to . . . to love someone whom you haven't known but a short while?"

He was silent a long spell before answering. "Molly, if you were a girl of seventeen or eighteen, I would have a very different answer for you. But you are not a girl. You are a grown woman. You are an educated woman who knows her own mind. You know what you want in life, and you have the internal fortitude to hold your ground when you know that what you are doing is the right thing. I have seen this in you more than once over the past decade. So my answer is yes. Yes, I believe it is possible to love someone whom you haven't known for long."

"Maybe I'm not confused. Maybe I'm afraid." She lowered her gaze again. "Maybe I'm afraid Jack will break my heart and I'll never recover."

"Without risk, there is no gain. Without struggle, we do not grow and change."

Did she dare risk her heart when she knew Jack didn't plan to stay in Killdeer? "I thought I knew exactly what my life was going to be. I thought I could give my all to the causes I believe in. But now . . ." She let the words fade into silence.

"Molly, the Bible tells us that the mind of man makes plans but God directs his steps. I believe what you need more than anything else is to understand God's plan for you. As His children, we must remain willing to let go of the plans we make, even the ones made with the best of intentions, and embrace His plans for us. It's an exciting way to live. Perhaps He has a great adventure in store for you too. Something unexpected. Something beyond your wildest imagination."

A great adventure. A glimmer of hope began to burn in Molly's heart.

The reverend offered another brief smile, then said, "Let's pray about it, shall we?"

CHAPTER TWELVE

ON MONDAY MORNING, JACK LEFT THE BOARDINGHOUSE
and walked to the corner of Birch and Main Streets. Once
there, he waited in the shade of a scraggly tree, hoping Molly
would come into town later rather than riding with her father
in the buggy. Relief washed through him when he saw Roland
Everton alone in the buggy. He stepped forward, as if just
arriving there.

His employer drew in on the reins. "Good morning, Jack.
Want to ride the last couple of blocks with me?"

"No thanks. I . . . I have something to do before I come
into the *Sentinel*. Hope that's all right. Shouldn't take me long."

"Of course it's all right." Roland slapped the reins against
the horse's backside and moved on.

Jack waited a few moments, then stepped back into the
shade and leaned a shoulder against the tree trunk. He didn't
mind waiting. Sometime during the night, peace had settled

over him. A peace unlike anything he'd felt before. He wasn't unfamiliar with the nudges of God, but this was something more than that.

This morning, he realized, all his plans for the future had gone out the window. He had been holding on to a dream for close to thirty years. He'd been determined to see it come to pass, no matter how long he had to wait or what he had to give up. But this morning, he'd opened his hand and offered that dream up to God. Whatever happened in the next half hour or the next day or even the next year, he was going to trust the Lord to guide him through.

As for Miss Molly Everton . . .

He saw her then, walking toward town in that straight, no-nonsense manner of hers, wearing a white blouse and dark skirt and vest, head held high. No hat. She often went without a hat, and even from where he stood, he could see strands of honey-brown hair had pulled free from the pins to dance around her face.

He loved her. Pure and simple. He'd never loved a woman before. Hadn't thought it mattered. It mattered now.

Jack moved out of the shade of the tree and stood watching her. When she saw him, she faltered a step or two before quickly regaining her stride.

When she was near enough, he said, "Good morning, Molly." No Miss Everton for him today. And he didn't care who heard him say it.

"Good morning . . . Jack."

Her use of his given name made him feel lighter than air.

She stopped a few feet away from him. "Were you waiting for Father?"

"No." He smiled. "I was waiting for you."

She didn't smile in return. In fact, she looked suddenly worried. "Is something wrong?"

"No, nothing's wrong. I'd say something's right. Very right." He took a step closer to her.

Her beautiful eyes widened.

"Remember on Saturday when I said I probably shouldn't have kissed you?"

She nodded.

"Well, I was wrong, Molly. Dead wrong. I'm glad I kissed you."

"You are?" The words were barely audible.

He laughed. He couldn't help it. She often made him want to laugh—and the rest of the time, she made him want to hold her in his arms. "I am," he answered when he could.

She mouthed the word, *Why?*

"Because I've fallen in love with you, Molly Everton. Hook, line, and sinker."

"How can that be? We haven't even known each other a month."

"I started loving you that very first night at dinner when you told me that noticing everything was a danger of your profession as well as mine."

She blushed, and Jack loved what the color did to her face.

"And I knew it for sure when you challenged me to name the twelve Caesars at your father's birthday gathering."

The rosiness in her cheeks deepened. "I was horrid to you."

"No, you weren't. You couldn't be horrid if you tried."

"I did try. I wanted to make you quit as editor and leave Killdeer."

"I suspected as much. But you still weren't horrid."

"I'm sorry all the same."

"Don't be sorry, Molly. I never want to make you feel sorry." He cupped the side of her face with his right hand. "All I want is for you to agree to marry me."

Molly couldn't seem to draw a breath.

Reverend Lynch's voice echoed in her memory: *"Perhaps He has a great adventure in store for you too. Something unexpected. Something beyond your wildest imagination."*

"Say yes, Molly," Jack whispered.

"Are you sure? You might regret—"

"I'm sure. Maybe it's crazy, but I'm more sure about this than I've been about anything before in my life."

She didn't want to cry, but she wasn't sure she could keep from it. "Then, yes."

"Do you think you could grow to love me too?"

"Jack Ludgrove, for someone who claims to notice everything, you should know the answer to that question."

He grinned. "Tell me anyway."

Was it possible for a heart to burst in one's chest from sheer joy? "I love you, Jack."

He laughed again. Oh my. How she loved the sound of his laughter.

"Perhaps we should go talk to Father now," she said, smiling back at him.

"In a minute." Then he pulled her into his embrace and kissed her.

CHAPTER THIRTEEN

Yellowstone National Park, September 1881

THE SMELL OF COFFEE DRIFTED THROUGH THE CANVAS tent and tickled Molly's nose. She tried to ignore it. She wasn't ready to wake up yet. She wanted to stay snuggled beneath the blankets until the sun had baked away the chill of night.

"You don't fool me, sleepyhead," Jack said.

She groaned but opened her eyes. Her husband looked at her through the open flap, a steaming mug in one hand.

"We need to get an early start. A lot of ground to cover today."

Molly sat up and shoved her heavy mane of hair back from her face. Sleeping in a cap would keep it from getting so tangled, but Jack liked her to leave it down and loose at night. And Molly loved to please him.

He handed her the mug of coffee. "Happy anniversary,

darling." He knelt beside her and kissed her, being careful not to jiggle the hot beverage in her hand.

"You remembered," she said when he leaned back from her. "I thought you might forget after all of these weeks on the trail."

"It'll never happen, Molly. The day you became my wife is the most memorable day of my life. I may forget every other day of the year, but never this one."

"Are you sorry we are on our way back to Killdeer? I know you've loved these last ten weeks, seeing all the things we've seen. Killdeer is going to feel quiet and uneventful in comparison."

He shook his head. "No, I'm not sorry. It's time. Winter will arrive in a matter of weeks. We'll want to be home again before that."

Home. Molly released a breath she hadn't known she held. She was so glad he thought of it as home.

His eyes narrowed. "Why do you ask?"

She'd meant to keep her secret until they made camp this evening, but Jack knew her too well. He would never let it rest, now that his suspicions were raised.

"Out with it, Molly." He leaned close again, a mischievous smile tugging at the corners of his mouth. "Tell me."

She touched his lips with her fingertips. "Was this trip the adventure you hoped it would be? Was it everything you imagined when you were a boy?"

"Better." He took the mug from her hand and set it aside, then he pulled her back down onto the bedding and drew her close. "I can't imagine seeing all that we've seen without you at my side. It wouldn't mean much alone. I know that now."

"And you won't mind not going off on another trip like this for a while?"

"No. I won't mind. Not as long as I'm with you. Besides, you and I have a newspaper to run. Time we got back to it."

"Oh. The newspaper. About that. I might not be as much help as you need."

"What are you talking about? I'm the dispensable one. You could run that paper with your hands tied behind your back."

Fighting a smile, she shook her head. "You're wrong this time, my dear. I won't have much time to write a weekly column."

Jack pulled back so he could look her more fully in the face. A frown pinched his eyebrows together. "Not have time to write? What do you mean?"

Laughter bubbled up from Molly's chest. When she was able, she said, "Can you really not guess, Jack Ludgrove? After all of these weeks of keeping each other warm in our bedroll?"

Confusion remained in his eyes several heartbeats longer.

Softly she quoted from *The Winter's Tale*, "He makes a July's day short as December."

Understanding dawned and it spread across Jack's face. "A baby? Molly, are you going to have a baby? Are you sure? Do you—" He broke off abruptly, pulled her close, and kissed her once again. When the kiss ended, Jack withdrew no more than a breath away. "When?"

"I can't be positive, but I think April."

Jack pulled the covers over them both and went right on holding her close. "Know what, Molly? I think I've finally learned what Reverend Lynch was saying to each of us back before I asked you to marry me. We can have all kinds of dreams. We can imagine all kinds of adventures. We can even experience some of them. But nothing will ever be as amazing as the life God has in mind for us, if we'll just follow His lead."

Fleetingly, Molly remembered the day she'd stormed into her father's office in a rage because Jack Ludgrove was coming to Killdeer. Now she couldn't imagine herself without him.

But then he kissed her again, more deeply this time, and all rational thought seemed to flee.

They wouldn't break camp quite as early as Jack had intended.

Dear Editor:

What a wonderful thing it is when a woman or a man releases what they are holding on to so tightly so they can take hold of something better. So they can take hold of what God wants them to have. My mother told me once that love can be a great adventure. Never has she been so right as she was about that.

William Shakespeare wrote in one of his sonnets, "Love comforteth like sunshine after rain . . . Love's gentle spring doth always fresh remain."

How right he was.

Sincerely,

Contented in Wyoming

A Cowboy for Katie

Debra Clopton

CHAPTER ONE

Midway, Texas, 1871

SHE MIGHT BE AS CRAZY AS THEY SAID, BUT KATIE Pearl had learned that most men were light between the ears. She wondered which one of them she was gonna have to shoot today.

It wasn't as if she wanted to, but if they came snoopin' around, she was willin' to oblige them.

"There ain't no sense pretending you like this, Katie Pearl, no sense at all," Katie told herself. From her perch on the wagon seat, she could see the dusty buildings of town. And as Myrtle May pulled the wagon 'round the bend in the road, Katie's insides tensed up.

"You're a good horse, Myrtle May. Yes you are." She was glad to have the comfort of her old horse with her as the fire in the pit of her stomach informed her trouble was near.

Town was trouble and there was no getting around it.

Most folks in town crossed the street and walked on the other side these days when they saw her. At least if they were smart they did.

Especially if it was any of them sodbusters who'd recently come callin' for her hand in marriage. "No siree, Katie Pearl," she spoke aloud again, her words reassuring to her. "Them sorry no-goods have seen your fingers itchin' on the pearl handles of your Colt, and some have seen the end of the barrel pointing at them too." It was true, fools. "You don't take kindly to none of the hogwash they've been trying to sell you."

Sighing long and hard, she shook her head. "No, I don't. Ain't that so, Myrtle May?"

Myrtle didn't answer, which didn't surprise Katie. Her horse was a little on the quiet side. And that was okay. Katie didn't mind the quiet—though she sure missed conversations with her pa. She just plain missed her pa.

It was just her now. And though things were fuzzy in her head since the tornado, she was making it. If only she didn't have to go to town for supplies.

She tugged her pa's hat low over her eyes and gritted her jaw down tight.

"You can do this, Katie Pearl. Yes, you can," she assured herself. "Long as you don't have to shoot somebody, you'll be just fine."

Almost there, Katie sat up ramrod straight and hiked her chin in the air. Clamping her brows down hard, dare in her eyes, she stared straight ahead and pretended her stomach wasn't so queasy that it threatened to give her back the ham and beans she'd fed it for breakfast.

A man's horse dropping dead in the middle of nowhere left a man with few options.

Treb Rayburn was that man.

His shoulder numb, he let the saddle that had been riding his back for the last three days slide to the ground as he stared at the pitiful excuse of a town. Midway, Texas, or so the sign read.

Not much to look at—not by a long shot—but his aching feet and sore back would attest that he'd never been happier to see a town in all his life.

Scanning the street, his gaze drifted past the clapboard hotel and diner that were by no means fancy and then on past the saloon, which appeared to be doing a fair business from the looks of the cowboys lined up outside. Treb wasn't interested in the saloon. He continued his survey, coming to rest on Crandon's General Store, sitting directly across the street from the saloon.

That'd be the place.

Hefting his saddle once more, he strode down the rutted, dusty street and stepped up onto the rough wood walk, purpose in his steps. He'd find work, earn enough money to replace his horse, and then he'd be on his way toward the next sunset, the next horizon. He had places to go and things to see: Galveston, New Orleans, and on farther along the Gulf of Mexico.

A few miles beyond Midway ran the Trinity River. Treb planned to cross the river as soon as he had a fresh horse beneath him.

His boots thudded along as he strode toward the store where he'd begin his search for work. A young woman in a blue gingham dress with a holstered pistol strapped around her slim hips caught his attention. She wore an oversized felt hat with a wide brim. He wasn't sure if it was the gun or the cornflower-blue eyes that met his briefly before darting off that drew his attention. After all, he'd seen women in the West packin' pistols and rifles before. This was still wild country and a person had to be prepared. He decided that what got his attention the most was that he'd never seen one quite so pretty and wary at the same time. Her eyes connected to his again, but she spun away and started studying the dry goods in the window like she was desperate to have what was there.

Treb rubbed his bristly jaw and figured he needed a shave. A bath wouldn't hurt either. The door was open and he walked inside, setting his saddle in the corner out of the way. There was a tall crane of a man with a pleasant smile helping two older women choose some thread. Treb didn't miss their curious stares as the man moved away from them and came toward him.

"Hello, I'm Marcus Crandon, proprietor. May I help you?"

Treb introduced himself as they shook hands. "I'm just passing through—" Movement distracted Treb when, out of the corner of his eye, he caught the young woman on the side-walk peeking around the door at him. Her face was small, her chin dainty, her cheekbones high, her expression suspicious. When his gaze met those blue, blue eyes, she scowled at him, tugged her hat low, and found the doorjamb immensely fascinating.

Curious for certain. Treb wasn't sure what to make of the snoopy young woman who seemed to be stuck to the boardwalk. He forced himself to focus on the proprietor. "My horse died about three days back, and I need to find some work. Nothing permanent, mind you. Just something so I can earn enough money to buy a good horse and be on my way."

Crossing his lanky arms, Mr. Crandon tapped his cleft chin with his index finger. "Got wanderlust in your veins, do you?"

"Like floodwaters," Treb said, grinning. "There's a big, vast land out there, and I aim to see most of it before I settle down."

Crandon grinned. "When I was younger, I got the itch myself. That's how I ended up here. I wish you all the best." He paused, briefly. "Tell you what, they might be hiring down at the Rattlesnake Ranch. That ranch is so huge they're always looking for cowpokes."

"Psst."

Treb heard the loud hiss and looked around.

"Psst!" It was the gal from the sidewalk hissing. She was peeking around the door, her brows crunched down hard. She waved to draw their attention.

"Katie," Crandon said patiently, as if talking to a child. "Hold on. Ernie is getting your order ready and will have it out to you soon. Your windows aren't here yet though."

She shook her head impatiently and glared straight at Treb. "Him. I want him," she said, motioning for Treb to come over.

He wasn't at all sure what to make of the woman. She couldn't be more than twenty, and she was pleasant enough to look at. But it was the wariness in her eyes that struck him as he stared back at her and poked a finger to his chest. "Me?" he asked, looking around just to make certain no one had come to stand behind him.

She nodded real fast, waving him over.

Treb shot a questioning glance at Crandon, who hiked a brow, his hawk eyes studying Treb. "Katie's not one to talk to strangers. Truth be told, she's not one to talk to most anyone. Least not lately."

Treb's neck started to itch from all the folks in the store looking at him with an interest that hadn't been there a few minutes ago.

Slowly, he strode toward the curious woman. She scuffled away from the door to stand in front of the big window. While no one inside would be able to hear what Katie had to say to him, they'd have a full view of the conversation.

Her hand rested ominously on her pistol as he walked toward her. But he was six feet two inches tall, and she had to crane her head back to look up at him.

"I'll hire you on at my ranch. Starting now."

His brows dipped, not sure he'd heard her right. But there was no mistaking her clear words. She shifted her pretty eyes from side to side. It made Treb nervous just watching her.

"*You'll* hire me?" he managed after those eyes came back to meet his. It was the first chance he'd had to look really close into them, and his gut did a funny thing—kind of dropped and rolled, end over end, the way it had three days earlier when his horse fell dead beneath him and sent him tumbling headfirst into the road. He wasn't sure what to think of the look in her eyes. They narrowed now, distrust edging them. Her eyes were beautiful, and his gaze dropped to the firm tilt of her kissable lips . . . What in tarnation was he thinking?

This woman looked like she'd just as soon shoot him before she'd even think about kissing him. Then again, she was offering him a job.

"You can't be more'n twenty," he said, not beating around the bush. "You telling me your pa would hire me?"

"My pa's dead. If you want to be hired on at my place then I'm the one you'd be hirin' on under. I'll pay you double what Rattlesnake'll pay you, and add a good horse to the bargain when the job is done." She shot off a wage that he'd be a fool to pass up. With a horse in the bargain—no doubt about it—it was too good to be true.

There had to be a catch.

"What exactly would I be doing?"

Her brows puckered up. "What do you think? Ranchin' cleanup and . . . ah, building."

He heard the hesitation in the last word. "Building? What would I be building?"

"A house. Mine was destroyed by the tornado three weeks ago, and I need help putting it back together. I've got windows ordered and will need some walls to hold them in place. I need the building more'n anything."

He was pretty certain he heard sadness in her voice. Treb didn't do sadness too well. He wasn't much on getting close enough to folks to care about their feelings, and he had no desire to experience it anyway. He'd had his belly full of emotion.

He wasn't real enthusiastic about the idea of working for a woman either. Especially one younger than him and who looked like she was itchin' to shoot a man rather than hire one. While standing there contemplating his situation, a scrawny cowboy with shifty, weasel eyes strode toward them. The cowboy halted abruptly and turned pasty white the instant he spied Katie. Poor fellow looked like he didn't know what to do.

Katie glowered at him—she might be small, but there was no never mind to that, not with the way her hand itched on that pistol at her hip. The man's gaze dropped to that pistol, then he spun and crossed the busy street as if someone had just lit fire to his pants.

Treb nodded toward the fella. "Friend of yours?"

Katie scowled. "Only if I needed target practice."

Treb nudged his hat back a notch and cocked his head to the side. "You plannin' to use me for target practice?"

Her soft lips twitched and her eyes lightened for a brief moment before she slammed her brows down and frowned. "Not long as you do your work and don't ask me to marry you."

He almost laughed—but held back, figuring if he did she might shoot him where he stood. "Marry you? I'm not marrying anyone, so you've got yourself a deal."

He could have sworn he saw relief in those distrustful eyes. But it vanished just as quickly as he saw it appear. "Good. Got my wagon right there. Soon as they finish loading up my supplies, we can head out to my place."

"I've got a few things to grab for myself inside the store, then I'll meet you back out here. How's that?" he asked, still not accustomed to having a woman for a boss. She gave a curt nod, and he headed inside only to stop in the doorway and turn back. "Can I ask you something?"

"Don't see why not."

"How do you know you can trust me?" It was a fair question. He wasn't sure why this girl of a woman was in the position she was in, owning a ranch and all, but it didn't sit right on his chest, her trusting a stranger. If she had been his mother or his sister, he wouldn't be too happy with her for just hiring some could-be-vagrant off the street.

Her brow hiked instantly. "I can shoot better than most men and I don't sleep much. If you're not to be trusted, I'll figure it out soon enough. Then you'll be the one turning pale and crossing the street before I lose my good humor and shoot you."

Treb's lip hitched up on one side. She had some spunk. He admired that in a woman. His mother crossed his thoughts again but he pushed that door closed. Some regrets were too hard to go back and think about. "I reckon you're right about that." He started for the store, then spun back again. "And thanks for the hire. You'll get a hard day's work out of me, and I can promise you there won't be any need in pointing that pearl-handled pistol my way."

"Then we'll get on just fine."

When he entered the store, the two women who had been buying thread were now almost standing at the door. They were concentrating on the molasses as if they were starving. He'd caught them spying on him, no doubt about it. *Women,* he thought with mild disgust.

"Ladies," he drawled, tipping his hat, then moved toward Crandon.

"Did I hear right?" Crandon asked. "Did Katie Pearl just hire you on at her ranch?"

"Yep."

Shocked gasps erupted from the molasses aisle. He spun to find the women in a tizzy.

"Crazy Katie Pearl has hired a *man*!" one said, her hand to her cheek.

Women he hadn't noticed before hurried from other parts of the store.

"A *man*," whispered a plump lady in head-to-toe purple. She flapped open her fan and began fanning herself.

Treb looked at Crandon and leaned in with a question for his ears only. "Why are they doing that?"

The proprietor shrugged a shoulder. "Ever since the tornado Katie hasn't been . . . herself. Her pa got killed in that tornado and she's been peculiar ever since. Don't want nothing to do with folks. And I mean nothing." Crandon shook his head. "It's a bad situation."

Treb didn't feel comfortable talking about the poor woman so he kept his mouth shut—but he was about to spend time out there with Katie Pearl.

"She was trapped under her house, you know," one lady offered.

"For *days*," the purple-clad one added. "Poor thing lay in the dark all alone talking to herself. It was just terrible."

Treb felt a knuckle in his gut thinking about it.

Another lady hiked a brow as she gave him the once-over. "She's done nothing but threaten to shoot every man who's looked at her twice since then, and heaven forbid one ask for her hand in marriage. Why, it's indecent, I tell you! A young girl like her needs a husband's protection. Don't you agree?"

"Especially if she's going to hire help all by herself," another added, her lips turned down in a frown.

Treb had heard enough. He tugged his hat down low. "Ma'am, I'm her hired help. I don't reckon it much matters what I think." With that said, he laid his money on the counter and picked up the tin of peppermints he'd come in to purchase. He had a mighty fierce sweet tooth, and he'd learned it never hurt to have a little something on him at all times.

A man never knew when he needed to head off trouble— sometimes it took a gun and sometimes it just took a treat. Suddenly there was a commotion out on the sidewalk.

"I told you to stay away from me, you lily-livered skunk!" Katie Pearl's voice, distinct and determined, erupted through the doorway. "Just stay right where you are. I want no part of you."

A flurry of women raced to the window and Marcus Crandon strode to the door. Treb followed, ready to step in if he needed to.

Katie had her gun out and aimed straight at a skinny, shiftless-looking cowpoke who was standing in the street. Treb figured *some* women might call the man handsome. He didn't like the man on sight. There was a calculating look in his eyes that instantly made Treb distrust him. And he was good at reading people.

Behind him, across the street, the gathering of cowboys outside the saloon had multiplied.

"Now, Katie darlin', put that firearm away. All I'm saying is I'd like the chance to court you. You need some help and I'm willing and able—"

"Ha! Willing and able to take my land right out from under me." She waved her gun at him. "Now move on back over there before I have you high-stepping across that road."

Anger, and something dangerous that Treb didn't like, flashed across the man's face. Lending support, Treb moved past Crandon and onto the boardwalk behind Katie. The cowpoke met his warning gaze, then he turned to storm back toward the other side of the street. He didn't stop till he'd slammed through the swinging doors of the saloon and several fellas followed him.

Katie had made an enemy today. Treb wondered how many others she'd made before he'd come into town.

She spun back toward the store, her expression grim, the gun still in her hand. A gasp went up behind him. He turned to see feathers and hands waving and ladies scurrying away from the window.

Glancing to see what his boss thought of that, he found wary, gleaming eyes watching him. In a sweeping motion, she holstered her pistol, leaving her hand resting on the pearl handle like a gunslinger. "I've spoke my piece. It's time to head out."

A young teen had loaded up the back of the wagon. He looked a little nervous, standing there, off to the side.

"Mister," he whispered low, "you best get on with it before trouble starts. That there fella won't take kindly to being talked to like that in public."

Treb glanced across the street, making sure no others were going to come calling on Katie. Who in his right mind would do that anyway? Hadn't they seen how she was acting?

Treb didn't pick up his pace as he took in the bewildered expressions on the men's faces. He had to agree, until he got a handle on what he'd gotten himself into, he planned on keeping his focus on doing the job he'd been hired to do, getting his money, and heading out on his new horse as soon as possible.

"You ready?" Katie Pearl asked as he rounded the end of the wagon. Those wary cornflower-blue eyes slammed into him and knocked the breath right out of him. "We're wasting daylight."

"You driving or am I?" he asked, not at all happy about the way those eyes of hers were affecting him. He'd seen blue eyes before, but there was something different about hers . . .

What was it about these eyes? *They're crazy, maybe?*

He ignored the echoing voice in his head. Maybe it was that behind their startling color and the warning to keep away, he saw a powerful lonesomeness. He knew about being lonesome, had learned to head it off at the pass when it tried to grab hold of him. For the most part he'd made his peace with it.

She didn't look like she had.

Grabbing the rail, she climbed up and sat down on the seat and looked at him. "Myrtle May's driving. She always does." She gave him a half grin that almost made him smile.

Almost. "Who is Myrtle May?" he asked, climbing up beside her.

She pointed at the gray horse hitched to the wagon. "Let's go home, Myrtle May. Hold on, Cowboy."

Her warning came almost too late because the horse shot off as if it were in a race. The jolt sent Katie and Treb slamming hard into each other. Katie bounced off of him and nearly toppled over the edge of the wagon. Treb threw his arm around her and yanked her back against him.

"Thank you," she gasped, her hat hitting him in the face. She grabbed for it as it went flying out toward the street.

Treb snatched the hat with his free hand while tightening his grip on Katie just as the silly horse ran straight into the path of an oncoming wagon.

Katie pushed away from him as if he were a hot coal, then grabbed for the reins as they barely missed colliding with the wagon.

"Watch out!" the grizzly-looking man yelled. He shot to his feet in his wagon and pumped a fist at them.

Katie shot to her feet. "Watch out yourself!" she yelled as the wagon careened across the rutted road and past other wagons heading their way.

Treb gripped her by the gun belt and yanked her down. Her backside hit the seat with a hard thud.

"Ouch!" she yelped, glaring at him, mouth open, eyes flashing. He pushed her hat at her and snatched the reins in one motion. Fuming, she fumbled to get a grip on her hat before it took another ride on the wind.

"Myrtle May's done driving today," he snapped, pulling firmly on the reins.

"Hey, give those back to me."

"Nope."

"You work for me," she huffed, looking madder than an angry prairie dog. "Give me those reins."

"Nope." Focusing straight ahead, he placed his elbows on his knees and gave a tug to let Myrtle May know he was in charge.

"Well," Katie huffed again. He could feel her eyes burning holes in his back. "I ought to—"

He looked briefly over his shoulder at her. "Fire me? Looks like you have plenty of men lined up ready to take my place."

Katie eyed him rebelliously from beneath the brim of the floppy brown hat.

He wondered if her hand was tickling the pearl handle of her Colt.

Probably. He could be a dead man in about half a second.

CHAPTER TWO

SERVES YOU RIGHT, KATIE PEARL.

Katie nibbled at her bottom lip, her hands holding tight to the reins the stubborn man handed over to her after they'd gotten out of town and into open space. Poor Myrtle May was moving at her own sporadic pace toward the ranch.

He hadn't said a word since he'd handed her the leathers. He'd arched one of his thick, dark brows, then slumped in the seat like a lump of lard. A handsome lump, but a lump nonetheless. He'd pulled his hat down over his eyes and leaned back against the oat bags that were stacked higher than the low seat back. Time for a nap.

Katie tugged her hat to the side to shield her eyes just a bit, then snuck a peek at him.

The dad-burn hat got in her way. But she could see that he was a huge, dark-haired mountain of a man.

She hadn't realized how big he was until he'd climbed up

and sat down beside her. And then when he'd grabbed her up against him! The man had muscles as hard as green pears. Almost knocked the breath out of her when he'd slammed her to him. To be fair, she might have leaned out too far when she stood up and waved her fist at the rude man in the other wagon. Not that she would have fallen out of the thing—she'd have saved herself before that.

She was good at saving herself.

Still, truth be told, Treb Rayburn had sort of rescued her . . .

"So, what are you mad about?" she grunted out loud before she could stop herself. She glanced at Treb and was relieved that he was still sleeping. Since the tornado, she tended to talk to herself—and it was plumb worrisome. But at night in the dark, it was a comfort, hearing the sound of a voice even if it was her own. It had been her *only* comfort when she'd been trapped in the dark for days, hurting and alone.

Katie stared out across the pastures.

She was so thankful her ranch was getting close. Going to town these days was a near intolerable strain, almost beyond bearing now that everyone there thought she was a lunatic.

You are a lunatic.

She tried to ignore the voice in her head, concentrating on the wildflowers blooming across this stretch of the road. But even their bright yellow faces and deep burgundy colors failed to lift her spirits.

Her life was a mess. Nothing helped her spirits since the tornado ripped across her home leaving nothing but disaster in its wake.

Her pa was dead.

Her home destroyed.

Sometimes she thought she was destroyed too.

She wasn't sure what to think of herself anymore. Honestly, she was scared.

Not that she'd let anyone know it. Forcing the thought away, she glanced at the good-looking lump. "What were you thinking, Katie Pearl?"

The old gray horse drove the buckboard over a rut, jostling everyone, including the lump—she'd been hitting ruts pretty regular on this trip. "Haven't had anyone but myself and Myrtle May to talk to for weeks, and now look what I've done. Hired a non-talker."

The words slipped out just like before. She shot Treb another glance.

He nudged his hat back and was studying her. Katie's insides dipped—even though Myrtle May hadn't hit a hole in the road.

"I talk. Just resting a bit. So, you know how to use that sharpshooter on your hip?"

That he thought she'd been talking to him was a relief. She relaxed, staring at him. She'd forgotten that his voice was as smooth as honey—she'd been having a little trouble with her memory lately. Forgetting things. And her head hurt something fierce sometimes. Of course there were a fair amount of things that weren't right about her since the tornado. She recognized it, but just couldn't seem to fix most of them. But she would.

"Better than most," she said. "It eases my mind a great deal, just like my pa told me it would when he taught me." She cut her eyes back to his. "Not many men find my ability to shoot a good thing. Especially when they find themselves staring down the barrel of my Colt or my long gun."

"Sounds like your pa was a wise man too."

Oh, that got her right in the heart. "He was." She sighed, giving Treb a grateful look. "Not the easiest man to know, but my pa was the best rancher around these parts. Wasn't anything he couldn't face straight on and win because of his mind working so far out in front of him. Just wasn't nothing he could do when the . . ." She couldn't bring herself to go on. She rubbed her temple as a pounding started. That day was fuzzy in her head, bits and pieces coming together in odd ways and none of it fitting quite right. Most times she'd wake in the middle of the night crying and with a fierce headache when scenes collided in her head. Her hands were damp just thinking about it. And the pain started throbbing in her temple like a sledgehammer hitting one of those spikes she'd seen workers hammering into a railroad track. She blinked hard and tore her eyes away from Treb's penetrating gaze.

"Sounds like you've had a tough situation out here."

His quiet words caused some calm to settle over her thoughts. She nodded and took a steadying breath. "Nothin' I can't handle. Except the building. I don't know a thing about building."

Silence surrounded them again as the blue sky and the

green meadows spread out before and behind them. *Progress.* That was what her pa was always saying. A person always needed to be making progress, moving forward. That was what she was trying to do. Even as dark as things were inside her head since he'd left her.

And he'd been more than right about the relief she got from making progress and being able to shoot her Colt. If she just kept pushing, things would get better. She hoped.

"So you've had your share of no-goods calling trying to get your ranch?"

"They call me Crazy Katie, and they might be right. But even I know that since my pa died and left me owner of the ranch, it makes me a prime prospect for marryin'. A bride they think they could make cower so they could claim my land for themselves. They've been crawling out of every hole in the ground since I was . . . found alive." She started to say pulled out of her grave, but the words stuck. "I've been running them off by using them for target practice, but they just keep coming. They're a dense lot, that's for certain. Isn't that right, Myrtle May? Some men just need a good kick in the head—that's what Myrtle thinks about the situation."

"I'm real sorry about what you've gone through. But it sounds like your pa would be real proud of you and Myrtle May. Sounds like you two have it all figured out."

They topped the hill and her gut tightened up knowing what lay on the other side. A wave of lonesomeness crashed over her as she met the deep gray eyes of Treb. Suddenly she was fighting back the urge to cry. She didn't have anything figured out. Her life lay in ruins over this hill, and try as she might, she just couldn't fit the pieces back together.

But looking at Treb calmed some of the upheaval inside her. For the first time since the tornado ripped her world apart, it was good to have someone riding beside her. He might be moving on when the job was done, but for now, there was comfort in his presence.

And his words.

The drive to Katie's place took half the day—especially with a horse that went whatever speed it wanted, *when* it wanted. The horse seemed at times to simply follow the grass trail.

It was no wonder, considering how far the drive was, that it took several days for someone to realize she and her pa had been in trouble after the tornado. Katie had talked to herself several times on the drive. He wasn't sure if she even realized that she was speaking sometimes. If he hadn't been forewarned, he'd have been disturbed by it.

He hadn't been prepared, though, for the extent of damage he was going to see until they topped a rise and there it was—or what was left of the house and surrounding grounds. The place was a disaster. The house had been nearly demolished. One side lay in rubble, the roof was torn off the other side, and the front side was missing too. This had been the home of a man who'd done well for himself and his daughter.

The extent of what Katie had been through hit Treb as he

realized she'd lain beneath all this rubble for days—with her father dead. There was no doubt that God had been looking out for her that day. The cross made of two sticks that marked the fresh grave on the hill belonging to her pa was evidence enough of that.

There was a chicken coop that leaned to one side and looked as if it had been somewhat repaired. A barn was still standing but part of the roof was missing. The corral was a pitiful sight—clearly Katie had attempted to repair it herself with a mishmash of materials. Surprisingly, though, it held a number of good-looking horses. How it held them in he wasn't sure, but it did. The makeshift concoction of wood looked as if it might fall down with the slightest wind.

Myrtle May took them to a spot beside the barn where a small grouping of supplies sat right out in the open. Even bags of feed and flour. Treb didn't understand why they were here, not with the barn sitting right there with half a roof to protect them from the elements.

"Unload everything here," she said, hopping from the wagon.

She was the boss so Treb kept his mouth shut, though it was hard to do. He got busy earning his wages.

Hefting the first bag of oats, he laid it beside the other bags of supplies already there in the dirt and watched as Katie unhitched Myrtle and led her to a small pen off to the side of the barn. Like the chicken coop, it was a pitiful thing leaning to one side—the loose posts shook as she tugged the gate open, and the entire pen moved.

Treb watched her lead the horse inside. With her back straight in her blue calico dress, Katie was silhouetted against the pale summer sky. The poor girl. It was her against the world. A sudden and unwanted wave of protectiveness washed over him.

"Don't go there," he growled to himself under his breath. He shook off the emotion and got back to work. He'd known Katie Pearl for the whole sum of half a day—best just to keep his mind on helping her get her house fixed, then get out of here as fast as he could ride.

Beyond that, helping her get her life in order was none of his business.

"Where have you been sleeping?" he asked, eyeing the campfire in the center of the clearing between the rubble that had been her house and the barn.

She came out of the stall, struggling to drag the pitiful gate closed before she nodded toward the campfire. "There."

Disbelief had him scrubbing the back of his neck hard. "Let me get this straight. You've been sleeping out here for a *month*?" And no one had come help her clean up this wreck? What was wrong with this town?

"Three weeks," she said defensively. "And that's where I'll keep sleeping. You, on the other hand, can bunk in the barn."

She was getting odder by the moment.

He reckoned he could understand her staying there a night or two. He enjoyed sleeping beneath the stars as much as the next man, and he did it often on his travels, but this was a woman. One used to living inside a nice home.

But that was her choice and none of his business, he reminded himself.

As soon as he finished unloading the supplies, he went to check out the barn. It had half a roof but it was a wreck inside. The splintered wood and shingles of the ruined roof still lay where it had caved in. Standing in the entrance, he spied two saddles among the ruins. "There's some good tack and stuff in here," he called to Katie. "Do you want me to clean some of this up?" She was over by a pile of limbs and cut wood.

"That would be a good thing for you to do for now," she said, distracted as she gathered an armload of wood. "We'll start the house tomorrow."

Glad to have a plan, he strode forward and pushed debris out of the way until he was able to pull the saddles free. How could she be so reckless with something so valuable? Tamping down his consternation, he moved the saddles to the side, then set out to save what he could from the rubble.

Before the sun started setting, Katie had a roaring fire going and was stirring a pot of beans as he took a break from working. His stomach growled, reminding him he hadn't eaten since the jerky he'd had that morning.

Moving over to the fire, he sat down on a log and watched her. Her hand shook as she stirred.

Unable to hold it in any longer, he put his elbows on his knees and leaned forward. "I was thinking it might be best to start the barn, get it cleaned up before we start on the house. You could have a roof over your head while we work on the house."

"I'm fine." She shook her head. "We've already settled

this. You can stay in there. I'm fine out here." Her voice shook slightly and she stirred the beans faster.

"But—"

"I'm fine," she broke in. "The open air suits me. Sleep where you want, but I hired you to help rebuild the house—not to tell me where I need to sleep."

"It doesn't make sense," he snapped, his irritation flaring.

"It . . . it's what I want. And that's all that matters." She grabbed a tin plate, dipped a large ladle of beans onto it, and stomped around the fire to hold it out to him.

Stubborn woman! He'd figured there'd be trouble working for her. "It isn't right," he said as he reached for the dish. His fingers brushed hers—his pulse jumped at the touch and a tingling sensation raced up his arm.

Katie yanked her hand away almost before he got a good grip on the dish. "It's right for me. I can't help if you don't like it. I didn't ask you either."

She stalked back to the other side of the fire before looking across the flames at him. The woman was small, but the fire in her eyes clearly said, *Back off.* He got the feeling she'd felt the same tingling sensation he had when they'd touched, and she didn't like it either.

"Fine, have it your way," he grunted. Tugging his hat low over his eyes, he held back further comments and dug into his beans. He wasn't here to talk sense into her, and he wasn't here for romance. He was here for a horse. And that was it.

This was going to be a long few months.

How bad did he need a horse?

He thought about Galveston and how much he wanted to see the ocean.

He needed a horse bad.

And the truth was, Katie Pearl needed his help.

Even if she was determined to sleep in the elements.

CHAPTER THREE

As the dark settled in, Katie added another log to the fire. The sky was clear with stars twinkling, and that at least gave her some comfort. Across the fire, Treb had stretched out on his bedroll and now lay there with his boots crossed and his hat pulled down over his face, his hands folded over his chest. Studying him, she thought about the way her pulse had reacted when their fingers had touched. It had almost taken her breath away. Infuriating man, made her mad, and yet she had reacted to his touch as if she . . . were attracted to him. She tried not to think about that, tried hard to put it out of her mind. He was irritating; still, she found a bit of peace looking across that fire and seeing him there. Her heart hammered relentlessly despite it, just as it did every night when the darkness sank in around her.

She prayed for the morning to come soon and the sun to peek over the distant horizon. She knew she would have to burn a lot of logs before that moment came. Sitting with her back against the large log she'd rolled into place that first night alone, she drew her legs up and wrapped the blanket around herself.

Leaning her forehead on her knees, she rocked gently, trying not to think about the darkness . . . "The morning will come soon enough, Katie girl," she whispered, keeping her voice low but needing the comfort she found in the sound.

"You just hold on, my girl. Hold on." Her heart ached for the sound of her pa's deep, reassuring voice. "You've got nothing to be concerned about, Katie girl. You've got help now. A strong man to lend a hand." She could see her pa even now, so strong.

"He'll be moving on, Pa. Soon as the work is done."

"Until then, you've got some comfort. Make a list, get it done. And calm down. Things will be all right. God has a plan."

Katie could feel her pa as if he were sitting right beside her having the conversation. He'd talked to her and comforted her that night. He'd been her saving grace during the nightmare of being trapped beneath the rubble of her home. Hearing his voice had kept her hanging on. As usual her head throbbed when she thought too much about the days she lay there. Things muddled together. She couldn't remember everything, and when she tried to bring it all back, the hurting in her head got worse.

Suddenly feeling weary through and through, she lifted her head and rested her chin on her knees. Her eyes grew heavy as her gaze settled on Treb in the flickering light. The throbbing eased and her nerves seemed to calm looking at him. Was it that for the first time in weeks she wasn't by herself? Somehow, knowing he was across the fire from her helped.

It felt good not to be alone.

Treb rubbed his eyes as the scent of coffee, and frying bacon had him sitting up to the rumble of his stomach. Katie was busy flipping the bacon in the pan. Her hair had escaped the plait and tendrils lay softly against her cheek. She looked tired—it was no wonder since as far as he could tell, she hadn't slept last night. He'd drifted off to the sound of her mumbling softly to herself.

At first she had mumbled in the same absent way she'd talked in the wagon on the way over. But this time his boss lady had been talking to herself. Not only talking—she'd held an entire conversation with herself as if there were another person sitting there talking to her, only Katie Pearl was doing the talking for both of them.

Crazy Katie, they'd called her. With every passing moment it was becoming a little clearer why.

"Mornin'," he grunted, rubbing his jaw.

"Morning." She poured a cup of coffee and held the tin out to him. "I was just about to wake you. We've got a long day of work ahead of us."

"Thanks." He took the offered cup, his fingers brushing hers for a moment. Instantly his insides seemed to jump again at the contact, and his eyes latched onto hers and didn't want to let go. He'd thought it had been because of the fight they were having last night. Not so this morning. "Did you sleep any?"

A blush tinged her cheeks buttercup pink. "Enough."

He sipped the hot coffee and let the bitter brew spread through him as he studied her. She was a puzzle.

Finally he couldn't help it. "Why won't you go in the barn?"

She heaved a sigh. "Because. I don't want to. That's your job. I don't want to get into it again today. So, what do you know about building a house?"

Prickly. Prickly. He understood prickly. He also understood a change of subject when he heard it. "I've helped build a few."

"Good. I mean, I could've done it myself. I just didn't know how sturdy it would be."

He nodded toward the makeshift pen that Myrtle May stood in. "If that's a sampling of your skills, then I can safely say you need to let me take the lead on the house building."

Uncertainty lit her expression. "It's not that bad."

"Is so. Your horse is only staying in because she wants to. She could walk out of there in a heartbeat."

Her shoulders slumped. "I suppose you're right." She sighed and then handed him a tin plate with a stack of bacon and a hard biscuit.

He was careful not to touch her as he took the plate of food. As they ate, he noticed her eyes went over to her handiwork on the corrals several times, and each time he felt worse about telling her she'd done a poor job.

When he finished breakfast, he went over to look at the

horses. Katie came to stand beside him. "The black one was my pa's, and the chestnut is my cattle horse. But the rest of them you can pick from. You can start figuring out which one suits you anytime you want."

"Thanks. They're a fine bunch of horses. Who broke them?"

She looked up at him, her brows crinkled over those pretty blue eyes. "I did."

"You?"

She crossed her arms. "Yes, I did. Not that we normally tell folks that because they might not want to buy them. But it's the truth."

Silence stretched between them and he found himself smiling in the end. She was a stubborn, unpredictable woman. "Did your pa raise you to be independent or did you fight so hard he had no other choice?"

The challenge in her expression eased. "It's a hard land out here. It killed my ma early—she was too soft to make it. So Pa toughened me up from an early age."

Treb thought of his mother and sister, and his insides twisted. "You took to it like a baby duck takes to a watering hole, didn't you?"

"I did." A faint smile bloomed across her face.

It was a small one but it took Treb's breath away. She'd been so serious and sad-looking the entire time he'd known her. For an instant he imagined her as she'd been before the tornado tore up her world. Then a flashback to a time before he'd lost his family slammed into him. Tragedy changed a person. It had changed him. Suddenly he wished with all his heart that Katie Pearl would not have suffered loss such as she had.

"Well, I best be getting to work on rebuilding your house, Katie Pearl. Maybe that'll make that smile show up more often. It looks right nice on you." He tipped his hat, spun on his boot heels, and strode across the yard to the barn.

It was time to get to work.

They spent the day hauling out the good wood from the ruins of the house for repurposing, setting the rest aside for firewood. From the look of last night's fire, he figured Katie was going to need a lot of wood. She'd burned that fire long and hot all night.

The sun was a scorcher, and by midday they were both soaked with sweat, but Katie never slowed down. She hauled wood like a pack mule. She also hadn't talked much—at least not to him. He'd caught her a time or two talking to herself when he'd come around a corner. After thinking on it he'd decided that given what she'd been through, she was due a few oddities. She was tough—he was learning that more and more. He didn't know all the details of what had happened, but after getting to know her a little better, he figured it had been bad. Probably would have broken a softer woman.

A man rode into the yard that afternoon.

Treb saw Katie's hand move to her gun as she watched him approach. "What do you need, Preacher?"

Treb wouldn't have guessed the solid-built man was a preacher. He looked more like a lawman.

The preacher smiled. "I came to see if you needed anything, Katie. And to see if we can expect you at Sunday services. That's all." His hands tightened on the leather reins as his shrewd navy eyes dug into Treb, giving him the once-over. "And to see if this man you'd hired was a decent sort. The kind who would respect your wishes."

Treb suddenly felt as if he were being judged by Katie's pa on whether he was good enough to court her.

Katie scowled. "I can take care of myself, Preacher Dawson. And I won't be coming to services."

"Have you reconsidered letting us come out here to help get things in order?"

"I don't want any help. I hired myself a man. And he'll do just fine."

The preacher didn't linger long, obviously having learned that there were times when it was best to retreat. But not before he let Treb know where to find him and that if he needed any help to let him know.

By the time the evening came around, black and ominous clouds gathered on the horizon and the wind kicked up something fierce. Katie had been carrying firewood when she paused to stare at the dark clouds rolling fast across the sky. Her blue dress billowed in the strong wind and her hair streamed out behind her.

"Don't you think we better move the supplies into the barn?" Treb asked. When Katie turned to reply, her complexion was ashen. "Are you okay?"

She blinked and took a deep breath, still looking alarmed.

He put down the wood in his arms, realizing something wasn't right. But before he could ask more questions, rain started coming down in sheets. He broke into action, jogging toward the supplies.

"I'm going to move your food supplies into the barn," he called over the wind. "It'll all be ruined if we don't do something."

She didn't move at first. Then seemed to snap out of whatever held her captive and followed him. "I'll help." She grabbed a bag of flour while he grabbed a large sack of oats and hurried into the barn. He set the sack in the corner where it would be safe and realized that Katie hadn't followed him. She was grabbing supplies and dropping them off at the entrance of the barn but not coming inside. He rushed past her to grab the heavier feed sacks, and when he was done with those, he took up bringing what she'd piled in the wide doorway.

Her dress was plastered to her and rainwater ran off the limp rim of her hat like a waterfall. She was drenched, but still she didn't step into the protection of the barn.

The wind whipped about them, howling as the storm moved in, fierce as a pack of wolves. Lightning flashed across the sky. Katie jumped but she remained rooted to the spot, frozen, staring at the sky.

"Come on." He had to raise his voice over the wind as he took her arm. "We've got to get inside."

"No!" she cried, yanking her arm free. Her eyes were wide with terror as she backed away from the barn, totally exposed to the storm. Rain was blowing sideways now. The wind was so strong she had to lean into it to stay upright.

"Katie, you have to get out of this."

She didn't seem to hear him.

"Katie, you have to come inside the barn," he yelled. He was beside her in two strides. Water dripped from her face. Her eyes were as big as dinner plates as she stared at him. "Come on, Katie."

She shook her head vigorously. "No! I don't have to do anything you say. I'll stay right here."

"You can't stay here," he yelled over a crack of thunder. "You could be hurt. Come on." He reached for her arm but she jumped away.

"Leave me be. I'm not going in there! I can't."

It dawned on him then as he looked from her to the barn why in all this time she hadn't set foot into the barn. She was afraid of being inside. He thought of the way she'd stood outside the General Store and hadn't entered the building. And who could blame her? She'd been trapped beneath her home when it had fallen down on top of her. The terror was clearly visible on her face. When the lightning lit up the night again, too close for comfort, he felt for her. There was no way she could stay out in this.

With no other options, and before she had a chance to shoot him, he reached for her.

"No," she cried, sounding like a wild animal.

Treb ignored her—he had to—as he scooped her into his arms, being careful to clamp his hands around her arms so she couldn't get at her gun. Good thing he did, since she turned into a wildcat.

"Put me down," she screamed, kicking and fighting.

Ignoring her, he strode toward the barn.

"Nooo! Not in there. Nooo!" she cried.

"You can't stay in this storm, Katie." He was losing patience. Fool woman should know this was the only way. He strode into the barn.

"You no-good, lily-livered skunk! Let me go!" Wiggling her arm loose, she walloped him on the side of the head.

"Ow! Hold still, you wildca—"

She got another wallop in. This time she managed to startle him so bad his hold on her loosened, and she flew out of his arms. He managed to snag her pistol out of its holder, though, and was sure he'd saved his own life in the process.

Stuffing it in the back waistband of his britches, he wondered how in the name of thunder he was going to get Katie calmed down. He was between her and the exit of the barn. Through the hole in the roof, lightning lit up the darkened sky. Thunder cracked instantly. Katie looked like a cornered animal, darting from side to side and looking for a way to get past him. "Let me out," she gasped, racing forward suddenly, so terrified that she tried to run right by him. He wrapped his arms around her. She elbowed him hard in the ribs, then kicked him in his knee with the heel of her boot.

"Umph!" he grunted, barely hanging on to her. She kicked him in the knee again, then twisted loose as he buckled in pain. Grabbing his knee, he watched her race into the storm.

For a little thing she made him feel like he'd just tangled with five of her. It was embarrassing. "Katie, come back," he yelled, his words disappearing on the wind just as she disappeared into the darkness.

What had he gotten himself into? The question came at him once more as he limped out into the rain calling his boss's name. It was a silly question, that was for sure, because ten minutes ago he might not have known—but now he knew exactly what he'd gotten himself into.

A mess. Pure and simple. One strange mess.

Rain rolled down his face and dripped off the brim of his hat like a river. Hanging his head, he stared at his boots. Water puddled about them.

Katie was terrified of being trapped. The realization hit him hard—shamed him.

She'd laid under her house trapped alive for days in a grave, basically. It all made sense to him. It wasn't that she didn't want to go in the barn. She couldn't.

And when he'd forced her, she'd gone wild.

She was probably afraid of the dark too.

That would explain the fires and the way her hand shook last night as dusk came and went. And talking to herself? It could very well explain that too.

Katie Pearl was afraid of the dark.

His little sister had been afraid of the dark. The memory came at him from a long way off. He remembered how he used to tease her about it. Even jumped out at her a time or two . . . stupid adolescent fun. It was a regret he'd lived with ever since she'd—since they'd all died nearly ten years ago.

He had to find Katie.

Had to find her and get her out of this. Get her safe.

"Katie!" he yelled to the wind, then took off jogging.

CHAPTER FOUR

KATIE RAN UNTIL SHE WAS OUT IN THE CENTER OF THE meadow and even then she kept running, her heart pounding. The storm—the terrible, awful sound of the tornado coming—rang in her ears. She stumbled and fell hard to her knees.

Her heart pounded louder than the sound of the tornado.

Only she wasn't sure if the tornado was coming now or if it was the one that had killed her pa she was hearing in her head. She would never forget that one, that night.

Crying, unable to move, she curled into a ball in a mud puddle, locked her arms around her legs, and buried her face in her knees. "Please help me, Lord," she cried. But God hadn't helped her that night. That horrible, terrible night that spread into days—so why would He help her now?

"Katie."

Her head jerked up at the sound of Treb calling her name. She wanted to call out to him, but he would force her into the barn again. She couldn't go inside. She huddled into herself more, hoping he wouldn't find her. She couldn't move if she wanted to. She shivered and her teeth chattered, and the raging roar in her head outdid the sound of the storm.

And then suddenly, tender arms gathered her up. "It's okay, Katie," Treb said, pulling her close.

"I can't go inside. I can't," she cried, trembling and too weak to fight, hating herself for it.

"Shh, it's okay. We won't go inside," Treb soothingly whispered against her ear. It dawned on her then that he'd dropped to the ground, pulled her into his arms, and was cradling her face in the crook of his shoulder. His strong hand cupped her head as he gently rocked her. "Shh," he whispered again, as if she were a child. "I'm going to sit right here in this wide-open space, and we're going to ride out this storm together."

Her throat was clamped up tight, and Katie could only nod against his neck as another crack of thunder made her jump. "Is it coming?" she asked, her hands clenching his shirt.

"Is what coming?"

"The tor-na-do." She managed the word in broken sobs.

His arms tightened around her. "No tornado. Just a regular Texas thunderstorm. A bad one, but no tornado tonight."

A terrified whimper of relief broke free of her. She hated the weakness it revealed but she couldn't stop it. Again, Treb's arms held her secure.

Though the storm raged around them, she began to feel safe . . . and it had been a long time since she'd felt that way.

Especially around a man. But she was so tired. So very tired. And Treb was here, holding her.

In that moment Katie felt everything would be all right.

Would it be? She didn't know, but she had hope.

The storm raged about them for hours. Treb ignored the mud he was sitting in and the rain pelting them in sheets, driven by a relentless wind with the strength of a bullwhip. He just sat there in the middle of the field with lightning striking in the distance—and sometimes so close he wondered how it didn't hit them, but the good Lord was looking out for them. He figured since Katie was an innocent victim of a cruel act of nature that the Lord might be making it up to her.

Maybe the Lord was giving him a chance at redeeming himself too.

As he held Katie, feeling her relax in his arms, he whispered words of reassurance in her ear. Somehow he felt that helping her out was a chance to make up for not being there when his family had needed him.

Not that he deserved a second chance . . . but the Good Book spoke of second chances often. His pa had believed in them, God rest his soul, and though the storm raged around them, a sense of hope eased its way through Treb.

Katie Pearl was all alone, and she needed help in more ways than he'd ever suspected until tonight. It was more than needing her house rebuilt. Katie needed someone to stand by her as she struggled through whatever was holding her captive in her mind.

He would be moving on once the house was finished. But for now, a determination struck him as fierce as the thunder and lightning breaking the night in half with its ferocity. Before he left he'd help Katie through this fearsome road she was traveling. He decided there in the middle of that storm, holding Katie in his arms, that by the time he left she'd be able to sleep inside the house she'd hired him to build.

It was a vow he made to the Lord. And maybe, in the process, he'd get some relief down deep in the dark corners of his heart where regret had eaten a hole clean through him.

"Are you okay?"

Treb's gentle voice penetrated Katie's sleep-fogged brain. She stirred in his arms, lifting her head. She found herself staring up into his concerned gray eyes. He looked terrible.

His hat was gone, his hair was plastered to his face, and his eyes were bleary from lack of sleep. She knew she looked no better.

Her heart tugged tight in her chest. She nodded. "Thank you," she managed, touching his face for just an instant. She was unable to believe how tender he'd been holding her during the storm, but right now she needed to move away from him, out of his strong arms. Her knees were stiff and her legs wobbly as she stood. He held her elbow and supported her as she straightened. And then he stood up too. He didn't say it, but she could see that he was even stiffer than she was.

"We're an awful sight," she said, feeling the heat of a blush spreading across her skin.

He grinned. "I'd have to agree with you on that, but I'm afraid you might haul off and kick me again."

She gasped, realizing she had kicked him last night! And jabbed him hard in the ribs too. "I'm so sorry. I just lost it."

His smile faded. "It's all right, Katie. After what you've been through it's understandable. I wouldn't have tried to get you in the barn if I had really thought about how something like that could affect a person."

Turning away, she wrapped her arms around her waist and hugged herself tight. Wishing she could hold off the truth but knowing now that she couldn't. Her shoulders slumped. "What they say about me is true."

Treb's hand on her shoulder turned her back to face him. "No, it's not. It's no wonder going inside a building terrifies you. Or that you talk to yourself sometimes. Time will help heal this problem."

His words hurt deep down inside. Hurt in a way she didn't understand—it was a good hurt. A dangerous hurt, knowing he believed in her.

"I am afraid," she admitted, "but I aim to fix it." She looked down at the ground, then back up to meet his watchful, kind eyes. Even all mushed and tired she decided the man was about as good to look at as a sunrise on a clear morning. "I'm very obliged to you for what you did last night. My pa would shake your hand, Treb Rayburn. And Pa didn't shake just anyone's hand."

Katie glanced at a patch of muddy grass to the side and noticed Treb's hat turned upside down in it. She walked over and picked it up, then went back and handed it to him. "Thank you," she said, again needing some space to think. She spun and headed back across the field toward the remains of the buildings. Her still-wet dress slapped against her legs, and her shoes made squishing noises as she trod through the mud. The sun was rising slowly in the sky, burning off the morning dew. The sunlight was wonderful to see, its rays warm on her clammy, damp skin. But when all the mud caked to her dress and her skin dried, her nasty predicament was only going to feel worse. Turning around she saw Treb walking at a much slower pace behind her. His soaked clothing looked worse than hers—still her heart squeezed looking at him. She'd hired a safe bet—a rambler who had no intentions of sticking around when the work was done. He was perfect for this job. Safe.

But last night, snug in Treb's strong arms, things had become complicated. He'd cradled her with such care . . .

Safe bet, ha! He'd come into the awful storm and sat smack down in the middle of a puddle of water and just held her tight. Held her all through the night, trying to protect her from the elements because he'd seen how hysterical being inside made her.

And being in the dark too.

The man had downright messed up her plans.

A girl had to fight holding back feelings for a man who would do that for her.

But she'd been too fearful to fight it. She'd needed what he offered.

Of course she would have made it, with no other choice.

Yet she couldn't bring herself to think of what the morning would have been like after the storm if he hadn't been there. She remembered how it was when they pulled her out of her grave.

She swallowed hard as the memory of screaming and whimpering like a hurt animal rushed at her like the wind. She'd been dirty and bruised and wild. Like last night in the storm.

"I'm going to the stream to clean up," she said, shaking off the memory, glad to have an excuse to be alone, to get away from what was eating at her. "When I'm finished, I'll show you the way." Changing directions she hurried toward the stand of trees off to the side of her homestead. She wished being normal again would be as easy as washing the mud off of her. But she knew that wasn't how it was. Treb might tell her she wasn't crazy, but she knew it wasn't that simple.

CHAPTER FIVE

"WHAT ARE YOU DOING?"

Treb looked up from planting a post in the hole he'd just finished digging. The sun was out as if there had never been a storm in the night. It was a scorcher even though it was only midmorning. Steam had risen from the ground as the water evaporated causing his wet, mud-caked clothes to dry stiff and scratch against his skin. Katie, on the other hand, had been gone so long he'd begun to worry. He hadn't been able to stop thinking about her. She'd been so fragile. So alone. So small in his arms. And when she'd looked up at him as he held her, he knew he would have walked through fire to help her.

Now, here she stood with her dress freshly washed and sun-dried, and her cheeks shone with the glow of having been scrubbed. Her deep brown hair glistened like mahogany in the sunlight, hanging loose around her face and shoulders. She was holding her hat and without it she looked extremely feminine. Her eyes sparkled despite the weariness he saw in them.

He swallowed hard as realization struck . . . Katie Pearl was beautiful.

His gut suddenly felt as if a family of grasshoppers had been cut loose inside it. "I'm making you a shelter. No more need for you to be caught out in the weather again." He'd spent the night holding her, listening to her mumble to herself when she'd fallen asleep in his arms. The woman had been so worn out that she'd slept through a blasting thunder and lightning display like he hadn't seen in ages. Only by the grace of God had they not been struck down sitting where they were. But somewhere in the middle of all that, Katie Pearl had closed her eyes against his heart and slept.

It was a disturbing thing to a man who didn't want connections. And he recognized this powerful, protective instinct as the dangerous kind, the kind that had the power to undo him. When she didn't say anything more, he met her wide gaze—not happy with what she was doing to him.

"Now, Katie, don't be lookin' at me with those big eyes of yours. I'll just attach some old wagon tarps I found in the barn to the top and sides of these poles. You'll have nothing but cloth over your head and daylight on two sides. Or all sides if you want. You can tie the sides to the poles, but if a storm blows in, you can at least keep dry."

"I—well," she stammered, studying the other poles with interest, "it might help. I can try it at least."

Good. She wasn't as stubborn as he thought she'd be. "I

figure if there isn't a heavy roof above you that could cave in, it will be a step forward. Progress, you know."

She clasped her hands together and a smile spread across her face. He sure liked her smiles.

"Progress. That's just what my pa used to say. I like the sound of that, Treb Rayburn."

"Good," he grunted and went back to work, trying hard not to let those eyes or that smile wheedle their way any deeper. Nope, this shelter would help keep her firmly away from any more chances of him having to hold her close.

"The water's good if you want to wash that caked mud off of you." She pointed toward the creek, then headed over and stood with her hands on her hips as she stared at the barn. "It gets all-fired irritating that I can't go inside a building." She spun toward him. "And when I get to talking to myself . . . You're as loony as they say, Katie Pearl." She mumbled the last words under her breath. Pure disgust directed at herself.

He threw the spade to the ground. "No, you're not. And I wish one of them name-calling old biddies would come call you that while I'm standing beside you. I'd let them have it. Now, stop spouting that nonsense and help me attach these tarps."

She scowled at him and that was just fine. It suited him in fact, much better than when she smiled at him. He didn't need her smiling at him anymore. No, sir, he did not.

"Don't you give me orders! I'm still your boss, and I was thinking I was hungry and thought you might be too since we haven't had breakfast. But my supplies are inside the barn."

Stalking inside the barn, he grabbed a pouch of beef jerky,

strode back out, and shoved it at her. "This should do us till we get some work done."

He figured the madder he made her, the safer he'd be. He planned to see New Orleans down in Louisiana and the Gulf before the winter hit. He had a whole list of places he was going to visit before he settled down, and the sooner he got Katie's life in order, the sooner he could ride out. His clothes were stiff and scratchin' his hide raw, and his insides were feeling just as raw every time she looked at him with that lost-little-girl look.

Keeping her mad at him and out of his arms seemed the safest way of getting back on the trail and making tracks.

Her blue eyes froze over and hit him with an icy blast. *Perfect. Good. Couldn't be better.*

"It's no wonder your horse up and died on you, you ill-tempered hunk of flesh." Jabbing her nose in the air, she strode past him and headed toward the pile of rubble that used to be her home. There she sat on a section of flooring that had remained intact. He watched her grudgingly pull a piece of jerky from the sack to chew on as she studied the disaster.

She needed to see progress and she needed to see it now.

With a grunt of irritation at himself, Treb went back to work. Katie would have shelter before nightfall, and that was a fact.

❦

Katie felt helpless enough, and she hated the feeling. She did not need Treb making her feel worse!

The man was infuriating. He was ornery, pushy, and arrogant.

Chomping on a tough piece of jerky, she watched Treb working on the structure that would keep the rain off of her and give her some shield against the night. Truth was she was grateful. She really, really was. But he was treating her like she was helpless, and it didn't sit well—not since she was fighting against giving in to it with everything she had.

Resentment settled over her like the stink of soured milk. Watching him, she knew exactly what it was. He'd walked out in that storm and held her, protected her, and shielded her with his body. She'd slept. She'd actually drifted off to sleep during the awful storm with the steady sound of his heart beating in her ear, giving her comfort.

She hadn't felt comforted in so long. But now he was taking over. And she didn't like it. It made her feel even more helpless than she already did, and that made her mad. Chewing on the jerky, she watched the man work. The muscles in his arms bunching with each movement reminded her that those arms had made her feel safe. She shoved the thought aside. It did no good sitting there daydreaming about falling in love with a practical stranger. He was going to be leaving before the summer was over, so the very idea of such a fanciful thought irritated her even more.

"You better get up and get busy, or before you know it you'll be beggin' this man to stay," she growled. "That's what you think."

Jumping up, she decided she needed to take charge. She

was sleeping in the shelter tonight, and she was sleeping on something other than the ground. Surveying the ruins, she saw a section of wall that would work just perfect. Stomping over to it, she wrestled the piece from the other wreckage. It was wider and taller than she was, but not overly big. Dragging it toward Treb, she dropped it in her tracks, then went back for some planks. This would soon be her bed. Raised about four inches from the ground, it would ensure that her bedroll wouldn't get wet if it rained again. Feeling much better about herself, she marched over, and with just a small hesitation, she stepped beneath the canvas canopy.

Her heart pounded but the space was no more threatening than a porch overhang, and she could handle that. Still, pride flooded through her. She'd made a step forward.

"Good for you, Katie," Treb said. His gentle words of encouragement flowed over her and eased the anger she'd felt toward him. "It's a beginning."

"Yes, it is."

"I still don't understand why no one from town has come out to help you clean up some of this wreckage."

Katie placed her hands on her hips, her fingers tapping on her hip bones. "After they pulled me out from under the house, I guess I was a little upset. I might have screamed at them and maybe waved a pitchfork around a little. When I found my gun . . . they scattered."

Treb was speechless, but she couldn't read his face.

"The townsfolk didn't come back after that. But then the fellas started coming around trying to court me, wanting my land, so I started shooting. They all stopped coming around after that. Better that way."

"Katie, you have got to stop waving that gun around. You could have friends in town who would come out here if you'd just holster that thing."

"They call me crazy. Why would I want their help?"

He raked a hand over his face. "I guess I see your point. Only, if you would stop shooting at people, then they wouldn't call you names."

"Ha, why would I want that? If it wasn't for me bein' crazy, I'd have more men than a dog has fleas out here trying to latch on to me for my ranch. Besides, I hired you and you're doing just fine." It was true, he was doing fine . . . when he wasn't making her mad.

It hit her again, looking at him, that soon he would be gone and she would be all alone once more. Her head started pounding just thinking about it.

CHAPTER SIX

TREB WONDERED WHAT KATIE HAD BEEN LIKE BEFORE the tornado. A week after hiring Treb, she seemed less skittish than she had been. They had worked side by side clearing the house and sifting through the materials, determining what was usable and what was useless. There had been times when he'd known it was hard on Katie digging through the leftovers of her life before the tornado. She'd grow quiet, her work would slow, and then he'd hear her talking to herself. It was as if talking to herself comforted her. And sometimes he'd watch her sit up on the hill by her pa's grave. When she'd come back, he could see she'd been crying. Treb always pretended he didn't notice this and he said nothing. What was he supposed to say anyway?

He didn't know how to comfort someone. He'd tried the night of the storm—he thought of that night often. Of holding Katie in his arms and of her sleeping soundly with her

cheek against his heart. Sometimes he'd find himself thinking about what it would be like to settle down with a good
woman and build a life.

And then he'd shake off the thought and get back to
work. His mother had always longed to see the world. She'd
talked of it often and told him of the places she'd seen and
the places she longed to see. After moving from the East and
heading west on a wagon train, she'd fallen in love with Treb's
dad and ended up marrying and having two babies quickly
thereafter. His father had been a farmer who just wanted to
work the land and put down roots. He'd been a good man,
but he hadn't ever understood his wife's desire to see more of
the world. It had put a wedge between them, and his mother
had buried her longing within her. But Treb had understood
it—he also understood how marriage affected dreams.

Tonight was a beautiful night. The stars were sparkling
radiantly against a pitch-black sky. Treb lay on his bedroll
with his arms behind his head staring up at it. A lonesomeness for his family took hold of him, and he wished they were
alive here beside him. He let his gaze fall to Katie. She was
quiet in her tent. She'd been that way all afternoon.

"Tell me about some of the places you've seen," she said,
startling him, as if she'd been reading his mind.

Shaking off the melancholy memories and always glad to
talk about his adventures, he sat up. "Well, let's see, I think
you'd like the Grand Canyon. It's out in Arizona Territory. It's
as big and vast as anything I've ever seen, and more stunning
than anything I could have ever dreamed of."

"I've heard of it. I heard it's so deep you can't hardly see the streams down at the bottom."

"That's true. From the rim of the canyon, the big Colorado River looks like a pretty ribbon you could tie your hair up with, that's how far down it is snaking through the gorge. And the colors . . . Katie, you haven't ever seen so many colors in a rock face. Reds, oranges, browns, and creams. Even golds. It's like God took the sunset and laid it down on the rock face that He cut out of the earth. The rock formations are huge and the drop-offs of the cliffs aren't for the faint of heart. But you can stand on the rim and watch the eagles soar out over the canyon that stretches as far as the eye can see. It'll make you believe in the Lord like nothing else could." It was true. He and the Lord had regained footing there on that rim after he'd lost his family. It had been rough, though, with all the guilt and bitterness Treb had felt for himself and the Lord.

"It sounds amazing," Katie murmured, placing her hands beneath her chin. She studied the fire. "Do you have any family, Treb? Anyone you left behind when you headed out to see the world?"

Was she reading his thoughts? He shifted uncomfortably in his bedroll. "Nope. No family—living."

"What happened to them? Did you lose them like I lost my pa?"

His heart ached and his gaze shifted to the fire flickering between them. "I lost them. But it was a long time ago." Talking about this was too hard. He needed to change the subject. "What about your mother?" he asked. "What happened to her?"

"She got sick with pneumonia when I was a little girl. I don't remember much about her, except I can remember her singing to me."

He remembered his mother singing to him too. "I'm glad you have that memory to carry with you."

She sighed. "Me too. It was awful lonely sometimes, but Pa taught me everything a girl needed to know. I can shoot better than most men, and I can ride and use a whip. And I can tend to my cattle too. Though they're so scattered out right now I might never find them all."

"Do you need me to help you locate them?"

"Maybe one day. There's enough grass right now. I know they're out there. I need the house more than anything."

Katie rubbed her temple. She did that a lot, he'd noticed. "Is your head hurting?"

"Sometimes. When I try too hard to remember things. Especially my pa."

"Did you see a doctor after the tornado?"

"I ain't having no doctor poking and prodding me. Why would I need to, anyway?"

"I was just wondering is all. You rub your temples a lot and sometimes your eyes look pained. Does the sunlight hurt them?"

"They hurt sometimes, but it's just the headaches." She closed her eyes. And the flicker of the fire cast soft shadows on her features. He'd found himself studying her face more than he thought was good. Sometimes he'd be working and he'd get distracted just watching her.

It wasn't helping him get the job done any faster and that was for certain.

"What happened to your family, Treb? I'd like to know."

He closed his eyes. "They had a wagon accident and died."

"I'm sorry," Katie gasped. "Were you in the accident? Did you get hurt?"

His throat clamped down and he couldn't speak for a second. "Nope," he said at last. "I wasn't there. Pa and I had had an argument. I was eighteen. He and I had been butting heads over me wanting to see the world and him wanting me to stay on and farm beside him there in the panhandle. I rode off up ahead that morning on our way into town, and when they never showed up, I backtracked and found them." It still ate at him that he hadn't been there.

That he was alive and they were dead.

"I'm so sorry," she whispered across the flame, her eyes so full of sorrow for him that they dug into his heart.

"Yeah, I struck out after that and haven't stopped. Every time I see something amazing, I think of my mother and I tell myself that I'm seeing it for her." He paused. "It gives me comfort . . . I should have been there for them, Katie. And I wasn't."

Katie came out of the tent to sit beside him. "I didn't mean to open wounds to your heart."

He'd never spoken of this to anyone, but suddenly he was glad he'd shared it with Katie. It made him feel better . . . like he wasn't alone. "I'm glad you asked. You'd have liked my mother and my sister. You'd have liked my dad too. He just wanted the best for me. I know that now. But he and I had different dreams. Still, it nearly kills me that I wasn't there to save them. What kind of son isn't there for his family?"

She placed her hand on his. Though she had calluses from all the work she did, there was a tenderness to her touch that sent his heart racing.

"You didn't know when you rode off that you'd never see them alive again. I didn't know when my pa told me to get under my bed that I'd never see him again either."

Looking into her caring eyes, he wanted to pull her close like nothing he'd ever wanted. But he didn't. Instead, he lifted his hand and gently caressed her jaw with his thumb. "You're more sane than most folks I've ever known, Katie. Only God knows when our time is up. When it is, there's nothing anyone can do to stop it. I just wish I'd been there. That my last words to my pa hadn't been words of anger."

"He was a good pa, right?"

Treb nodded.

"Then he knew, and I'm sure in the end he didn't hold it against you."

Treb swallowed hard, but the lump in his throat was lodged tight. His eyes burned. Tears were for women. Still, when one slipped from the corner of his eye, there was relief in it. Somehow what Katie said was true. His pa knew he loved him. Despite the angry words.

"Has time healed your wounds, Treb?"

Her question slammed into him, and he knew he had better think long and hard about his answer. "It's numbing my pain, Katie. I don't think the hurt ever goes away. And I don't reckon I want it to. The hurt tells me they were real, that my love for them wasn't made-up. It's been almost ten years for me, and not a day goes by that I don't have regret about them not being here. I wish it had been me instead."

"I feel the same way, Treb. Why couldn't it have been me and not my pa? Or my mother before that? Why am I still here and they aren't?"

"I guess it just wasn't our time. But that doesn't make the regret any less, or the pain any smaller."

"No, it doesn't." She stood and moved back to her bedroll, looking at him across the fire. Her eyes glistened bright with tears in the light of the flames.

"Katie, you're not crazy," he said, finally saying what he'd been about to say earlier before she'd started asking him about his family.

"I sure feel like I'm crazy. I feel fuzzy in my head a lot and I can't remember things very well. And the talking to myself, I thought it would go away but it hasn't. I—"

"You have symptoms of a concussion, Katie. If that's the case, then you'll get better and better. The doc could tell you for sure, but I figure this far along you are probably over the worst of it."

"You really think so?" The relief was thick in her voice.

"I'm not a doctor but, yeah, that's what I think. And I know you're not crazy. The sooner you stop worrying about that, the better."

"I hope you're right," she said. "But if I can't make myself go into the barn or the house—"

"You will. You've been through a lot. Give yourself time."

"I'll try," she said, and the wistfulness in her voice had him wanting to hold her and whisper more reassurance to her. That alone kept his mouth shut.

"Thank you, Treb," she said softly. "For everything."

"You're welcome," he said, ripping his gaze off of her and pinning it on the flickering flames.

They didn't say more, just watched the flames. He realized not too much later that Katie was sleeping.

She'd fallen asleep peacefully, talking to him and not to herself.

He smiled as a warm sense of contentment nestled deep inside of him.

It was a dangerous feeling for a drifter like him. A dangerous feeling for certain.

CHAPTER SEVEN

DAYS PASSED, AND HE AND KATIE WORKED. THEY DIDN'T talk about the night around the campfire when they'd spoken of their families. It was as if they'd opened up more than they were comfortable with there under that starry sky with that crackling fire between them. But she did seem to relax some, and there were no more references from her about being crazy.

They got a routine down. He'd work straight through the day, and Katie would fix the meals if he got the supplies out of the barn. He sure hoped that she'd start venturing inside the building soon, but it had been two more weeks, and she'd made no attempt to even stick her head in the door. Her hands still shook if she got a late start on getting the fire going, which didn't happen often. Sometimes, though, despite his reassurances to her, he wondered if he was building a house for nothing. What good was a house if she couldn't walk into it?

The canvas structure that he'd built her was helping, and

he was glad the idea had come to him. There had been some rain showers since the storm, and he'd retreated to sleep in the barn on those nights. But no storms had come through, and for that he was grateful. Sometimes at night as they sat around the campfire, Katie would ask him to tell her more about the places he'd seen. He liked telling her about them and seeing the excitement on her face as he talked. He'd never really had anyone to share stories with since he'd lost his family. He figured relationships got in the way of his plans, and if he ever got close to someone, he would lose them. He didn't plan on having to deal with that ever again.

His heart had lost all it was going to lose. It ached just thinking about it.

If Katie's affection for her pistol was any clue to how she felt about the subject, he knew that she understood. She'd lost everything too. The only problem he had was that he'd begun to think more and more about kissing Katie. It had been almost two weeks since that storm when he'd held her close, and try as hard as he could to forget, the memory lingered. The feel of her soft in his arms. The trusting look in her eyes when she'd glanced up at him there in his embrace.

He'd tried to shove the thoughts out of his mind but they'd come charging back, relentless. It was getting so he couldn't keep his eyes off of her.

And sometimes he'd catch her looking at him, and he wondered if she was thinking similar thoughts. But then she'd frown and go back to work.

Just as well. He had places to see and she had a ranch to run.

He was nailing up the last of the interior walls between the three rooms that Katie had decided on. She wanted a house much smaller than the original one, but the rooms were still spacious. He was on the ladder pounding nails when he noticed a movement out of the corner of his eye. A man was approaching in a wagon that looked as if it carried something. He glanced toward Katie who was helping hold the frame steady as he nailed it to the floor.

"We have company."

Katie swung around toward the approaching wagon. "It better not be one of those lily-livered skunks again."

"Don't shoot till we find out what he wants. And let me finish pounding these nails before you let go and reach for your gun." Treb had already decided if he ever met up with the men who'd come calling on Katie and made her feel like she was nothing but a crazy woman who needed her ranch taken from her, he'd make certain they understood to never bother her again. How he was going to do that after he was gone was unclear, but then Katie thought she could take care of herself, and she probably could.

"I haven't killed one of them yet, so don't get all worried."

Chuckling, he slammed the three nails into place, then he climbed down the ladder and set the hammer down. "Good. I told you, folks might stop by if you stopped shooting at them. Might even have some offering to help you."

She glared at him. "Why do I need them? I have you."

"Can you just be nice this one time, for me?"

The wagon pulled into the yard and a grizzled, older man

drew it to a halt. "Howdy, folks, I got an order of windows for Katie Pearl. Would that be you, ma'am?" He looked warily at Katie as if he expected her to whip out her pistol at any moment.

Katie's smile bloomed large, and she jumped down from the house's floor to the driveway. "Yes, that's me. You brought my windows?"

"Yes, ma'am. Mr. Crandon said to get them out to you as soon as possible."

"Did you hear, Treb?"

He followed her to the wagon, then reached up to shake the older man's hand. "Thanks for bringing these out. We'll put them to good use."

The man gave a tobacco-stained grin as he climbed down from the rig. "Well, I got to admit I weren't too sure what I'd find out here. You know, I heard all kinds of things about getting shot at. But you folks are right nice."

Katie frowned, but Treb placed his arm across her shoulders and pulled her gently to his side. She met his gaze, her face upturned, and Treb suddenly had a desire to kiss her. He swallowed the notion and looked quickly to their guest.

"Katie had reasons for insisting some folks get off her property. Anyone with the right intentions is welcome anytime. Isn't that right, Katie?"

"True." Katie paused, measuring the man with her gaze. "I suppose I like company. What's your name, sir?"

Treb's heart was racing. What was coming over him?

"Well, Miss, folks call me Dooley."

"Then, Mr. Dooley, would you stay for dinner if I were to get started fixing it right now? You could still get back to town before nightfall."

That won her a wide smile from the visitor. Treb dragged his thoughts back to the conversation and away from thoughts of kissing her.

"I'd be mighty honored to share a meal with you folks. Mighty honored. I'll just help your husband here unload these windows while you're preparing the meal."

Katie and Treb both stiffened. Treb dropped his arm from around her shoulder and Katie stepped away.

"Thanks for the help, Dooley," Treb managed, his heart hammering in his chest something awful. "The name's Treb. I'm Katie's hired man. I'm just here building her house for her."

Dooley looked from him to Katie, rubbed his jaw for a moment, then grinned again. "I guess I just saw the closeness and misread it. Sorry about that. Didn't mean no disrespect."

Treb knew he had been out of line placing his arm around Katie and drawing her close. Katie hadn't spoken up and was just staring at the both of them. "I've been working here for almost three weeks," Treb finally went on. "We've become friends so it was my instinct to be protective of Katie when a stranger drove up. It's my fault for giving you the wrong impression."

Katie's brows met as she scrunched her forehead deep in thought. Her fingers twitched a little next to where her pistol usually hung on her hips. But her pistol wasn't there.

At the moment he thought it was a very good thing. She looked upset.

"I'd be much obliged if you'd help Treb unload those windows, Mr. Dooley," she said. Then she spun on her boots and strode off toward the barn for supplies. Treb's mouth was dry as he watched her go. What was she so upset about? He'd fixed the misunderstanding.

He waited to see what she would do when she got to the barn. He prayed she'd be mad enough that she'd go inside.

"She's a right pretty little filly," Dooley said beside him. "Kind of reminds me of my sweet Edith Ann, God rest her soul. Got spunk, that one does."

Treb couldn't help smiling. "Yes, sir, she does. Spunk enough to fill up Texas, I reckon." As he spoke, she halted at the barn entrance. Her hands were on her hips as she studied the interior like it was a wall before her. Then she poked her foot across the line and Treb held his breath. "If you'll excuse me for a minute." Hurrying forward, he covered the distance in record speed.

"What do you want me to get for you?" Treb asked, coming to a halt beside her—but far enough away not to make Dooley think he'd overstepped his boundaries again.

There was anger and fear and a whole heap of emotion tangled in her eyes when she looked up at him. "I need all the usual stuff. The flour and meal. And some backbone if you see any in there."

He chuckled, then sobered. "It'll come, Katie. You made some progress just by thinking about entering the building, so don't let it beat the dust out of you."

Her eyes calmed a little. "I guess you're right."

Wanting once more to pull her into his arms and whisper that everything would be all right, he clenched his fist and strode inside the barn. What was wrong with him? Why was he suddenly thinking of things he had no business thinking about?

Grabbing a fresh bag of meal, he headed out of the barn, and stalked to the campfire area, his mind reeling. Katie had gone after a chicken, so he set the bag down and went back to unload windows. He had plans for these windows and wanted to get a good look at them.

Plus, he needed to put distance between himself and Katie.

And get a handle on the thoughts pressing a hole into his chest.

They spent an enjoyable afternoon meal with Mr. Dooley. Katie kept having to pull her eyes away from Treb. Ever since Mr. Dooley had assumed they were married, she'd had a deep hankering for it to be true.

It pained her something fierce and she wished it weren't so. Oh, how she wished it weren't so. They'd spent several long days together and long nights across the fire from each other too. Her heart ached terribly when she thought of how far he'd come on the house, and that within just a few short weeks, he'd be gone. Someday soon he would hop on the horse he'd chosen and ride out of her life on his great adventures.

Her gut twisted at the thought.

She had land and a home, yet she found herself longing for adventure, too, wishing she could see what Treb would see on his travels. Longing to be with him wherever he was going . . .

But she wouldn't be going anywhere.

"You take care of yourself, little lady," Dooley said, pausing before climbing up into his wagon. Over lunch, they'd explained a little about what had happened in the tornado because he'd asked. His watchful eyes studied her, and Katie felt concern in them.

"I will." A powerful lonesomeness swept over her. "You too."

"That there is a good man." He nodded toward Treb, who'd already said his farewell and gone back to work. "One worth keeping around, I 'spect." He winked, tipped his hat, and climbed up into the seat. "My Edith Ann? She had spunk like you, spunk that nothing could knock down for long. You'll get your feet under you again, Miss Katie. Just push forward through the darkness. There's always daylight on the other side, thanks to the good Lord and His faithfulness."

With that, he slapped the reins and set the horse team forward in an arching turn, then off they went down the track. Katie stood with her hand protecting her eyes against the sun as Dooley's words echoed in her head. *That there is a good man,*" he'd said. She could not stop herself from turning to watch Treb with his hammer, building her house.

If only I could keep him.

The wistful thought trickled through her like a sigh, but she cut it off at the pass.

What was she thinking?

Nope, she might still be off-kilter, but she knew she'd be a fool to fall for a man with leaving in his plans.

"What you need to do, Katie Pearl, is march over to that barn and go inside." Her stomach rolled when she took a step and then another in that direction, only to stop after a couple.

"You can do this. You are not a coward."

But she was. Her head started thumping, her vision blurred, and she knew she couldn't go inside the barn.

But that wasn't her worst fear anymore.

Most of all she feared that when it came time to wave good-bye to Treb . . . she wouldn't be able to do it.

And that scared her more than anything.

CHAPTER EIGHT

FOR TWO WEEKS, TREB WORKED ALMOST NONSTOP ON the house. A desperation churned inside of him that he didn't totally understand. All he knew was that he had to finish the house. Katie worked beside him hammering away and helping him hold windows in place. They got the walls up, and he'd grouped the windows in pairs—the large glass panes creating the illusion that even when they were inside, it felt like outside.

Now he was working on the roof. From his vantage point he could see Katie riding a horse and working with it like she was born to train. He paused to watch her. There was nothing crazy about Katie. She was smart and stubborn, and the more he was around her, the more he wanted to be around her. He felt for her though, every day when she strode to the barn and stared inside, standing there like a feather balancing on the wind waiting for the next gust to blow it a new direction. She would hover as he held his breath, hoping she could conquer the fear holding her. But each time she would spin around and stomp away, either to ride the horses or to head to the stream. He could see that she didn't like to be beat and it was eating at her.

She was so determined to fix herself, and each day that she couldn't do it frustrated her more.

He didn't know what to do for her other than to do what she'd asked of him, which was to get her home built.

And he was almost done. That was the best thing, he told himself. He needed to get done. He was getting attached to Katie even though he tried not to. Ever since Dooley had mistaken him as Katie's husband, he found himself wondering what it would be like to call her his own. He thought about kissing her and holding her more and more and it was driving him wild.

So there it was. The problem plain and not so simple—he was falling for Katie.

The protective feelings held him captive. She was out here, isolated and alone.

And he was going to ride off into the sunset and leave her.

He had to.

He needed to.

He was driven to. But right now, he wanted to ride horses with Katie.

Climbing down from the roof, he strode across the yard to the arena. "Do you want to go for a ride?"

Katie pulled her horse to a halt and smiled. "I would love to do that."

He grinned, grabbed his saddle, and opened the gate. He chose the good-looking buff-colored horse he'd settled on and within minutes, they were riding across the pasture, with Katie talking excitedly about the ranch and the beautiful land that she owned.

He might regret it tomorrow, but for now, Treb let himself relax and enjoy the afternoon.

He'd think about tomorrow, tomorrow. For now, he was enjoying himself too much.

Since the day he'd gone riding with Katie over a week ago, Treb had done nothing but work. It had been a lovely afternoon they'd shared, but Katie was upset by how much she'd enjoyed his company.

Now he acted as if he couldn't get the house built soon enough. He hardly took time to eat, much less time to ride horses with her again.

She was acutely aware that each strike of the hammer took him closer to leaving.

And her closer to watching him ride away.

Angry at herself for being a fool, she tried to keep busy. And as far away from him as possible. If she wasn't swinging a hammer, she was riding her horses. Work steadied her nerves. Her headaches had stopped for the most part, and she'd started feeling more like herself. Though she still hadn't brought herself to enter a building.

"Katie, would you come here please?"

Treb was standing beside the door of the house. He'd done such a good job on it. He was amazing. Her stomach flip-flopped, all shaky-like, every time she got near him. She stopped stirring the lunch soup, wiped her hands on her apron, and warily headed his way.

"I have an idea. How about we try going inside together?" He raked his hand through his long hair. Katie had been watching him sweep it out of his face for a week, and she had the hankering to reach up her hands and touch the waving, dark mass. Thinking about that, her stomach tilted oddly, and her heart squeezed again. She was thinking about things she couldn't have.

"Katie."

She swallowed hard and met his beautiful eyes. "You don't need to be worrying about me, Treb Rayburn," she snapped, disgruntled by all the emotions grabbing hold of her. "I'm going in there, and that's for certain. That's why I had you build the place."

His lip lifted slightly. Her mouth went dry just looking at those lips.

"Katie, I'm not leaving here until you can sleep in the house I built for you."

Her eyes narrowed. "I don't need a nursemaid. I'll go in, but I don't need you going in with me."

She couldn't let herself get used to him always being by her side—because he wouldn't be. If there was one thing she'd learned in this life, it was not to count on anyone sticking around. If the Lord didn't call them home, then something else called them away.

"If you don't need me, then let me see you go in there," he said, irritation flashing in his eyes.

She hiked her chin and shot daggers at him. "I aim to do just that. Stand back." Her palms were wet as she glanced inside the open doorway. What she wanted more than anything on earth was for Treb to take her hand and walk with her through that door. But she had to do this on her own. She had to.

Her heart squeezed tight in her chest, just like it always did when she stood in the doorway looking inside of the barn or any building.

But today she'd come to fight. She'd had it!

She rammed her booted foot across the entrance and slapped it down on the floor. It took every ounce of strength she had to hold it there when she wanted to swing around and run for the hills. Her knees started trembling, then her whole body. It made her so mad she wanted to scream. Or shoot something!

"Katie." Treb stepped up beside her, placed his finger beneath her chin, and lifted her face so that he was staring down into her eyes. "You don't have to do this on your own. When are you going to get that through your thick, beautiful head?"

His voice trailed off and the air just disappeared around them. Katie knew that if he hadn't been cupping her face between his big, strong hands, she probably would've sunk to the ground. Looking up at him made her so weak.

He bent his head and his lips met hers.

Treb's kiss was firm but so tender that it had Katie's heart turning to mush. Her arms went around his neck of their own accord, and she stepped into his embrace, his strong arms tightening around her, drawing her close. The world, her worries, her fears—everything just faded away in that moment at the touch of his lips against hers.

Her heart thundered against her ribs as he moved the kiss to her temple, then whispered her name in her ear and held her close. Katie hadn't ever felt these emotions racing through her. How did someone fall in love so quickly? And yet she knew that love was what she was feeling. And this kiss, this tenderness that she felt in his arms, undid her.

"You don't have to do this alone," he said, hugging her tight before pulling away and taking her hand. "I'm here and we're going in together."

She blinked back tears. Holding his hand, she stared at the interior of the home he'd built. It was empty, but spacious. No furniture yet. First she had to go inside.

"I'm ready." Gripping his hand so tightly she thought her own would break in half, Katie stuck her foot inside and froze. She looked up at Treb. That gave her courage. She hated needing someone to help her when she knew she had to do this on her own. Despite the kiss, he wasn't hers. She had to stand on her own feet. But even knowing that didn't stop her from needing his support.

"Tell me about the Grand Canyon again," she said.

He smiled and stepped inside the house, holding her hand across the threshold. She didn't move, just kept her foot on the porch and her hand in his.

"The canyon is as wide open as anything I've ever seen. As far as the eye can see, there's rock and sky mixing together over gorges so deep it seems like you're seeing the center of the earth. Come on in, Katie. Think of wide-open spaces. The sun is shining outside. It's streaming through the windows in here and sunbeams are dancing on your new floors. You can do this."

She forced her other foot forward and stood in the door frame. He was right. The sun was bright and streaming across her new floors. There was nothing dark and suffocating here. And yet panic clawed at her; fingers tightened around her throat.

"Look at me, Katie."

She did. He smiled. Oh, how she'd come to enjoy that smile. And that kiss. Her mind pulled back from the panic a little as she thought of the feel of his lips against hers and the sweet security of his arms around her. It steadied her.

"Katie, you have the freedom to go and to come as you like. I'll even let go of your hand the minute you tell me to. There is nothing trapping you. Nothing holding you down."

She took a small step forward. But her head started shaking of its own accord.

"Stand firm, Katie. Stand firm."

Her heart lifted. "That's what my pa always said. He said the Bible was full of verses that said we were to stand firm and wait or watch for the Lord's deliverance. Or telling us to stand firm in our faith. Or stand firm and be courageous." She pushed her shoulders back, knowing this was a time to stand firm and be courageous. Her gaze locked with Treb's and she took a trembling step into the house. Every bone and every ounce of flesh quivered with fear, but she refused to retreat. She held her ground. Stood firm. Treb gave a small nod, and just a hint of a smile tickled the edge of his lips. His eyes encouraged her to take another step.

She felt as if she were a child learning to walk to her parents for the first time in her life. But Treb was no parent.

No, he was the man she'd fallen in love with.

CHAPTER NINE

HOLDING KATIE'S GAZE, TREB'S HEART FELT FULL TO bursting. Pride filled him as he watched her. She was a fighter. She came one hesitant step at a time into the house. He'd never seen a more beautiful, stronger woman—or man, for that matter. The courage it took for her to make these steps humbled him. After witnessing her fear the night of the storm, he knew the depth of control the tornado held over her.

He wanted to reach for her. To pull her close again and take these steps with her, but the kiss had cost him too much.

He was leaving. *He was.*

He'd never planned on staying. He wasn't the kind of man to stay and give his heart away . . . Because what if he lost her?

He couldn't bear it.

So instead, he smiled and he waited and willed her to hold his gaze and hopefully draw strength from him, too, as he prayed for her to conquer the fear.

She'd made it four steps into the room. A sunbeam danced across her and she looked so very lovely. Her eyes never wavered from his but suddenly she halted, and the saddest look he'd ever seen crept across her expression. Her eyes hardened.

And then she spun and stalked from the house.

What just happened?

Katie was sashaying across the yard toward the barn. He jogged after her.

"What's wrong, Katie? You were doing great, darlin'."

She stalked straight over to the coiled whip that hung around a nail on the outside of the barn. Startled, Treb yanked to a halt as she took the ominous weapon into her small, competent hands. "What are you doing, Katie?"

Chin up, she walked to the back of the barn where a tree stump for chopping firewood sat. She picked up a tin bucket and sat it on the stump, then backed up and swung the whip wide.

Treb knew to stand back. With the precision of a master, Katie snapped the whip and the tip pinged against the bucket and sent it flying. She repeated the action again and again. He stood back and watched.

Finally, breathing hard, she spun, her gaze fierce. "I thank you for coming to work for me, Treb. You have helped me in more ways than just building my house. You got me inside it. Our deal was for you to build my house in return for wages and a horse. Now that the house is done, I'll pay your wage. You go on and saddle up your horse and get on your way toward Galveston or New Orleans—or *wherever* you plan to go. I don't want to hold you up any longer."

That speech delivered, she marched over to where a heavy rock sat against the barn and she pushed it hard. The rock moved, and there beneath it was a hole. From the hole she pulled out a tin can. Treb was speechless as he watched her pull money from the can, count it, then march over to him.

"This should cover your wages. And the horse is waiting and ready. You go now."

He pushed the money back at her. "Whoa, hold on to your money. I'm not done yet," he snapped, finding his voice at last.

Eyes flashing, she shoved it right back at him. "I'm the one who did the hiring and now I'm telling you the job is done. Go. I don't need you here any longer."

"But you do."

"I don't." She spun away, grabbing the whip again. She strode back around the barn, the skirt of her yellow dress flouncing with each step.

Treb slowly trailed her, his thoughts rolling like a tumbleweed. Myrtle May eyed him sharply as he passed by her pen. He started to tell the horse not to look at him that way. That he was trying to talk sense into the stubborn woman in front of him—then he realized that would mean he was talking to a horse. He clamped his mouth shut and quickened his steps.

Katie was strapping on her gun when he rounded the barn. What had gotten into the woman?

Hadn't she liked the kiss they'd shared? From her reaction

it sure seemed like she had when she'd joined in the moment his lips touched hers.

He'd felt as though he'd died and gone to heaven.

Treb had never felt so good as he had in that moment kissing Katie. And Katie kissing him back.

"See, I don't need you anymore, Treb. I can take care of myself. I'm not the same batty woman who hired you over a month ago. I've got a roof over my head—thanks to you—and now I have a ranch to run. And you—you have places to go and things to see." Her eyes softened. "It's what I want. It's why I hired you, because I knew you would be leaving."

He'd forgotten that. Completely.

Forgotten that his leaving was the main reason she'd hired him. "I thought you might have changed your mind." His words were softer. "I hoped—"

"Nope. I don't need you around any longer, and I don't need any more kisses. I'm not the marrying kind—I told you that early on—and neither are you. So kissing won't do anything but blur the line I've got drawn for my life."

What she said was true. That was their arrangement. What could he do but honor it? Torn, he nodded and went for his saddle. His mind was twisting like a tornado as he went into the pen and saddled his horse.

Katie watched him but she said nothing more. She was right in saying he wasn't the marrying kind. Even if he loved Katie—and had for a while, the stubborn woman. It would break his heart to lose her like he'd lost his family. All the more reason for him to ride out of here today.

He headed straight over to her, cupped her face with one hand, and looked deep into those amazing, cornflower-blue eyes. "You—" His voice cracked. "You're right, Katie Pearl. You're doing good." He dropped a gentle kiss on her lips, backed up, and swung into the saddle. "You take care of yourself."

That said, he drank in one last look, then turned his horse and rode out of the yard for open ground, focusing his eyes on the horizon.

It was better this way, and he knew it.

Folks might have called her crazy, but she had more sense than anyone he'd ever met. And more heart too.

He made it over the rise, and it hit him that he needed to go see the preacher. He needed someone to check on her every now and again and make sure she was okay. Her being out there all alone needed to stop, and worry pressed in on him. What would happen to her? The preacher seemed like a decent sort, and it seemed—with his influence on his congregation—that he was the right person to get the town to change. Surely he would check on her some. Treb couldn't leave until he had asked.

It was the least he could do.

❦

It took every ounce of willpower Katie had to watch Treb ride out toward the horizon. Though her heart was breaking in half, she wanted him to move forward with his dream.

She was torn with loving him, wanting to hold him, and

wanting to see him go. Wanting to see the world with him. And wanting to carry on with her ranch.

A person shouldn't have to make choices like that. Then again, when two people were involved, there were different wants . . . and if Treb had wanted her more than he wanted to see the world, her whip and her gun wouldn't have stopped him from staying.

She stood there for the longest time watching the spot where he'd disappeared over the horizon. The breeze ruffled through her hair and she touched her lips, thinking of his leaving kiss. It had been as soft as the breeze.

Her heart twisted and her throat clogged. She blinked back tears. "Don't you cry, Katie Pearl, don't you dare cry."

CHAPTER TEN

"She sent me away." Treb paced across Preacher Dawson's parlor floor, raking a hand through his hair as he clutched his hat in his other hand. "She strapped her gun back on and told me to leave."

"She always had a mind of her own. So why are you so upset? Seems to me the two of you had a plan going into this, and Katie's just doing what y'all agreed to."

Treb stared at him for a moment before he muttered, "That's true, I guess. Listen, can I ask a favor? Could you and maybe some of the women folk from town go by every once in a while and check on her? She'll get lonesome out there and, well, she needs to know that everyone doesn't think she's crazy. She's not gonna shoot anybody, unless it's some no-count with bad intentions, and she has the right to scare them off."

The preacher studied him hard. Then, like the first time they'd met, Pastor Dawson struck Treb as more lawman than preacher. "I'll go by," he said, "and now that we know she's not going to shoot every living thing that moves, I'll make sure the ladies' group gets out there to see her. Maybe we can get her to join us on Sundays again."

"I'd appreciate it," Treb said, wondering what Katie was doing right now. "That's what she needs." He reached across the desk and they shook hands. Then he turned to leave.

"Do you love her?"

The preacher's words stopped him at the door. He couldn't lie. "I do," he said, then turned back. "To tell you the truth, Preacher, I didn't want to. I've lost too many people in my life who I loved and felt responsible for. I don't want to go through that again. But . . . Katie." He dropped his chin to his chest and stared at his boots, thoughts whirling. "It doesn't matter anyway. Katie isn't the marrying kind. She told me that. I knew it and I . . ." He faltered, then started pacing the floor.

"You fell in love with her anyway," the preacher finished for him.

"I tried not to," Treb said.

"Did you tell her how you feel?"

"Are you kidding? She wouldn't let me."

"Did you want to?"

The preacher's question had Treb's boots skidding to a halt.

"Sure I did. But it wouldn't have served a purpose. She didn't want it."

"Are you sure about that?"

"She made it clear on several occasions."

"Treb, sit down, please. I'd like to tell you something."

Doing as he'd been asked, Treb sank to the edge of the chair and stared across the big desk.

Preacher Dawson took a deep breath as if nervous.

"I've been the preacher here for a long time. And I watched Katie wear her heart on her sleeve as a young lady. There was one young man in our congregation she had her eye on and everyone knew it. But he had eyes for another young lady, and they started courting as soon as they were old enough. I performed their wedding ceremony soon after, and I believe it hurt Katie deeply." He took a deep breath, his expression solemn.

His heart heavy, Treb waited, anticipating more was coming. He was right.

"There were a couple of young men who did start courting Katie, but it was over before it got started both times. Maybe it was because Katie had been raised by her pa and she wasn't one to know how to . . . to attract a fella. A fella wants to be needed, and I don't think any man ever thought Katie would need him, much less love him or be easy to love herself. Does that make sense?"

Treb nodded slowly.

"I watched Katie see every young woman her age marry. Finally she quit wearing her heart on her sleeve. I think she decided it was safer to decide never to marry. And then to have these four or five worthless cowboys offer to marry her right after the tornado . . ." He hiked a brow.

Closing his eyes, Treb hung his head.

Katie had been hurt far more than he'd ever known. And he'd almost hurt her again.

She'd been right to send him away.

Treb stood. "Thank you for telling me. But still, if you'd look in on her I'd be obliged." That said, he hightailed it out of there like a yellow-bellied coward. He and Katie both knew how hard it was to love and lose.

Leaving was the best thing he could do for both of their hearts.

"What are you doing here, Silas Pruit?" Katie's tears had barely dried when the aggravating cowpoke came riding over the ridge and straight into her ranch yard. Her eyes narrowed and her hand tightened on her whip, the other on her gun. If he knew what was good for him, he'd turn and run out of there because she had a hankerin' for some target practice in the worst way.

"I've come to give you another chance to accept my offer." The cowboy thumbed his hat back, looking cocky and trying every last nerve she had.

The cowpoke might be nice to look at, but he had shiftless eyes and a no-good heart. She wouldn't trust him as far as she could spit. "Don't even think about getting off that horse."

"Now, Katie, I don't mean any harm." He swung out of the saddle.

She whipped out her pistol, then thought about him going back to town to tell everyone that she was crazy. The thought made her hesitate. During those moments, he took three strides and was standing closer than she wanted.

She aimed her pistol at his boots. "You take another step my direction and I'll shoot off one of your toes."

Silas's jaw jerked and his eyes hardened. One minute he was glaring at her, the next he'd lashed out and grabbed hold of her pistol.

"You loco, fool woman. Your pa is gone and I aim to have this ranch. You'll be nice and do as I ask or you'll be sorry. I'm losing my patience." He wrenched her gun from her hand, then backhanded her across the jaw. The blow shocked her, and she stumbled backward a few feet before landing on the ground with a thud.

"I knew you were a worthless skunk, but I didn't figure you for this," she snapped, her jaw throbbing. She didn't hold with a man who would hit a lady—even a lady who was itching to shoot off his toe. She'd shoot them all off if she had her gun.

"You'll play along or you'll regret it."

"I'll never marry you," she said, too angry to be afraid.

He glared down at her as he shoved her gun into the waist of his pants, then cracked his knuckles. "Oh, believe me, I aim to have this ranch. And I'll do what I must to get it. When I get done with you, you'll marry me and be glad to be alive to do it. Or else . . ."

From her makeshift stall Myrtle May snorted and pawed at the ground. Would the horse charge Silas? He'd think nothing of putting a bullet into the animal. Katie's hand tightened on the whip she suddenly realized she was still holding.

"You want to turn around here and pick on someone your own size?"

Treb!

Katie gasped as he stepped from behind the barn, his pistol aimed at Silas. Fear clutched her heart as Silas whirled around and yanked her pearl-handled pistol from his waistband. Treb's eyes were full of fury. He must've witnessed Silas strike her. He wouldn't like seeing a man strike a woman. Something terrible was about to happen. If she didn't stop it!

One quick flick of her arm and the whip snaked free of its coil as she sprang to her feet. She whipped it through the air. It reached out and grabbed Silas's wrist. He yelled in pain and surprise as she yanked him to the ground.

Everything worked beautifully until the pistol fired.

CHAPTER ELEVEN

PAIN SURGED THROUGH TREB AS THE BULLET KNOCKED him to his knees. Feeling the warm flow of blood running down his arm, he kept his gun steady on Silas. Katie, white as snow, raced forward, grabbed her gun from the ground where it had dropped, then took Silas's from his holster.

"How bad are you hit?" Katie's voice trembled as she backed toward him, keeping her gun on Silas who had suddenly lost his tongue. He was holding his wrist and blood dripped from his fingers where she'd yanked him to the ground like he'd been no more than a willow branch.

"I'll live," Treb said. "Can you grab some rope?"

She nodded, her gaze flicking once to his wound before she ran. Only after she was gone did he remember that the rope was in the barn. Within moments, she returned carrying the rope, and he watched her push Silas to the ground. Treb marveled. She hadn't even hesitated to go into the barn, and for that he was so very happy for her. As if she were working cows, she placed a knee in his back, grabbed both of his wrists, and hog-tied him within moments.

The sound of hoofbeats sounded, and to Treb's surprise Pastor Dawson rode into the yard. He swung himself from the saddle, rifle in his hand.

"You folks all right?" He shouldered his rifle when he saw Katie hog-tying Silas.

"We're fine, Preacher," Treb said.

"No you're not," Katie said, kneeling at his side. She grabbed the hem of her dress, and gently covering his wound on his upper arm, she applied pressure to both the entry and exit wounds. She was staring into his eyes and he forgot everything. Everything but her.

"You came back," she said softly.

"I couldn't leave. And I'm so glad I got here when I did. I came over the ridge and saw Silas knock you down. I wanted to charge in here as fast as I could, but I knew if he shot me I would be useless to you. So I rode through the woods and came in behind the barn."

She kept pressure on his arm, her eyes softer than he'd ever seen them. "But why did you come back?"

He touched her cheek gently, loving the feel of her skin. "I came back because I love you, Katie. And the preacher here made me realize that the only thing that matters to me is you. I want to marry you, Katie Pearl."

Katie stilled, searching his eyes with her beautiful blues. "But what about your dreams?" Her voice quivered. "Seeing the Gulf?"

He smiled. "You are my dreams. I've been traveling around, adrift with no anchor until I wandered in here and found you. God knew exactly where I was wanderin' to all along, and for that I'm eternally grateful."

Katie's eyes misted, and his heart nearly burst with his love for her.

"Will you marry me?"

That smile he loved so much spread across her face and dug deeper into every dark corner of his life. "Oh, Treb," she said softly, "you're the only one I'd ever marry." Her sweet lips trembled as tears began to stream down her cheeks. "And"—she hiccupped, her words catching—"of all"—hiccup—"people, I went and shot *you*. Oh, Treb, I almost killed you."

The last words were barely audible.

He couldn't help it. He threw his head back and laughed.

"This is serious, Treb. Why are you laughing?" She stopped crying and her eyes were flashing fire again.

"Because I love you, and if the preacher is up to it, we're fix'n to have ourselves a wedding to stop all this nonsense."

"I'm fine with that," Preacher Dawson said, grinning, "if Katie says she wants the same thing."

Katie smiled. "Oh, I do." She leaned in and kissed Treb, right there in front of the preacher. "It sounds wonderful."

"I don't want to watch a stinkin' wedding," Silas growled.

The preacher shifted his rifle from one arm to the other. "I don't think you have a choice. Especially since I'm going to throw you over a saddle horn and take you to the jailhouse soon as we're done. After all the trouble you've caused and from the looks of that bruise on Katie's cheek, you better be on your best behavior."

Katie jumped up and went to a chest of clothes that sat among the things they'd salvaged from the house. She opened it and pulled out a length of muslin. She came back and wound it around Treb's wounds. When she was done, she grinned. "Preacher, would you marry us now, please? The sun is going down and I want to spend the first night in my new home with my husband."

Treb grinned. "I do love the sound of that."

"And I love you," Katie said, helping him stand. "But, Treb, if I agree to wed you, do you promise to show me some of the places you were planning to see?"

"Katie Pearl, I'd love to do that." And he would. She would love it.

"Then let's make this official."

Treb looked into Katie's eyes. He'd come to her ranch hoping to earn enough money to leave town to see the world. He never expected he'd be the man who would tell Katie he loved her and then stick around to prove it.

But he would. For the rest of his life.

Courting Trouble

Margaret Brownley

CHAPTER ONE

Lone Pine, Colorado, 1882

BROCK DANIELS SCOWLED AT THE LEGAL BRIEF HE'D BEEN studying for more than an hour. *Obstreperous conduct?* It took thirty-two pages to list a complaint that added up to little more than one shop owner calling another a name generally reserved for crooked politicians and stubborn mules.

Hardly a week went by that a similar freewheeling lawsuit didn't cross his desk. No wonder Lone Pine was on litigation overload. They sure didn't do things here in Colorado like they did back in Philadelphia.

Tossing down the brief, he reached for his dip pen. No sooner had he dunked the nib in the inkwell and started to write than a slight sound made him lift his gaze. A boy of eleven or twelve stood in front of his desk, staring at him with big, rounded eyes.

It wasn't the first time someone had sneaked up on him while he was working at his desk. The two-room office had been his for six months, and he still hadn't gotten around to attaching a bell to the front door.

Brock stuck the pen in its holder and reached into his vest pocket for his watch. The gold case opened with a flip of his thumb. It was nearly ten p.m. Too late for someone so young to be roaming the streets. He snapped the watch shut.

"May I help you?"

Instead of answering, the lad placed four coins on the desk with such care that the money had to have been hard earned. The coins added up to fifty-six cents.

"I want to hire you," the boy said.

There wasn't enough money there to hire a mule, but the boy's youth demanded special consideration.

Brock slid his watch back into his pocket. "What's your name, son?"

"Jesse Morris."

Brock was pretty sure he'd not seen the boy before. Certainly he'd never seen a more sorrowful pair of trousers. Innocent of anything resembling the original fabric, they were patched so thoroughly that they resembled shingles on a roof. The child's shirt didn't fare much better. The thin cotton was more suited to hot summer days than cool spring nights.

"What kind of trouble you in?"

"No trouble," Jesse said. "It's my ma."

Brock's eyebrows shot up. "Your ma's in trouble?"

Jessed nodded. "She's in jail."

Far as Brock knew, the only woman in jail was the one they called the Black Widow. From what little he'd heard, it sounded like an open-and-shut murder case. What he hadn't known was that she had a son. More's the pity.

The boy twisted his porkpie hat in his hands. Reddish brown hair reached his shoulders and curled around his neck and ears. "The sheriff said she killed her husband and that ain't true."

Husband, not father. Brock pinched his forehead. It was late and he was tired.

"I'm sure the judge has appointed your mother's legal counsel."

The boy nodded. "Her lawyer's name is Mr. Spencer."

David Spencer was one of three lawyers in town. Far as Brock knew, the man had no formal education in law. But neither did the others, which explained why the Lone Pine legal system was such a mess and, in some cases, a joke. The closest any of them had been to "passing the bar," which consisted of a simple oral exam, was to walk past a saloon.

"If your mother has a lawyer, why do you want to hire me?"

Jesse set his hat on the corner of the desk and pulled a piece of paper from his trouser pocket. With as much care as he'd afforded the coins, he unfolded it and straightened out the creases.

"Mr. Spencer loses most of his cases," he said. He placed the paper on the desk and pointed to the names carefully printed beneath a hand-drawn gallows. "Those are the men he let hang last year."

Half a dozen names were on the list, including a gang of horse thieves. The boy had done his research. "I admit that doesn't look good but—"

"Reverend Fields said you're the best lawyer in town. Said you were almost as good at law as Moses."

"Did he now?" *Moses?* If only the reverend knew . . .

"I handle mostly contracts and land disputes," he explained. Not only was business law more lucrative than criminal law, it was less risky; no one was likely to die if he messed up. "I don't handle criminal cases."

"Ma's innocent, so this ain't no criminal case."

"Jesse—"

"Please."

When Brock showed no sign of relenting, the boy's eyes filled with tears. He apparently thought that if he tugged on enough reins, one would eventually give. He wasn't that far off in his thinking.

"I don't know that there's anything I can do," Brock said. He could well imagine the town's reaction if he stuck his nose in the high-profile case. Not many liked his big-city ways, but then he didn't much like what passed for justice in this town.

"You could talk to Ma." Jesse swiped a tear from his cheek. "Then you'll know she didn't do the awful things people say she did. Please, Mister."

Brock grimaced. Law school had not taught him how to turn down a pleading youth. Giving up the fight, he said, "All right. I'll talk to your mother."

A corner of the boy's mouth curved upward, and Brock had the feeling the boy didn't laugh much. Probably didn't smile much either.

"Where you staying, son?"

"With Reverend Fields."

"The pastor and his wife are good people." They would do right by the boy. "Do you like it there?"

He nodded. "But I'm not sure Reverend Fields likes me."

"What makes you say that?"

"He asked me if I was Methodist or Presbyterian."

Brock arched an eyebrow. "And?"

"I told him the truth. I'm a Democrat."

Brock grinned. What he would have given to see the preacher's face upon learning he was housing a member of the party he so bitterly opposed.

"I have a feeling the reverend likes you just fine."

"So when are you gonna talk to Ma?"

"First thing tomorrow." He leaned forward. "I said I'll talk to her. That's all I'll do." His voice was gruff. He didn't want to discourage the boy, but neither did he want to give him false hope. "Now, take your money. I don't charge for consultations."

Jesse scooped up the coins and jammed them into his pocket. "Thank you, Mister." With that he grabbed his hat and dashed from the office into the waiting room. The outer door slammed shut with a bang.

Brock groaned. Now look what he'd done. Promised to look into a case he had no intention of pursuing.

With a weary sigh, he stood, plucked his hat off a hook, and turned off the kerosene lamp. From the recesses of his mind came the memory: *With the authority given me by the state of Pennsylvania, I condemn you to hang till death.*

CHAPTER TWO

"You've got a visitor, ma'am."

"Jesse?" Grace jumped to her feet and grabbed hold of the iron bars.

Instead of her son, Deputy Sheriff Parker led a stranger to her cell—a man who seemed to fill every inch of the jailhouse corridor with his wide shoulders and tall, straight form.

Fighting disappointment, she studied him with wary regard and quickly brushed wayward curls from her face.

The stranger thanked Parker and waited for the deputy to leave before walking up to her cell, black leather satchel in hand.

He acknowledged her with a tip of his bowler. Thick, tawny hair framed a handsome, square face, and sun slanting through a single barred window picked up the blue of his eyes. In his fancy clothes, he sure didn't look like a local. His gray flannel trousers, frock coat, and vest could only have come from one of the big cities in the East. Boston, perhaps, or New York.

His gaze lingered on her for a moment before he spoke. "Mrs. Davenport, I'm Brock Daniels. I'm an attorney."

She curled her hands into fists. If the judge thought she needed *two* lawyers, she was in even worse trouble than she knew. On the other hand, that court-appointed attorney was long of tooth, hard of hearing, and he walked with a cane— none of which gave her much confidence in his abilities.

"I already have a lawyer."

"I'm aware of that, ma'am." His gaze held hers and she realized with a start that she must look a dreadful sight. She'd tried her best to appear presentable, but without a hairbrush and only a basin of water and bar of lye soap at her disposal, not much could be done.

"Your son asked me to talk to you."

"Jesse?" Just the mere mention of his name made her heart skip a beat. She inhaled and it was all she could do to find her voice. "Is . . . he all right? The sheriff won't let me see him." After the sheriff caught Jesse trying to smuggle in a file, he laid down the law and said no more visits.

"Seemed all right to me."

His assurance offered small comfort. Each moment away from her son seemed like an eternity. "I already told the other lawyer everything I know." Unfortunately, the man was deaf as a nail, forcing her to shout until hoarse. Even then she couldn't be certain how much he'd heard.

"I just have a few questions." He hesitated. One corner of

his mouth quirked up in a slight and attractive smile. "That is, if you don't mind. It seems to be important to your boy. He offered me fifty-six cents to talk to you."

"That's all the money he had."

"Well, he's still got it. I don't rob children."

She moistened her lips. She didn't miss how his gaze momentarily dropped to her mouth before he looked away and cleared his throat.

"I haven't got much more money than he has." Some miners still owed her for doing their wash, but it wasn't enough to fill the toe of a sock. "Sure ain't got enough to pay for a fancy lawyer."

"I don't charge for consultations."

She regarded him with curiosity. Never had she met a man so refined. His offer was tempting and his smile wasn't half bad either—not that she'd ever be taken in by another man. Still, it might not hurt to see what he was made of. "That's a mighty fancy word for asking a few questions."

He chuckled, smiling. "Lawyers never use a dollar word when a five-dollar one will do."

"Don't you know I'm guilty? Least that's what everyone says."

"In Philadelphia, a person's innocent until proven guilty."

"In case you haven't noticed, this ain't Philadelphia. Here they hang 'em first and worry about justice later."

"The law is the law."

She scoffed. Not only was he too young to be a lawyer, he was woefully ignorant of the town's reputation. He'd find out the error of his ways soon enough. Still, the man seemed sincere and Jesse had asked him to talk to her.

Well, pox, what did she have to lose? "Fire away."

He hesitated as if surprised she gave in so readily. "It won't take long," he said. He reached into his satchel and drew out a notebook. After leaning the leather case on the floor next to the cell, he straightened and riffled through the pages.

"According to witnesses, you and Mr. Davenport were seen arguing in public before he turned up dead." He looked up, all serious like, but for some reason the memory of his smile still lingered. "Is that true?" he asked.

"It's true, all right." Everyone in town knew about that, so no sense denying it. "That wasn't the first time I had to drag him out of a saloon kickin' and screamin'." She ran her hands up and down her arms to ward off a sudden chill, adding angrily, "But I didn't kill him. I didn't kill nobody." She and God might not always be on the best of terms, but she obeyed His commandments. Especially the one about not killing.

"What happened next? After you . . . uh . . . dragged him out of the saloon."

She didn't like to think about that night but she forced herself to continue. "Not much. I made him empty his pockets, and all he had was an empty money clip and his lucky coin. According to him, that old, dented gold coin saved his life during the war."

"I see."

"No, you don't." She frowned. "Billy-Joe would let his family starve to death before parting with that coin."

The lawyer considered that for a moment before asking, "Then what happened?"

"I got on my horse and rode home." She grimaced at the memory. "I had to tell Jesse there wouldn't be no new leather for his birthday. He had to keep wearin' the old boots with the holes."

"And your husband? Did he follow you home that night?"

She shook her head. "Never saw him again after that." For six long months she'd wondered what had happened to him. "Figured he took off, leaving me and my boy high and dry."

His gaze sharpened. "Did you report him missing?"

"Yes, but the sheriff didn't seem concerned. Said it wouldn't be the first time a henpecked husband ran off."

Mr. Daniels stared at his notes. "How long were you and Mr. Davenport married?"

"Three years, five months, and two weeks," she said. His eyebrows lifted to half-mast, but he said nothing, so she kept talking.

"Just before we got hitched, his uncle died and Billy-Joe took over his uncle's saddle shop." Her mind wandered back in time. "Everything seemed to fall into place in those first early months of marriage. Even his uncle's old chicken coop–sized cabin seemed like a gift from God."

Billy-Joe's resolve to do right by her and Jesse turned out to be just as flimsy as the thin cabin walls. Instead of working in the saddle shop, he spent his days at the saloons. After he lost the business, he worked at the mine. He hated the job and blamed her and Jesse for his ill fortune.

"I never should have married him," she said. If God judged her solely by the number of mistakes made through the years, she'd be in even bigger trouble than she was in now.

The lawyer held her in his gaze. "Do you mind if I ask why you did?"

She rubbed her forehead. "Jesse needed a pa. He needed someone to take him hunting and fishing and show him how to become a man. Billy-Joe promised he'd be a good father. Said he always wanted a son." She fell silent for a moment before adding, "That was another lie he told."

His brow drew forward in a frown. "The record also states that your"—he checked his notes—"*second* husband died under suspicious circumstances."

She shook her head. "Nothing suspicious about it. Harry had a full-grown case of booze-blindness and was thrown from his horse." She sighed. "We'd only been married a month. He was a schoolteacher. A good man he was, 'cept he sure did love his whiskey. Taught Jesse about faraway lands and how to work with numbers."

After a moment's pause, she added, "I thought that once he had a home and family, he'd stop drinking. I thought wrong."

The lawyer considered her answer with narrowed eyes. "The record also states that your *first* husband was poisoned."

"He was poisoned, all right." His name was Geoffrey Morris and he didn't have the brains God gave a grasshopper, but she'd always have a soft spot for him if for no other reason than that he was Jesse's pa.

"I was only fifteen when we got hitched. My parents had eleven children and couldn't afford to feed us no more. Papa said I either had to get married or hop on an orphan train." She often wondered what would have happened had she taken the train. But then she wouldn't have had Jesse.

As an afterthought, she added, "I *told* Geoffrey not to eat them mushrooms."

Mr. Daniels's eyebrows rose to meet the strand of dark hair falling across his forehead. "I have to say, ma'am, you're either the unluckiest woman alive or . . ." His voice trailed off.

She curled her fingers around the iron bars until her knuckles turned white. "Sounds like 'innocent until proven guilty' don't apply in my case."

As if caught remiss, he made an obvious attempt to compose his features behind a noncommittal expression. "It applies to every case." He reached for his satchel and slipped his writing tablet inside.

"Is that it?" she asked. "Is that the end of our consultations? Aren't you gonna ask me if I did it? If I killed my husband?"

His gaze met hers and she was in terrible danger of drowning in the depths of his eyes. "Did you?" he asked.

"Would you believe me if I said no?"

He inclined his head. "Would you believe me if I said yes?"

She thought for a moment. "I've believed a lot of men in my life and they all came to a bad end. Are you sure you want to take that chance?"

"I'm no stranger to bad endings." He studied her a moment before rattling the ante door leading to the sheriff's office. "But I have to be honest, ma'am. Your situation looks particularly worrisome."

Brock left the jailhouse with long, hurried strides. The clear blue sky and bright yellow sun hardly seemed to belong with his dark thoughts.

He didn't know what he'd anticipated, but it certainly wasn't anyone like Grace Davenport. She was a whole lot younger than he'd expected, somewhere in her midtwenties, though she looked like she was barely out of her teens. Now he knew where her son got his big blue eyes and reddish gold hair. Mother and son also shared the same combination of vulnerability and strength that could easily work its way beneath a man's skin . . . if he let it.

Could the redheaded beauty really be guilty as charged? It didn't seem possible, but he knew better than to judge a person on appearances alone.

He let himself into his office and stood in the small reception area. A leather couch was centered against one wall next to a potbellied stove. Dust mites spun in a ray of golden sunlight.

If she really did kill her husband, her best defense might be a plea of temporary insanity—in fact, that might be her only defense. That particular plea worked quite nicely for the man accused of killing Francis Scott Key's son, a case he'd studied in law school.

Then, too, crimes of passion often resulted in acquittal. Of course, Mrs. Davenport's unhappy marriage would probably make such a defense suspect.

Self-defense?

Surprised to catch himself considering Mrs. Davenport's options, he shook his head. He'd promised the boy to talk to his mother, nothing more. Having given up criminal law, he had no intention of repeating past mistakes.

He'd simply tell Jesse that her current lawyer was doing all that could be done and leave it at that. He owed the boy no more or no less. The decision not to get involved was easy to make. The hard part? Forgetting the sadness in Mrs. Davenport's big blue eyes even as she smiled.

The door flew open and the prosecutor barreled in to the office.

Brock grimaced. "Mr. Ambrose. What a surprise." An unpleasant one, at that. He hadn't expected news of his jailhouse visit to travel through town so quickly.

"Why are you sticking your nose in the Davenport case?" Ambrose was so incensed he fairly sputtered. As wide as he was tall, he barely reached Brock's shoulders. With his slanted forehead and carrot-colored hair brushed straight back, he looked even more lion-like today than usual.

"I see the rumor mill is at full tilt."

Ambrose's face grew redder. "Answer me!"

"Why is the location of my nose any concern of yours?"

Ambrose's gold-flecked eyes glittered with obvious dislike. "It's an open-and-shut case. I don't need no Philadelphia lawyer pulling courtroom theatrics."

Brock had been accused of many things in his career but never theatrics. He started to explain why he had visited the prisoner, but the memory of big blue eyes stopped him. Or maybe it was the sadness he'd seen in their depths.

Resting his elbow on his arm, he tapped his chin with a knuckle and studied Ambrose. Sweat ran down the side of his bloated red face. It looked like he'd run here all the way from his office. Why? If Mrs. Davenport's case really was that clear-cut, what was he so worried about?

"I consulted with the defendant by family request," he said.

Ambrose sneered. "She hasn't got a family. She killed them all."

Brock rubbed his chin. Apparently the prosecutor discounted Mrs. Davenport's son—a mistake. "Why the death penalty?" Far as he knew, a woman had never been hung in the county. Probably not even in the territory. "If she's found guilty, why not just send her to prison?"

"We're not talking one dead husband; we're talking three."

Brock's jaw clenched. "When I read the court papers, I didn't see anything in the way of real evidence against her."

Ambrose drew back as if surprised. "I don't need evidence; I've got facts."

"All you have is circumstantial at best."

"All?" Spit sprayed from Ambrose's mouth. "I have witnesses who saw her not only arguing with her husband but threatening him."

"But no one actually saw her pull the trigger."

Ambrose practically foamed at the mouth. "If that was the criteria for judging guilt or innocence, every murderer would walk free."

"And if you had your way, everyone charged with a crime would be ruled guilty. Why don't you just do away with the not guilty plea altogether?"

"And why don't you go back to Philadelphia where you belong?" Ambrose stabbed Brock's chest with a thick index finger. "I'll get my conviction, don't you worry about that." Without another word, he stormed out of the office. The slamming of the door rattled the windows, and Brock's Harvard diploma crashed to the floor.

He picked up the frame. Not having a hammer to replace the nail, he walked through to his office and set the frame on the desk. That was when he noticed the coins lined in a neat row on the ink blotter. The money totaled fifty-six cents.

CHAPTER THREE

THE NIGHTS IN JAIL WERE THE WORST. ALONG WITH the darkness came icy-cold fear—as cold and as penetrating as a winter storm. Grace missed her son, missed fixing his meals and mending his clothes. Just thinking of Jesse filled her with such loneliness that even her whispered prayers failed to bring comfort.

Drunks were hauled into cells with alarming regularity and told to "sleep it off." Their slumped bodies and loud snores offered no cure for her loneliness.

It was the fifteenth night in that horrible place, and she had just settled on her cot when the door to the jail rattled opened, followed by men's voices. Thinking it was yet another prisoner, she was surprised to recognize the cultured bass voice of the Philadelphia lawyer. The Southern drawl belonged to the sheriff.

The lawyer stepped into the corridor outside her cell. "Mrs. Davenport?"

She slid off the cot. It was too dark to see his face, but his form was outlined by light shining through the open door of the sheriff's office.

Even in the dark she could feel his restless energy, sense his strength and vitality.

"I didn't expect to see you again, Mr. Daniels," she said.

"Likewise." He stood only a few feet away, and the pleasant smell of bay-rum hair tonic overcame the whiskey odor wafting from the other cells.

"If you're happy with your current lawyer, I'll leave." He studied her intently as if trying to read her thoughts. "But if you want me to represent you, there's something you need to know."

"I . . . I think there's some sort of mistake, Mr. Daniels. Like I said, I can't afford to pay you." She shuddered to think how much a fancy lawyer like him would cost.

He brushed away her concern with a wave of his hand. "We'll discuss that later." He stepped closer to the cell, and the warmth of his body offered a welcome relief from the cold. "Right now you need to know that I haven't been in a courtroom for nearly three years. I currently specialize in business and real estate law. The last time I defended someone charged with murder, I lost and he was sent to his death." He blew out his breath and his voice thickened. "He happened to be my best friend."

A soft gasp escaped her. Without thinking, she reached between the bars and her fingers brushed against his arm. "I'm so sorry."

He surprised her by taking her hand in his, and she couldn't remember feeling so safe and protected as she did at that moment.

"Now that you know my history, I wouldn't blame you if you wanted nothing more to do with me." He released her hand, but the thread-like bond between them remained intact. "However, if you so desire, I'll represent you."

"What would be the advantage of that, Mr. Daniels?" Other that the fact that he was a whole lot more pleasant to look at than her current lawyer and wasn't hard of hearing.

"I know the law."

"And the court-appointed lawyer, Mr. Spencer? What does he know?"

"He knows the judge."

"Bail?" Judge Herbert J. Hackett peered at Brock from behind the bar of the Golden Nugget Saloon. The town had no access to a courthouse, and trials were usually held at the Grande Hotel. But that was before a guest set his bed afire, damaging the entire second floor. The saloon made a poor alternative, but it was the best that could be done on short notice.

"You want me to set the Black Wid—" Hackett caught himself and chomped on his cigar. His jowly face was framed by sideburns. Smoke circled his head before rising to the tin ceiling. "You want me to set the defendant free?"

"Temporarily," Brock said.

"Objection!" Ambrose shouted.

"It's not necessary to raise your voice," Brock said mildly. It was just the two of them standing in front of the polished wood bar. Regulars scattered among the tables in various stages of inebriation paid little heed to the proceedings and the faro players were too intent on their game to care.

Ambrose glowered. "The charge of murder makes her not eligible for bail." His finger raised orator-style, he continued, "And furthermore, the trial begins tomorrow so setting Mrs. Davenport free makes no sense."

The judge reached for a bottle of whiskey and refilled his glass. "Mr. Daniels?"

Brock rested his foot on the brass guardrail. "My client needs privacy to prepare for trial."

"She's in jail," Ambrose bellowed. "How much more privacy does she need?"

Ignoring the question, Brock continued, "It's also in the best interests of the town to release her."

The judge's bushy eyebrows formed a V. "How so?"

"The sheriff has limited space for prisoners and the other two cells are full. Putting a man in the same cell as the lady creates a management problem and puts her virtue in jeopardy."

Ambrose practically choked on his words. "Virtue! Is that all you're worried about? The woman's on trial for murder!"

"Enough!" The judge banged the butt of his Peacemaker on the bar. Glasses shook and whiskey bottles rattled.

The man known as Tall Pete lifted his head from a nearby table and slurred, "Objec-shun."

"You can't object, Pete. You're not part of the proceedin's." The judge banged the butt of his gun a second time. "Bail denied. Now if that's all—"

"I also ask that the case be heard in front of a jury," Brock persisted.

"A jury, eh." Hackett raised a finger and pointed to the group of men playing faro. "Hey, you in the red shirt." The old-timer looked up. "You and your friends there are on jury duty. I expect to see you all in court."

The man shrugged and went back to his game.

"Satisfied?" Hackett asked.

"That's only six," Daniels said. "We need twelve."

Annoyance flitted across Hackett's face and he turned to Ambrose. "Round up six more bodies before trial begins." He shifted his gaze back to Daniels. "Anything else?"

"I do have one more request," Brock said. "I'm new counsel and have not had adequate time to review the evidence against my client. I request a postponement until next week." Since the judge was one of three who rode circuit and was only in town for a short time, there was little chance of having his request granted, but it never hurt to try.

Ambrose threw up his hands. "Your Honor—"

The judge clamped down on his cigar. "I'll give you until the day after tomorrow and not one minute more. Now git, both of you."

Ambrose stopped Brock on the way out. "You might have won a point or two, but the trial's gonna be a whole different story."

"I'm not worried," Brock said. "The judge seems fair enough."

"Hackett?" Ambrose's smile lacked humor. "Don't be fooled. He might be short on words but, believe me, he's long on sentences." With that he walked off.

❧

The outer jail door clanked open and Grace bolted upright on her cot. Seeing her son's grinning face, she jumped to her feet. "Jesse!"

The deputy jingled his keys. "You got fifteen minutes."

Jesse ran to her cell and stuck his arm through the bars. "Ma."

"Oh, dear heart . . ." She held his hand in both of hers. "How did you get in? The sheriff said no visitors 'cept for my lawyer."

"Mr. Daniels talked to him."

"He . . . he did that?" A vision of a handsome, square face came to mind. She tucked the memory away and studied her son.

Jesse nodded. "But only if I promised not to sneak in any more files."

"And that's a promise you have to keep." She had so much she wanted to say to him she hardly knew where to start. "You should be in school."

"My teacher let me out early for noon break. I'll be back in plenty of time."

She bit her lower lip and nodded. "The other kids . . . they aren't bothering you, are they?"

He shook his head. "Reverend Fields told the class that anyone who gives me a bad time would have to sit in school all day and listen to him preach."

She laughed. "I guess no one wants to do that." She gazed at his new shirt and trousers. "You look real good. And, heavens to Betsy, look at your hair!" It was cut short and neatly combed to one side.

"Reverend Fields took me to the barbershop."

"Did he, now?" Never had she been able to afford such luxury, and a feeling of inadequacy washed over her. Her son never looked this good while in her care.

Jesse wrinkled his nose. "The barber made me smell like a girl."

Grace laughed. "You look mighty handsome and so grown up." *Too* grown up. Her heart ached with a combination of pride and despair.

"Are you keeping up with your schoolwork?"

The rumors about her being a Black Widow had begun after the death of her second husband. The other pupils said such horrible things to Jesse she had been forced to pull him out of school. She'd done her best to teach him, but having so little education herself, it had been difficult.

He nodded. "Reverend Fields has more books than the lending library. Ma—he's teaching me Latin."

"Oh my, Latin. Never knew anyone who could speak Latin. Sounds like the reverend is treating you well. Got you new clothes and all."

"He said I had to look presentable when I testify."

She tightened her hold on the bars. "I don't want you nowhere near that courtroom. You hear?"

"But I have to! Mr. Daniels said he needs me to tell the court what a good ma you are."

She reached through the bars to smooth away the worried frown on his forehead. Glory be, was that peach fuzz on his upper lip? And it seemed as if he'd shot up another inch since she last saw him two weeks ago. At nearly twelve, he was already tall enough to look her square in the eye. Lately, it was hard to see the boy for the man and that worried her. How much longer before he grew restless and deserted her like everyone else?

"Mr. Daniels kindly agreed to be my lawyer, but that don't mean our troubles are over."

Jesse's eyes blazed with earnestness. "That's why Reverend Fields said we have to pray."

"God doesn't always—" She fell silent.

"You were gonna say He don't always answer prayers, right?"

She pushed a strand of hair from his forehead. "He does sometimes. I prayed for a healthy baby boy and He sent you." Maybe a person was entitled to only one answered prayer in a lifetime, but just in case God saw fit to favor her again, she'd never stopped praying, for all the good it did her.

Jesse's eyes watered. "I . . . I prayed that Billy-Joe would go away because he made you cry. But I didn't want him to die."

His tears nearly shattered her tightly held control. "I know you didn't, Jesse."

Church bells rang out the noon hour and Jesse knuckled

his eyes. "Reverend Fields said those bells are the voice of God," he whispered.

The chimes seemed to have a calming effect on him and she smiled. "And the voice is saying that none of this is your fault."

He lifted his gaze upward, eyes glistening. "Mr. Daniels will prove you're innocent," he said. "That's what God is saying."

Her heart squeezed tight and for a moment she believed it was true. Believed that Mr. Daniels really was an answer to prayer. But all too soon the chimes faded away, taking the last of her hopes with them.

The outer door to the jailhouse opened. "Time's up," the deputy sheriff called.

"You better go," she whispered. They hugged each other through the bars. "Take care, you hear? And don't give the preacher a hard time."

Jesse backed away from her cell as if trying to hold her in his gaze until the last possible moment.

Her eyes burned, but not wanting to worry him, she forced a smile. "Don't forget to tell Mr. Daniels that you won't be testifyin'—"

Jesse turned and shot past the deputy sheriff before she could finish her sentence.

CHAPTER FOUR

LATER THAT AFTERNOON MR. DANIELS APPEARED IN front of her cell. "We have work to do," he said. "The trial begins tomorrow." He held up a package. "I brought something for you." He slipped the package through the bars.

Their fingers met as she reached for it and a spark seemed to pass between them. His gaze held hers for a moment before he backed away.

"Open it," he said. He looked slightly uncomfortable . . . or maybe embarrassed.

She set the package on the cot and eagerly pulled off the string. The paper separated, revealing a garment. Lifting it from its wrappings, she held the frock in front of her. The black floral-print dress had a fitted bodice and slightly flared skirt. Not only was it the prettiest dress she ever did see, but it was also store-bought—a luxury she'd never been able to afford.

She raised a questioning gaze to find him watching her.

His eyes clung to hers as if to analyze her reaction. "It's the only black dress I could find on such short notice," he said as if to apologize. "I hope it fits."

"I think it will fit just fine," she said. The thought of him picking out a garment her size made her blush. "But—" She refolded the dress and placed it back in its wrappings. "I can't accept this." It was enough that he'd agreed to defend her, but gifts too?

"You don't have a choice," he said, his voice brusque. He was all law wrangler now, all businesslike. "You have to look like a mourning widow when you take the stand."

"I *am* a mourning widow," she said. Despite Billy-Joe's many faults, she never wanted to see him dead.

He fixed his gaze on her as if to weigh her sincerity. "You'll be judged on your appearance and demeanor." As if he'd suddenly realized he'd been staring, he lowered his gaze and pulled his writing tablet from his leather satchel. "You'll also be judged on the way you answer questions and—"

"Jesse blames himself for Billy-Joe's death," she blurted out. He looked up from his notes. "If you let him testify, that's what he'll tell the court, and I don't want to put him through that."

"He's the only character witness we have."

"I don't care!"

His brow furrowed. "I don't think you fully understand the seriousness of your situation."

He was wrong about that. She understood all too well. "I said no," she snapped. "He's not testifying!"

The following morning Brock breathed in the clear, pine-scented air as he hurried to his office. He had a dozen things on his mind—all having to do with the case for which he was now in charge. Knowing Mrs. Davenport's future was in his hands had kept him twisting and turning all night. What was it about her that affected him so? He couldn't even close his eyes without seeing those big blue eyes of hers. Seeing that smile.

He shook his head. Getting too close to a client could be dangerous. A clear and objective mind was essential for defending a client. Personal feelings would only get in the way. If he'd learned anything from failing his friend, he'd learned that much.

He forced himself to focus on his list of things to do. Colorado lacked court transcribers, and though mechanical shorthand machines had been introduced to Philadelphia courtrooms, no such instrument existed out west.

He was obliged to hire his landlady's daughter to take on the recording chore with pen and ink. Miss Watkins, a thirty-year-old spinster, could read and write, but had no knowledge of shorthand. Whether she could adequately record testimony remained to be seen.

The street was deserted, businesses still closed. The rising sun cast fingers of light through piney branches and turned the scattered clouds into pink cotton balls.

Located in the Rocky Mountains, Lone Pine was named after the tall tree that stood smack in the center of town. Since gold was first discovered there in the 1850s, the town had known more busts than booms, but it never lacked for action. Since Brock's arrival six months previous, the town boasted more than a dozen drunken brawls, three shoot-outs, two knifings, and a dogfight.

Today, however, all looked peaceful as he made his way down Second Street. Only a thin, young voice broke the early morning silence: "Extra, extra! Read all about the Black Widow!"

Frowning, Brock pulled a coin from the pocket of his frock coat and handed it to the newspaper boy. After giving Brock a copy, the boy continued on his way, shouting at the top of his lungs.

Brock tucked the paper beneath his arm to be read later, though he could pretty well guess what it said. The *Lone Pine Herald* read more like a dime novel than serious journalism.

Shouts greeted Brock as he turned the corner to Main. Stepping off the boardwalk, he dodged a delivery wagon and ran to the other side. A fistfight was in progress, and onlookers yelled from the sidelines.

Brock gave the crowd a cursory glance. Probably a couple of miners fighting over a pretty woman. Or maybe drunks. At least this time they were using fists and not guns.

A man he recognized as Jim Clover waved his hat and yelled, "Come on, kid. You can't let the Black Widder's boy get the best of you!"

Brock stopped cold in his tracks. Jesse? He quickened his steps. Holding his portfolio like a shield, he pushed his way through the crowd. Grabbing one boy by the shirt, he jerked him to his feet and pulled Jesse off the ground.

"What do you think you're doing?" His rough voice was enough to make the spectators back away.

Jesse shook with anger but said nothing.

Brock grabbed him by the arm and hauled him down the street to his office.

Jesse had a bloodied nose and one puffed eye had already started turning blue. That was the extent of his injuries.

Brock pointed to a chair. "Sit!" He poured water from a pitcher onto a clean handkerchief and handed it to the boy. "What happened out there?"

Jesse dabbed his nose and flinched. "He started it."

"Who's he?"

"Freddy Ambrose. He called Ma names. Said she didn't deserve to live and that his pa would make sure she didn't."

Arms folded, Brock regarded the boy. "You can't solve problems with your fists."

"So what should I do?" Jesse's blue eyes held a suspicious gleam, but he stubbornly held his tears in check. "Let people say bad things about her?"

"If you want to fight for your mother, fine. But do it where it counts—in a court of law."

"How am I supposed to do that? Ma won't even let me testify."

That posed a problem, but Brock hoped to change his

mother's mind once the trial began. Jesse was the only one willing to stand up for her character. Without his testimony, Brock had little from which to work.

"Can you read?"

Jesse nodded. "Read every book in the lending library."

"How many is that? Two?" Brock regretted his thought-less words the moment he saw Jesse's crestfallen expression. "Tell you what. See those books over there?"

Jesse eyed the shelves crammed with law books. "Yeah."

"Those books contain information about statutes and commentaries on various court cases. They also have several transcripts from Mr. Abraham Lincoln's trials." No trial record-ers existed in Lincoln's day, so the transcripts were probably not all that accurate. But much could still be learned from them. "Did you know he was a lawyer before he was president?"

Jesse shook his head.

"He'll be remembered for his presidency, but his real genius was law. His cases provide lawyers like me with information on how to prepare for ours. When I was in Philadelphia, I had an assistant who searched for what we call precedents. A precedent provides a model for lawyers to follow and to see how similar cases were handled. Now that I'm here—"

"I can be your assistant," Jesse said, his eager voice offer-ing an odd contrast to his swollen eye.

"The book is full of Latin terms," Brock cautioned.

"Reverend Fields knows Latin. He can help me."

Brock stepped toward the bookshelves and reached for a hefty tome that he placed in Jesse's lap. Law books didn't make for compelling reading; Jesse probably wouldn't get much past the first page or so. But having something to do might help keep the boy out of trouble, at least for a while.

Since the heavy book commanded both of Jesse's arms, Brock opened the door for him. "Let me know if you find anything similar to your mother's situation that I can use."

"I will, Mr. Moses."

Brock shut the door with a shake of his head. *Mr. Moses?*

CHAPTER FIVE

ON THE FIRST DAY OF THE TRIAL, GRACE SAT AT A square saloon table. She watched warily as Mr. Daniels took his place by her side. He gave her a quick, reassuring smile before opening his leather case.

She twisted her hands nervously on her lap. He'd spent hours going over her testimony and explaining law procedures, but nothing had prepared her for the actual trial.

The saloon was packed, and not a single inch of standing room remained. Spectators lined the staircase and hung over the flimsy second-floor railing. It was a wonder the thing didn't collapse. The air hung thick with the smell of alcohol, smoke, and unwashed bodies. Grace's stomach churned.

That morning the sheriff had taken her to his house where his wife helped her bathe and tame her unruly red hair into shiny curls that cascaded down the back of her head. Jesse, visiting the jail on the way to school to wish her luck, had hardly recognized her. Even Mr. Daniels, upon entering the jail to escort her to court, stopped and stared at her.

She smoothed the soft fabric of her skirt and sighed. It sure did seem like a waste to wear her pretty, new dress in such an unforgiving place.

The court watchers hooted and whistled and made disparaging comments. "Hey, Daniels, watch out. You could be the Black Widow's next victim!" someone yelled, followed by raucous laughter.

Ignoring the hecklers, Mr. Daniels covered her hand with his. His touch was tentative, yet more reassuring than any spoken word. He leaned close and a pleasant smell of soap drifted toward her like a breath of fresh air.

"Are you all right?" The concern in his voice was mirrored in his eyes.

She nodded and tried to draw from the strength of his touch. "Thank God Jesse's not here to see this." It was bad enough that he had a black eye from fighting. He didn't need the added trauma of defending her in court.

"Jesse's a big boy," he said. "He wants to help."

She shook her head. She didn't want Jesse testifying. *Please, God, don't let it come to that.*

Daniels removed his hand from hers and wrote something on his legal tablet.

A man dressed in a wrinkled, dark suit perched on a stool behind the bar like a crow on a telegraph wire. He took a swallow of whiskey, wiped his mouth with his sleeve, and lit a cigar.

"Is that Judge Hackett?" she asked.

Daniels looked up from his notes. "It's him."

She'd expected someone more refined, more like her new lawyer. But as she glanced around the courtroom, she realized that Mr. Daniels didn't belong there any more than she did.

The judge picked up his Peacemaker and Grace drew back in her seat. It took three loud raps with the butt of his gun before the saloon grew quiet.

"Court will now come to order. Anyone caught throwing turnips, eggs, or cigar stubs will be asked to leave."

Tall Pete lifted his head from a table and peered around the crowded room with bloodshot eyes. "Objec-shun."

The judged ignored him. "Who wants to go first?"

Mr. Daniels rose, his long, lean form seeming to command every eye in the place. His broad shoulders filled his neatly pressed frock coat.

"Your Honor, I believe it's customary for the prosecutor to go first."

Judge Hackett looked at him much like a schoolmaster regarding a wayward schoolboy. "So we're going to run things like a Philadelphia courtroom, are we?" Without waiting for a reply, he gave the bar another whack with his pistol.

"Mr. Ambrose, you may proceed."

Mr. Daniels sat and Ambrose stood.

Stomach clenched, Grace leaned forward. "He better not go telling any lies about me," she murmured beneath her breath. "That's all I got to say."

"Don't worry. We'll have our turn," Daniels whispered back.

"Thank you, Herbie." Catching himself, Ambrose cleared his throat. "Uh . . . I mean, Your Honor." He walked around the table and faced the twelve jury members.

Never had Grace seen such a motley group of men. One was reading a newspaper and his floppy, felt hat was all that could be seen behind the bold Black Widow headline. Two were playing cards and another was dozing.

"Gentlemen of the jury," he began.

The small, birdlike woman Mr. Daniels hired to record the trial sat at a table by herself. Tongue between her teeth, she wrote furiously to keep up with the fast-talking prosecutor.

"I will prove beyond a reasonable doubt that Mrs. Davenport not only killed her husband, a man who was loving, kind, and—"

Grace slammed her hand on the table. "Overruled!"

Daniels leaned sideways in his chair. "Only the judge can overrule."

"But he wasn't loving and kind," she argued.

The judge gave the bar a sharp bang with his gun. "Mr. Dan-iels," he said, stretching out her lawyer's name with a nasally twang. "Can you not control your client?"

"Let me do the talking." Daniels's breath caressed her ear like a summer breeze and she pulled back.

"B-but what he said was a bald-faced lie."

"We'll get our chance." His dark, earnest eyes sought hers, and again he covered her hand with his own. "Trust me."

Trust him? She snapped her mouth shut . . . for now. But she'd trusted the last man she ever intended to trust—ever.

Brock idly snapped a pencil in two as he listened to Ambrose's opening statement. Not only had the prosecutor managed with diligent effort to overcome all but the slightest regard for law, his oratorical flourishes were better suited for the stage. And to think Ambrose had accused *him* of theatrics.

The prosecutor went on at great lengths about Grace Davenport's three husbands and their untimely deaths. Brock voiced several objections based on prejudice, each of which the judge overruled.

"No favoritism there," he mumbled after the fifth such ruling. His objections, however, did serve one useful purpose; they allowed Miss Watkins time to catch up.

Mrs. Davenport remained silent throughout the long discourse, though Brock could hear her seething breaths. But when Ambrose suggested that Jesse's life could be in mortal danger, Brock had to hold her down physically.

"Don't let him get to you," he whispered. "That's what he wants."

He felt her relax beneath his touch, but the lost look in her eyes almost broke his heart. Satisfied that she had gained control, he drew back.

After that she held herself exactly as he wanted her to: head high, shoulders back. Wisps of red hair framing, softening the angles of her face. Her new dress followed the intriguing peaks and valleys of her feminine form in a way he'd not intended. He wanted her to look like a grieving widow, but he doubted that any of the men behind the covetous yet cautious stares saw her quite that way.

Her complexion was pale but it was complemented by the deep blue of her eyes, as it was by her rosy pink mouth. She sure did look fetching, but it was the way she tried putting on a brave front that won his admiration.

"*Psst.*"

Brock swung his head around to find Jesse on hands and knees by his side. The boy tried to escape notice by keeping his body down and hat pulled low.

Brock leaned sideways. "What are you doing here?" The boy's mother was adamant about him staying away from that courtroom.

"Somnambulism," Jesse replied, mispronouncing the word for sleepwalking.

"What?"

The boy pulled a piece of paper from his pocket and read it in a whispery voice. "In 1846 and again in 1879, somnambulism was used as a defense against murder. In both cases the defendants got off." He looked up. "Said so in that book you gave me."

Brock's eyebrows shot up. Never in a million years did he think the boy could read, let alone understand, anything in that tome. He glanced over his shoulder. Grace never took her gaze off Ambrose, and she appeared oblivious to her son's presence.

Brock turned back to Jesse. "Those two men were actually guilty of the crimes for which they were accused," he whispered. "Your mother's innocent."

"No one believes that," Jesse said, though his determined look began to fade.

Daniels glanced at the jurors lapping up Ambrose's opening statement like kittens at a bowl of milk. Even someone as young as Jesse knew the odds were against them.

"I'm not giving up and neither are you. Understood?"

Jesse nodded.

"All right, then. See what else you can come up with."

Jesse crawled away on hands and knees, leaving a trail in the sawdust and disappearing through a forest of dusty boots and canvas-clad legs.

At long last, Ambrose sat down and Brock stood and faced the jury. One man had written the word *Guilty* on the writing tablet in front of him. Brock considered having the man thrown off the jury, but that would mean having to replace one prejudicial person with another.

His opening statement was short and promised one thing: to prove beyond a reasonable doubt that the accused was innocent of the charge of murder in the first degree.

He sat down, but Grace's questioning glance did nothing for his self-confidence. Obviously she didn't think much of his carefully prepared opener.

"A lawyer never shows his full hand before it's time," he said in an effort to relieve her mind.

"I'd feel better knowing you had an ace up your sleeve," she whispered back.

That made two of them. Not wanting to worry her, he forced his tight expression into a smile. No sense letting on that the only thing up his sleeve was prayer.

Opening comments concluded, Mr. Ambrose called Sheriff Bower and questioned him at length on the condition of Mr. Davenport's body.

"Did you find any incriminatin' evidence on the corpse?"

"Found a couple of bullets," the sheriff said. "The bullets came from a twelve-gauge double-barrel shotgun, just like the one Mrs. Davenport owns."

"Thank you, Sheriff." Ambrose turned to Brock, his eyes full of challenge. "Your witness."

Brock rose. "How many similar shotguns would you say are in Lone Pine, Sheriff?"

Bower shrugged. "I dunno. Couple hundred maybe."

"What about in the county?"

"I guess I'd have to say 'bout a thousand or more."

"What about the territory?"

"Objection," Ambrose roared. "Speculation."

"No more questions," Brock said and sat.

Mr. Ambrose rose like a male lion rising from his nap. "I call to the witness stand Mrs. Davenport."

Brock jumped to his feet so quickly his chair flew back. "Objection. A prosecutor can't call a defendant to the stand."

"I'm not calling Mrs. Davenport to the stand as a defendant. I'm calling her as a witness. She was the only one present during the shooting. That makes her a witness."

"You have no proof that she was present during the shooting," Brock argued.

"Yeah, well, we all know she was," Ambrose countered.

"Objection." Brock turned to the judge. "May we approach the . . . um . . . bar?"

Hackett finished lighting his cigar. "Oh, why not?"

Brock won the argument that followed but it was only the first battle. He had a very bad feeling that he was losing the war.

Ambrose's accusations became more outrageous as the day progressed, but by then half the jury was asleep and the other half three sheets to the wind.

The sun dipped behind the mountains and a brisk breeze blew off the snowy peaks. The batwing doors swung back and forth and a noticeable chill crept into the makeshift courtroom.

Just as the saloon keeper began to light the gas lanterns, Judge Hackett pounded his gun. "Court adjourned till tomorrow."

Mouth tight, Brock shoved papers into his portfolio. His client's hand on his arm made him pause. She pulled her hand away, her eyes rounded in apology. Only then did he realize he was scowling.

"I . . . I guess my new dress didn't help, did it?"

He slammed his portfolio on the table. "It was only the first day," he said a bit too brusquely. She flinched and he immediately regretted showing his frustration. He purposely softened his voice. "Tomorrow will go better," he said, hoping to erase the worry lines from her face. A smile replaced her frown, bringing a smile to his own face.

They might have sat there smiling indefinitely at each other had the sheriff not appeared at her side to take her back to her cell. "Ready?"

She nodded and stood. "It'll go better tomorrow, Mr. Daniels. Don't you worry none, you hear?"

Guilt rushed through him as the sheriff led her away. It was his job to encourage her, not the other way around. From now on he intended to keep his worries about her case to himself. He gathered his frock coat from the back of his chair and swung it over his shoulder. It had been a long day and it looked to be an even longer night.

CHAPTER SIX

BROCK GULPED DOWN TWO CUPS OF COFFEE THE NEXT morning before grabbing his satchel and leaving the two-story brick boardinghouse. He dashed down the porch steps and hurried along the street toward his office.

"Mr. Moses, Mr. Moses . . ."

Brock stopped and turned. Jesse ran toward him, waving his arm. "Wait!" The boy caught up to him but was too winded to speak.

"What are you doing here? Why aren't you in school?"

The morning sun had yet to warm the air, and white puffs escaped Jesse's mouth as he tried to catch his breath. "Twins," he said between gasps.

Brock frowned. "Excuse me?"

"D.K. Jenkins claimed his twin robbed a bank, not him. Said so in your book."

Brock vaguely remembered the case. "Does your mother have a twin?"

"No, but . . ."

"Jesse, I'm not going to lie in court."

The boy wrinkled his nose. "But we don't have anything else."

Feeling sorry for him, Brock laid a hand on his shoulder. "We have the truth on our side. That means we have God with us too."

Jesse's eyes opened wide. "Does that mean our side will win?"

"What it means is we have to use all the tools God has given us. We just have to use them in the right way. So you need to keep reading and I need to keep working. And we both need to keep praying. Understood, Mr. Lincoln?"

Jesse saluted. "Understood, Mr. Moses." He turned and ran down the street, schoolbooks swinging from a leather strap. Then he vanished around the corner in the direction of the little brick schoolhouse.

Brock stared into the face of the rising sun. A vision of Grace Davenport came to mind and intense determination flared deep within, followed by doubt. What if he couldn't save Grace? *What then, God? What then?*

Before reaching his office, Brock bought the morning paper. The headline read: BLACK WIDOW TO CHANGE PLEA. He quickly scanned the article.

"What the—?" Tossing a coin to the paperboy, he raced down the street, reaching the sheriff's office just as Reverend Fields walked out. Salt-and-pepper sideburns hugged a well-used face, giving him a comical look that didn't belong with his formal black frock coat and high-top hat.

The preacher tucked his Bible into his coat pocket and greeted Brock with a grave nod. "This business about her changing her plea—" He shook his head and his jowls wobbled. "Maybe you can talk some sense into her."

Brock grimaced. "I'll try but there's no guarantee she'll listen."

Fields's eyebrows rose. "She's innocent, right? At least that's what Jesse believes."

"Yes, she's innocent. She didn't kill anyone," Brock assured him.

"That's a relief." The reverend studied him. "So why do you look so worried? Is there a chance you can't get her off?"

Brock hesitated. He seldom spoke of the past, but today his burden weighed heavier than usual, and the preacher's concern was hard to resist. "The last criminal case I handled turned out badly . . . an innocent man was sent to his death." He thought a Harvard law degree would guarantee his friend got off on a self-defense charge, but his youth and lack of experience were no match for the clever prosecutor. He'd been too dumb or maybe too proud to admit he was in over his head. In his arrogance he hadn't even thought to ask for God's help.

"I gave up criminal law and moved here. I always thought God wanted me to be a trial lawyer, but I messed up. I messed up bad."

The preacher commiserated with a shake of his head.

"Fortunately, God doesn't judge us by our failures. If He did, we preachers would be in a whole peck of trouble. I'm afraid we lose more than we save."

"I guess you can say the same about lawyers."

Fields chuckled. "That puts you and me in the same boat."

Brock nodded. "Yes, and that boat seems to be leaking. Before coming here, I was told that no law existed west of Kansas City, but I didn't want to believe it."

"Don't feel bad. I didn't want to believe that Sunday wasn't even on the calendar past the Missouri River either, but we can't give up. That would be the real sin. The only Israelites who made it to the Promised Land were the ones who didn't give up."

Was that what he'd done after failing his friend? Given up? Brock drew in a deep breath. "I'll do whatever it takes to defend her." The old fighting spirit that had long ago deserted him was back in full force.

"Good to hear." He laid his hand on Brock's shoulder. "Saving Grace might well be *your* saving grace."

With that the pastor walked away, whistling to himself. Puzzled, Brock watched him. What made the reverend think *he* needed saving?

With a shake of his head, he entered the sheriff's office. Bower looked up from his newspaper and tossed a nod toward the back. "It's unlocked."

The blazing headline on the sheriff's newspaper stoked Brock's anger. He strode past the sheriff's desk and through the door that led to the jail cells.

Mrs. Davenport whirled about to face him. Already

dressed for court, she looked as fragile as a porcelain doll. The half-moon shadows beneath her eyes told him she'd had a hard night too. Had he invaded her sleep as she invaded his?

Irritated at such wayward thoughts, he waved the newspaper in front of her. "What does this mean?" he demanded. His loud voice caused the prisoner two cells over to stir in his sleep. "You're changing your plea?"

Her lips quivered. "Thinking about it."

He glowered at her. "Why would you do such a thing if you're innocent?"

Her eyes blazed. "I *am* innocent!"

"Then act like it!" he shouted. She flinched and the prisoner in the cell next to hers rolled off his cot and landed on the floor with an audible thump.

"Hey, keep it down in there!" the man slurred.

Grace ignored him. "What am I supposed to do?" she cried.

"You do what I tell you to do. From now on you don't say a word to anyone without first consulting me. Is that clear?"

She glared at him. "I don't know much about the law, but I was raised in the South. I know a losing war when I see one."

He ran his hand across his chin. "We haven't yet begun to fight."

She closed her eyes as if the very thought of fighting was too much to bear. "The sheriff said he would ask the judge to sentence me to prison if I pled guilty. That's better than hanging."

"Some trade-off!" Prison conditions were abominable, even for men. He paced back and forth in front of her cell. He knew Grace Davenport enough to discern she didn't do anything—even marry—without consideration of her son.

"This is about Jesse, isn't it?"

The resigned look on her face told him he'd guessed right even before she answered.

"Have you seen him lately?" she asked.

"I've seen him."

"Then you know that Reverend Fields and his wife are doing right by him. Jesse never looked so good. He's got himself a real haircut. And two new pairs of trousers—two! And he's learning Latin."

"Grace . . ." He stopped himself. "May I call you Grace?"

She lowered her lashes and nodded, her silken cheeks pink. He studied her a moment before continuing, "Jesse is a fine lad. The finest I've ever met. He doesn't care about fancy clothes and haircuts. He just wants his mother. With God's help, I aim to see that he gets his wish."

She lifted her gaze to his. The liquid blue depths of her eyes awakened something inside that hadn't stirred since his friend's death. His professional façade deserting him, he was in dire danger of being drawn into forbidden territory.

"Why do you care so much?" she asked, her voice barely audible.

He did care, though in the beginning he hadn't even wanted to take her case. Wanted no part of it. But that was before he came to know her, came to see her basic goodness. He grimaced. Why was God testing him? He'd been perfectly content practicing business law and handling an occasional civil lawsuit. He hadn't given up as the reverend suggested; he'd simply traded one specialty for another. Now he was obligated to see this trial through to the end. God help him!

"You didn't kill anyone. That's why I care." Even as he said it, he knew that was only part of the truth, but he didn't want to think of the rest. If this really was a second chance, he prayed he wouldn't fail Grace as he'd failed his friend Philip.

"You said you wanted Jesse to get his wish." She bit her lower lip. "What is *your* wish, Mr. Daniels?"

He sucked in his breath and rubbed his chin. What he wished was to take her in his arms and comfort her. What he wished was to kiss away her worries and make her troubles disappear. But he couldn't say any of these things, shouldn't even be thinking them.

"Right now," he said with feeling, "I wish you had a twin."

CHAPTER SEVEN

A STRING OF PROSECUTING WITNESSES TOOK THE STAND that morning, one right after another. Dr. Matthews testified that the cause of death was a chunk of lead in Billy-Joe's heart. "And that's a calcified fact," he said.

A farmer testified that he'd found Billy-Joe's horse in his field. "But when nobody claimed it, I figured it was mine to keep."

Next, the man who spotted Billy-Joe's body at the bottom of a dry well took the oath. "I spotted something shiny and thought it was gold. Decided to take a look. Turned out it was Billy-Joe's watch."

Men with questionable reputations gave glowing accounts of Billy-Joe's moral character. "Finest man I ever caught cheating," one man claimed.

His testimony brought scattered laughter from spectators, and the judge immediately called for order.

Mr. Benjamin Haddock took the stand next. After placing his hand on the Bible and swearing to tell the truth, the whole truth and nothing but the truth, he introduced himself as a friend of the victim, Billy-Joe Davenport.

Mr. Haddock was a thin, nervous man who looked like he'd rather be anywhere but in that courtroom.

Mr. Ambrose questioned him about the night Billy-Joe was killed. "You said you and him were playing faro. Is that correct?"

"Yep. Just like we did every Friday."

"And did you see Mrs. Davenport on the night in question, which I believe was September ninth?" Ambrose asked.

"I saw her, all right. She was madder than a peeled rattler."

"A peeled rattler," Ambrose repeated for the benefit of the jury. After a dramatic pause, he asked, "And then what happened?"

"They went at it hammer and tongs and she stormed out of the saloon."

Ambrose turned toward the jury as if to make sure they were paying attention. "And what did Mr. Davenport do?"

"He . . ." A scuffle in the back of the saloon drowned out his voice.

Brock swung around. Two men were punching each other. Catching a glimpse of Jesse watching the fight, he glanced at Grace, but she didn't seem to notice. She'd have a fit if she knew her son was here, but there was no keeping him away.

Soon as the sheriff restored order, the judge yelled, "I'm fining you both ten dollars for contempt of court."

One of the two rowdies reached into his hip pocket. "It just so happens I have a ten spot right here."

"Well, while you're digging see if you also have thirty days in that pocket." The judge waved his hand. "Take 'em away!"

After the sheriff dragged both men out of the saloon, Ambrose continued questioning Haddock. "Let's see, where were we . . . ? Ah, yes. Did you see Mr. Davenport after September ninth?"

"Nope. That's the last time."

Ambrose turned to Daniels. "Your witness."

Daniels stood and waited for Miss Watkins to signal that she was ready to record. "Didn't you think it odd that your friend had suddenly disappeared?"

Haddock shook his head. "Didn't think it odd a'tall. If I was married to the Black Widder, I'd disappear too."

This brought laughter from spectators and jurors alike. The judge banged his weapon and Tall Pete's head shot up. "Object-shun."

The judge glared at him. "Order!"

Brock waited for the room to grow quiet before he continued. Something about Haddock didn't sit right. Nervous as a dog with fleas, he kept putting his hand in his vest pocket.

"Going back to the last night you saw him . . . did Billy-Joe say anything that led you to believe he feared for his life?"

Haddock gave a derogatory laugh. "He didn't have to. I could see his life was in danger with me own two eyes."

"You do know you're under oath to tell the truth, is that correct?" Brock asked.

"I don't need no oath to tell the truth. I've been wedded to the truth since the day I was born."

"Oh?" Brock gave him a wry smile. "And how long have you been a widower?"

"Objection!" Ambrose shouted.

"That's all the questions I have of this witness." Daniels took his seat.

Just before the church bells struck the noon hour, Ambrose rested his case.

It was nearly two o'clock before the trial got underway again. Hackett called the court to order. "You may call your first witness, Mr. Daniels. And make it quick. I'm due in Denver day after tomorrow."

"Here we go," Brock said under his breath. Grace felt a lurch of excitement. Maybe now the truth would come out. But as each witness testified, her spirits sank. Her lawyer would have gotten better results had he questioned a knothole.

After questioning Myron Johnson, the owner of the mine where Billy-Joe worked, Daniels leaned over the table to whisper in her ear. "Ready?"

Grace's heart pounded but she managed to find her voice. "Yes." No sense letting on how scared she was or that her knees were knocking.

Brock winked at her, but that only made matters worse, for it made her heart pound faster and her knees tremble more.

"I call to the stand the defendant, Mrs. Grace Davenport."

She rose and wiped her damp hands down the sides of her skirt. All eyes followed her to the ladder-back chair used by witnesses. All that could be heard were shuffling feet as spectators moved in to get a better view.

Brock waited for her to be sworn in.

"Please state your full name for the court," he said. He stood directly in front of her, effectively drawing her gaze to him.

"My name—" She cleared her throat and started again. "My name is Grace Elizabeth Davenport." The room was so quiet that only the scratching sounds of Miss Watkins's pen could be heard.

Brock had gone over the questions prior to the trial, but testifying in the relative privacy of her cell was a whole lot easier than facing a crowded courtroom.

"Opposing counsel has made much of your earlier marriages. Would you care to tell the court exactly how your two prior husbands died?"

It was hard to talk about Geoffrey and Harry, but she forced herself. She doubted it would do much good; the townspeople preferred wild rumors to the honest truth, and nothing she said would convince them she wasn't a killer.

Daniels whispered for her ears only, "You're doing great." He then led her gently step–by–step through her marriage to Billy-Joe up to the night he was killed. "Why was that particular night so important to you?" he asked.

"It was Jesse's birthday and I promised him a new pair of boots." She turned to the jury. "The ones he had were so full of holes he might as well have been going barefoot. Billy-Joe promised as soon as he got his pay, he'd pick up the ones we ordered." She twisted her handkerchief in her lap. "Instead he lost all his money gambling."

"So your son didn't get new boots for his birthday?" Daniels said, facing the jury.

"No, he didn't," she said. He told her to answer the questions honestly but not to say more than necessary.

"Did you see your husband after the night of September ninth?" he asked.

"No, I didn't."

"That's because you kilt him!" someone shouted from the balcony.

"Ob—" This time Tall Pete wasn't able to get the whole word out before his head flopped back down.

The judge pounded the bar with his gun. "One more outburst and I'll charge you all with contempt."

Daniels continued as if no interruptions had occurred. "Did you think it odd that your husband didn't come back to the house? To collect his belongings?"

"I figured he was too ashamed to face me after what he had done. But after a couple of days I went to the mine to talk to him, and the mine owner told me Billy-Joe hadn't shown up for work."

"Did that surprise you?"

She nodded. "That's when I got worried. Billy-Joe was real proud of his property. Said it was worth something now that Colorado was a state. It didn't seem right that he would walk away from it. That's why I went to see the sheriff."

"What did you say to the sheriff?"

"I told him what happened the night I last saw Billy-Joe."

"And what did the sheriff say?"

"He said he'd ask around. See if anyone knew where Billy-Joe might have gone."

"And you never saw nor heard from your husband again. Is that correct?"

She nodded. "That's correct."

Daniels turned to the prosecutor. "Your witness."

Ambrose rose and rubbed his palms together as if preparing for a feast. His questions started at a slow cadence, like a funeral march. He went into great detail about her two prior husbands and tried to poke holes in her testimony.

"You expect us to believe that a man who spent his life on a farm wouldn't know how to pick out a poisonous mushroom?"

"You can't tell just by looking at them," she said.

No sooner had she gotten the words out than he was on to the next question and the next. He hammered her until she felt like her most intimate thoughts had been turned inside out and laid bare for all to see.

"In your testimony a few minutes ago, you mentioned your husband's property. Who stands to inherit the land now that he's deceased?"

"Objection," Daniels said, rising. "The property has no bearing on this case."

"'Course it does," Ambrose argued. "I'm attempting to show motive."

The judge clamped down on his cigar. "Overruled."

Ambrose turned back to her. "Shall I repeat the question, Mrs. Davenport?"

She stared at his predatory expression. "I inherit the property." And with those four words she could feel the rope tighten around her neck.

CHAPTER EIGHT

THE TRIAL LASTED FOR THREE WHOLE DAYS—THE longest trial anyone in Lone Pine could recall. At last, the moment everyone had been waiting for arrived; the jury had reached a verdict.

Judge Hackett gave the bar a quick rap with his pistol, and a hushed silence filled the saloon. "The court will come to order. And hurry up. I've got a train to catch."

The jury had been out for less than forty minutes. Now they staggered into the saloon single file. Grace's stomach knotted. She'd never spoken to any of these men, yet they would decide her fate.

She gazed at Mr. Daniels's stony profile. "It's not a good sign, is it?" she asked. "The jury coming back so fast, I mean."

His gaze locked with hers and he squeezed her hand. "Whatever happens, we won't give up. I promise."

He seemed sincere; probably was sincere, but so were

Geoffrey, Harry, and Billy-Joe. At first. So, for that matter, was her father when he assured her that marrying at fifteen was the right thing to do. It wasn't until much later that she learned money had changed hands. Her father hadn't just given her away; he'd sold her like livestock.

Quickly she banished the thought and focused on the jury. They refused to look at her now, just as her father had refused to look at her then. She clenched her hands and forced herself to breathe.

The judge gulped his whiskey and ran the back of his hand across his mouth. "Has the jury reached a verdict?"

"Yep." Buzz McGinnis, a thin, wheezy man with a rounded back and concave chest, stood. His pince-nez glasses kept slipping down his nose. "We got ourselves a verdict."

A shudder ripped through her and Daniels's hand tightened on hers.

She absorbed the strength of him and prayed. Somehow she had to be strong, for Jesse's sake.

McGinnis took a raspy breath and looked down at the paper in his hand. "We the jury"—he pushed his glasses up his nose—"find the Black Wid . . . uh . . . the defendant . . ." He dropped his paper and stooped to retrieve it.

"Would you get on with it?" The judge's voice was thick with impatience. "Just tell us if she is guilty or not guilty so I can get outta here!"

"Not guilty," Tall Pete slurred, waving his arm in a circle.

"What's that? What did he say?" a voice called from the second floor.

"He said not guilty!" someone else yelled.

"How can that be?" another called out. "We all know she done it!"

McGinnis checked the paper in his hands and blinked. His glasses fell and he stooped to pick them up. He arranged them on his nose, but before he could read the correct verdict, someone yelled, "Done it or not, I say drinks on the house!"

The floor shook beneath the onslaught of stampeding boots. McGinnis looked around, startled. Recovering quickly, he scrambled to reach the bar before the other eleven jurors.

Grace sat rooted in place. She didn't dare move for fear of waking from a dream.

An incessant voice rose above the din. "Let me through." The newspaper editor elbowed his way through the crowd and dashed out the batwing doors.

From outside came the popping sound of gunshots—three to signal acquittal. The signal for conviction was only one.

Still she didn't move. Had she really been found not guilty? Ambrose apparently didn't think so. He and Daniels stood arguing in front of the bar—arms flailing, faces red, voices drowned out by sheer pandemonium.

Daniels finally made it to her side. Never had she seen such a wide grin. "Come on, let's get you out of here." He put his arm around her shoulders and guided her through the mass of heated bodies and overturned chairs.

Outside, she stopped to inhale the fresh air. Never had it tasted sweeter. And the sun . . . Closing her eyes, she lifted her face toward the sky and absorbed its welcome warmth.

"You okay?" Daniels asked.

She gazed up at him. At that moment, his nearness was the only thing that seemed real. "What . . . happened?"

His grin widened. "A miracle!"

She still couldn't believe it. "I'm free, right? I don't have to go back to jail?"

"Not if I can help it." He glanced around. The street was crowded with people rushing toward the saloon to see if the news was true.

"Let's go." With a protective arm around her, he led her along the boardwalk to his office.

Away from the public eye, her brave front deserted her. Weeks of tension begged for release. Tears swam in her eyes before slowly rolling down her cheeks. Sobs wracked her body. Daniels pulled her into his arms and, trembling, she clung to him.

She buried her head next to his throat and her eyelashes fluttered against his warm skin.

"It's all right," he whispered, rubbing her back. His lips brushed against her brow as he spoke; his breath mingled with hers. Cupping her face in his hands, he thumbed away her tears until her sobs subsided.

"What . . . what happened?" she whispered. "Why am I free?"

"When Tall Pete called out 'not guilty,' everyone assumed at first that the jury had spoken. Fortunately for us, the judge is leaving town and didn't have time to straighten out the mess. So he ruled in our favor."

"But . . . but that means that everyone still thinks I'm guilty."

"I don't. Jesse doesn't. God knows you're innocent."

She looked at him with tear-filled eyes. "But the others—" She started to sob and suddenly found herself in his arms.

"It's okay, Grace. Don't cry."

His breath warm on her cheek, he held her close. For several moments he rocked her until the tears had run their course. Tipping her chin upward, he kissed her, his mouth warm and sweet on hers. His kiss chased away the last of her dark thoughts. She flung her arms around his neck to deepen the kiss and waves of pleasure reached all the way to her toes.

The door to the office suddenly flew open. "Ma!"

At the sound of Jesse's voice, they pulled apart like two children caught stealing candy.

Grace quickly wiped away the last of the tears, but nothing could be done about her burning cheeks or her pounding heart. Or her mouth that still trembled with the memory of Brock's sweet, tender kisses.

Jesse ran into her open arms. "I heard the gunshots. Is it true?"

"It's true," she said, smiling.

"This calls for a celebration," Daniels said, grinning. "How about I treat you both to a meal at Mrs. Wilson's Inn?"

"Thank you, but I just want to go home." She didn't want to hurt his feelings, but the thought of spending another minute in the public eye was more than she could bear. Especially now that it looked like she'd gotten away with murder—yet again.

"You can come to our house for supper," Jesse said to Brock as he pulled away from her. "Ma's a good cook."

More heat rushed to her face. "I'm sure Brock . . . Mr. Daniels has something more important to do." Suddenly she felt shy, worried that their kiss a moment before meant nothing to the man.

Daniels shook his head. "Nope, not a thing." He gave her a meaningful look. "That is, if you don't mind the company."

"We don't mind," Jesse said. "Do we, Ma?"

Grace ruffled her son's hair. "Of course not."

Daniels smiled. "Allow me to bring something. I'm not much of a cook, but I can pick up some groceries."

She did a quick mental check of her pantry. It had been weeks since she'd been home, but she could still recall every item on her shelves. Johnnycake would go nicely with roast chicken. So would the canned string beans left over from last year's harvest.

"I think I have what I need," she said. If the birds hadn't eaten all the berries, there might even be enough left to make a pie. They settled on a time just as Reverend Fields popped his head through the open door.

"Heard the news," he called. "Do you and Jesse need a ride home?"

"Thank you, Reverend, that would be most helpful." It would also give her a chance to express her gratitude to him for taking care of Jesse.

Daniels walked them outside and helped her up the side of the wagon. Her hand in his felt almost as intimate as his kiss and her heart fluttered. She pulled her hand away as if it were on fire. He raised a questioning gaze but said nothing.

Reverend Fields took his place in the driver's seat and the wagon rolled forward. Jesse waved and Daniels called, "See you tonight."

People stopped to stare as they drove by and someone called out, "Hey, Black Widder. We know you done it."

Jesse opened his mouth to yell back, but she grabbed his arm. "Shh, don't say anything."

"But, Ma—"

"Your mother's right, Jesse." Reverend Fields snapped the reins to pick up speed. "The Bible tells us if we argue with a fool, we'll end up just like him." He paused for a moment before adding, with a twinkle in his eye, "And unlike someone I know, I have it on good authority that the man yelling his fool head off is not a democrat." He frowned. "Not much of a Christian either."

The savory smell of roast chicken wafted from the kitchen as Grace checked the three place settings on the table for perhaps the eighth or ninth time. The cabin contained only three rooms, a kitchen, a parlor, and a bedroom. The wood-block table took up half the parlor.

Jesse and the reverend had taken good care of the animals in her absence, and Mrs. Fields had even arranged to have groceries delivered to the house once the verdict was announced. Never had Grace known such kindness.

Jesse had picked purple and white columbines for the centerpiece, but no amount of wildflowers could hide the mismatched dinnerware or the frayed tablecloth. A fine gentleman like Mr. Daniels deserved so much more than their humble home could offer.

Just thinking his name made her heart pound and her knees quiver. And the kiss. Heavens to Betsy, how the man could kiss! His weren't the first kisses to cross her lips. Oh my, no! So why did it all seem so new to her? No man had ever affected her like he did, that was why. No man had ever made her feel so alive.

She glanced at Jesse stretched out in front of the fire, nose buried in a book. A feeling of inadequacy swept over her. Not only was she the wrong woman for Mr. Daniels, she was the wrong mother for Jesse. Much as she hated to admit it, he was better off with Reverend Fields.

Shaken by the thought, she dropped a glass and it shattered on the floor. Jesse looked up. "You okay, Ma?"

She nodded and he quickly returned to his book.

She grabbed the broom from a kitchen cupboard and tried to steady her nerves. What was wrong with her? She'd just been given her life back and she was feeling so out of sorts. What did it matter what others thought? Or the names people called her? What was that ditty they sang in school? Sticks and stones . . .

Sighing, she quickly swept the broken glass into a dustpan. A log rolled over in the fireplace, sending sparks flying up the chimney like little fireflies.

"Do you know what *habeas corpus* means?" Jesse called to her.

Jesse had been quizzing her on legal terms all afternoon. "It has something to do with a dead body, right?" she asked.

He laughed. "*Habeas corpus* means a person under arrest has to be brought before a court."

She stood the broom in a corner and gazed at her son in wonder. All those strange Latin terms. And goodness gracious! Never had she seen such a thick book.

A knock sounded at the door and Jesse jumped to his feet. "I'll get it."

Surprised by the sudden thump of her heart, she patted her hair and smoothed her apron.

Mr. Daniels ducked beneath the low door frame and entered the house. "Hmm, something smells good," he said, offering gifts: a book for Jesse and a bouquet of red roses wrapped in newspaper for her.

"Oh! They're beautiful," she said, sniffing the pleasant, sweet fragrance. She couldn't remember the last time anyone gave her flowers.

"My landlady is from England. Evidently growing a rose garden is a requirement of being British," he explained.

She laughed and hurried to the kitchen to find an empty canning jar. The two male voices floated from the parlor as she arranged the roses and put the finishing touches on their meal.

"I want to be a lawyer like you, Mr. Moses," Jesse said.

"Well, Mr. Lincoln, a lawyer requires a good education. A good school helps and . . ."

With a growing sense of dismay, Grace listened to them talk. She'd prayed for someone to come along and be a real father to Jesse. But a Philadelphia lawyer? *What are You thinking, God? You know this won't work.*

Jesse was fond of the man and that worried her. It worried her a lot. It was bad enough fighting her own feelings. Now that the trial was over, he was bound to lose interest in her son, lose interest in her. Once again, she and Jesse would be alone in the world. No sense wishing that this time things would be different. No sense praying for it either.

CHAPTER NINE

AFTER SUPPER, JESSE AND BROCK SAT IN FRONT OF THE fire playing a game of draughts. The clock on the mantel struck nine and Grace couldn't believe it. Where had the time gone?

"You have school tomorrow, Jesse," she said, though she hated to end his fun. "You better get some shut-eye."

Jesse looked surprised. "You mean I gotta go back to school?"

"You heard what Mr. Daniels said about getting a good education." If nothing else came out of the whole terrible experience, she knew that she could no longer give Jesse what he needed. She couldn't teach him anymore. Not like when he was ankle-high to a june bug. He needed a real teacher. She just hoped the rumors didn't get to him. Children could be so mean. Adults too.

Jesse made a face, but he picked up his book and left the room with a murmured good night.

Mr. Daniels placed the wooden game pieces in the tin box

but made no move to leave. "He's really something, that boy of yours."

She smiled and her heart swelled with pride. Jesse was something—the best thing that ever happened to her. "Would you like some tea?" she asked. "Or coffee, Mr. Daniels?"

"No, thank you." He hesitated. "Isn't it time you called me Brock? I'm no longer your lawyer."

"No, I reckon you're not." She'd call him by his front name if that was what he wanted, even if it did make it more difficult to keep her emotions in check. She moistened her lips and dropped to her knees on the rug in front of the fire, careful to keep a safe distance between them as she tended the flames. "I owe you a lot. I'll try to pay you back but it might take awhile."

He snapped the tin game box shut. "I don't want your money, Grace. The trial's over. We don't have to think about it anymore."

"It's over for you, maybe, but not for me." Even the orange flames seemed to mock her like wagging tongues. "It will never be over for me."

He turned his head to study her. "How can you say that?"

She replaced the poker and pulled away from the fire. "I'll always be the crazy woman with three dead husbands." She hugged her knees. "The woman everyone calls the Black Widow."

"People have short memories. In time, they'll forget."

"People don't forget that easily." She studied him. "Have you forgotten what happened in Philadelphia?"

A muscle tightened in his jaw. "That's different. I let a friend down. He depended on me and I failed him."

"Maybe it wasn't you that failed. Maybe it was justice."

"Actually, it was a clever prosecutor. I was fresh out of school and thought I knew it all. I didn't know enough to ask for help. I should never have defended him." He grimaced at the memory. "I probably shouldn't have even taken on your case."

The urge to smooth back the lock on his forehead was almost too much to bear. "Why did you?" she asked softly, her eyes narrowing.

"Have you ever tried to say no to Jesse?"

She laughed. "Oh yes."

His gaze lingered for a moment on her mouth and she quickly looked away. "Actually, he reminds me of a story Jesus told about the importance of persistent prayer. It's about a widow and a corrupt judge. She kept pleading for her rights and finally her persistence wore the judge down."

"Is that what Jesse did? Wear you down?"

"His persistence told me how much faith he had in your innocence. Just as persistent prayer tells God how much faith we have in Him."

She stared into the fire. What did she do to deserve such a fine, loving son? "When I was six, I asked my pa why my brothers got new shoes and I didn't. He said I was a girl and had no right to expect anything new or good to happen to me."

"Your father was wrong, Grace."

He scooted closer. Memories of his warm embrace flooded back, forcing her to look away.

He ran a knuckle along the side of her face. "If you let me, I aim to show you just how wrong."

A shiver ran through her and she hugged her legs tighter.

He sat back with a questioning look. "Do I make you nervous?"

"No." *Yes.* "Why would you think such a thing?"

"You hardly looked at me all through supper. Is it because . . . of what happened after the verdict? When I kissed you?"

She looked at him now. The kiss that had worked its way into the deepest regions of her heart seemed to stretch between them like a bridge begging to be crossed.

"Of c-course not," she stammered. "You were just trying to comfort me." She wanted him to deny that was the only reason he kissed her. When he didn't, she added, "I don't want you making promises you can't keep."

He raised an eyebrow. "What promises are those?"

"All that business about helping Jesse with his education. That was just polite talk. It don't mean a thing."

Flames from the fire flared in his eyes. "I don't say things I don't mean."

"All men say things they don't mean."

"I don't."

She wished with all her heart she could believe him, but that would only open her up to more pain.

"It must be difficult," he said, "raising a child on your own."

She nodded. "Things are different now. I don't need a man to take care of us. I've got this here property. I'm sure to get a handsome price for the land . . . at least enough to put Jesse through lawyer school, if that's what he wants."

"You aren't thinking of selling, are you? Of leaving?"

"Thinking about it. Maybe go where no one knows my past."

A muscle twitched in his jaw. "I meant what I said about helping Jesse. He can work in the office with me after school and have full access to my law library."

"That's kind of you," she said, "but it won't change nothing. Long as we stay here, he'll always be the son of the Black Widow."

"Not if we find the real killer."

She scoffed. "How we gonna do that?"

He stared into the fire as if the answer could be found amid the burning logs. "I don't know. But I'll do whatever I can to find him, and that's a promise."

He sounded so sincere she almost believed him. Wanted to. Wished with all her heart she could. But sad experiences taught her that even promises made with the best of intentions were seldom kept.

She yawned; she couldn't help herself. It had been weeks since she'd had a good night's rest. The warmth of the fire and Brock's smooth, velvet voice had a lulling effect.

Taking the hint, he stood and pulled her to her feet.

"Supper was great. Thank you." He held her hands and his gentle grip made her tremble. She pulled away, but his gaze on her lips felt like a kiss, had the same impact on her emotions.

As if catching himself staring, he turned abruptly and reached for his hat.

Desperate to fill in the strained silence, she blurted out the first thing that came to mind. "T-thank you," she stammered. "For everything. I wish I could do something to show our appreciation."

"Maybe you can." A look of excitement flashed in his eyes. "I'm thinking about running for judge this fall. Maybe Jesse will agree to be my campaign manager."

She covered her mouth and stared at him over her fingertips. "Judge Daniels. Oh my. That sounds important."

"I don't know about that, but I think I can make a difference. At least see that everyone gets a fair trial, guilty or innocent."

"Innocent like your friend," she said softly.

"And you." He nudged a strand of hair away from her face with a fingertip and her pulse quickened.

"I think it's a g-grand idea," she stammered. It was yet another reason why their kiss could never be repeated. Not only was she afraid to trust another man, she was also afraid she would cause him trouble. "But you best get another campaign manager. No one's gonna vote for you long as your name's linked with the Black Widow."

"Don't say that. You're not—"

"To the town I am!" Not wanting him to see her sudden tears, she whirled about and opened the door. A blast of cold air brushed against her heated cheeks. "It's late. You best go."

He hesitated a moment before walking outside. "Grace..."

CHAPTER TEN

SPRING TURNED INTO SUMMER AND STILL THE WHIS-
pers persisted. They greeted Grace like buzzing bees whenever
she drove into town. Sometimes at night while lying in bed,
she imagined that the breeze whistling through the trees and
brushing against the windowpanes was actually voices judging her, judging Jesse.

Sundays were the worst. Jesse had promised Reverend
Fields that he'd attend worship, and if she wanted to teach
her son anything, it was to keep his promises. So every week
like clockwork, Grace drove the horse and wagon to the little
white community church on Third Street.

People stared at her and whispered behind gloved hands.
Fearing what they might say aloud, she kept her distance. But
it wasn't the whispers that bothered her. It was the sideways
glances and questioning looks. As if they were convinced they
had a killer in their midst.

Mrs. Fields always greeted her and Jesse with warm regard. She had even invited them to attend church socials, but Grace continued to shy away. The preacher's wife was only trying to be kind, and Grace didn't want to cause her or the church any trouble.

Jesse never complained, but neither did he mingle with other boys his age. He stayed clear of the swimming hole outside of town and never joined in a game of rounders. After school let out for the summer, he did his chores in the morning and rode into town to read law with Brock. Despite her concerns, he also made "Brock for Judge" handbills and posted them all over town.

Not only had he passed her in height, but also she hardly understood what he was talking about much of the time. All those big words he used . . . five-dollar words, Brock called them.

During all that time, she tried keeping a respectful distance from Brock, even at church. It was as much for her peace of mind as for his career. Men had been the source of all her problems; it was better to stay away from them. Stay away from Brock. Better for both of them.

But the decision didn't come easy, and more than once Jesse caught her pacing the floor at night, struggling with herself. She didn't want to hurt Brock, but neither did she want to lead him on. The only way she could trust herself to do right by him was to turn down his constant invitations.

Jesse accepted her lame excuses for the late-night pacing without comment, but his eyes told her he knew better.

Brock collapsed into the chair behind his desk on that hot August day. Every bone in his body ached. "How many crying babies did you rock this time?"

Jesse raised his head off the back of his chair and wiped his sleeve across his damp forehead. "Three. How much butter did you churn?"

"Enough to cover every slice of bread from here to Boston."

Jesse giggled. "Never thought being a campaign manager would be so much work."

Brock sighed. It was work, all right. No one could get himself elected so much as a dogcatcher in Lone Pine without beating the bushes for every last vote. The locals weren't interested in his Harvard degree. They wanted to know what he knew about mining and if he could milk cows, plow fields, and repair fences. In other words, he had to prove he was one of them.

He held out his newly callused hands and groaned. The problem was that his opposition, Joseph Maxwell, was one of them. The man also had no qualms about bribing voters with liquor. Brock didn't think much of Maxwell's methods, but plying whiskey had to be kinder to the hands than wielding hammers.

"Mrs. Albright said she'd ask her husband to vote for you," Jesse said.

"You did good, Jesse. Now, if they would all do what they say . . ." He still had as much chance of winning the election as a grasshopper surviving on an anthill.

Jesse frowned. "You don't think they'll vote for you?"

"You can't always go by what people say. That's the first thing I learned as a lawyer. You can pretty much count on at least a quarter of the statements made by eyewitnesses to be false."

Jesse thought for a moment. "Is that why Mr. Haddock lied on the witness stand?"

Brock's gaze sharpened. "What are you talking about? Lied?"

"He said Billy-Joe picked up his winnings and left the saloon." Jesse hesitated.

"Go on."

"But Ma said he lost all his money."

Brock sat forward, his muscle aches forgotten. He knew what Grace had said, but Haddock?

"You must have misunderstood."

"No, I heard him say it. It was right when that fight started."

"The fight?" He'd never forgotten his promise to Grace to find her husband's killer. But so far his efforts had revealed nothing. Now, thinking back to Haddock's testimony, he jumped out of his chair and reached for a file-cabinet drawer.

Miss Watkins had done such a poor job recording testimony he'd given her notes only a cursory glance. Now he carried the file over to his desk and sat down, quickly thumbing through the pages until he came to Haddock's testimony. There were gaping holes where she'd missed large sections of what each person had said but, praise the Lord, she got that part of his statement down. There it was, clear as day: *He picked up his winnings and left.*

The most essential part of the testimony and he'd missed it. He couldn't believe it. The question was why had Haddock lied?

"You're brilliant!" he exclaimed.

Jesse grinned. "Like Moses?"

"No, that's me. You're brilliant like Abraham Lincoln." Brock pressed his fingers together and an idea began to form. It was a long shot, but it was all he had.

"Did I ever tell you about the time that Mr. Lincoln cross-examined a witness who testified to seeing a murder committed by the light of a full moon?"

Jesse shook his head.

"Mr. Lincoln pulled out an almanac and proved that there was no full moon on the night in question. The witness immediately confessed and was arrested. Rumor had it that Mr. Lincoln substituted an almanac from another year in order to show the jury there was no full moon that night."

"Do you think that's what he did?"

"Probably not. After all they did call him Honest Abe. Still, it's a good trick if you can pull it off." He tapped the desk with the palm of a hand. "A very good trick."

CHAPTER ELEVEN

GRACE LOOKED UP FROM THE WASHTUB AS JESSE DROVE the horse and wagon helter-skelter into the yard. Dirt flew from beneath the wheels and squawking chickens scurried out of the way.

She glowered up at him. "Jesse, what in the name of heaven is the matter with you? You came charging in here like buckshot."

Jesse was out of breath and sweat poured down the side of his face. "Mr. Moses," he said and stopped to correct himself. "I mean, Mr. Daniels wants to see you."

She stuck the plunger into the tub and wiped her hands on her apron. "If he wants to see me, he can come here." She'd promised to deliver Mr. Porter's wash to him first thing the following morning and she was already behind.

"No, he can't." He jumped from the wagon and raced to her side. "Come on, it's important." He practically dragged her away from the washtub. "Hurry!"

"Wait!" She dug her heels in. "I can't go into town looking like this." The front of her frock was wet and strands of hair had fallen from her bun.

Jesse tugged on her arm. "There's no time to waste."

Grace threw up her hands. "This better not be one of your tricks." She pulled off her apron and tossed it into the back of the wagon before climbing into the passenger seat. "And I won't have you driving fast! You hear?"

She had barely settled in before Jesse grabbed the reins and urged the horse forward at such a quick pace that she was thrown back against the seat.

They made it into town in record time. No thanks to Jesse, they also made it without mishap. Brock stood waiting for them in front of the sheriff's office.

Mercy, just the sight of him made her quiver inside. Nevertheless she managed to scramble down the side of the wagon without letting on how he affected her.

"What's all this about?"

"You'll see." Winking at Jesse, Brock caught her by the elbow and escorted her into the sheriff's office.

Bower greeted the three of them from behind his desk and tossed a nod at the empty chairs.

"Sit." Brock released her arm. "Don't say a word. And that includes you, Mr. Lincoln."

Grace's stomach tightened. "Am I in t-trouble?" she stammered. She had nightmares about going back to jail.

"Not you," the sheriff said. "But someone is."

Brock nodded. "I think we know who killed your husband."

Her mind froze on his words. Could it really be true? Had she heard right?

The door flew open and she clenched her hands tight. Mr. Haddock walked into the office and glanced at Grace before turning to the sheriff.

"I was told you wanted to see me."

Bower lifted his feet off the desk and sat forward. "Sorry to trouble you, Haddock. Daniels here needs some clarification on your testimony."

Haddock's face paled. With his protruding lips and stony-eyed stare, he looked like a fish about to take its last breath. "I thought . . ." He cleared his voice. "I thought the trial was over."

"Oh, it's over all right," Bower assured him. "But you know how these Philadelphia lawyers are. Have to dot every *i* and cross every *t*."

Mr. Haddock sat down on the only empty chair and fidgeted with his collar. The chair had been arranged in such a way that he faced the four of them, much like a witness on the stand.

Brock leaned forward. Elbows on his lap, he rubbed his hands together. He looked relaxed and all friendly-like. "You said in your testimony that Mr. Davenport was playing faro when Mrs. Davenport approached him. Is that correct?"

"Yep. That's right."

"After exchanging a few words with her husband, she then left. Is that correct?"

He nodded. "That's . . . uh . . . correct."

Brock slapped himself on the knee. "I guess that's it then. I just wanted to clarify the timeline."

That was it? Grace barely managed to hold her tongue. He dragged her away from her wash for this?

Mr. Haddock stood, clutching his felt hat. "I'm glad I could be of help."

Brock stopped him with a raised hand before he reached the door. "Just one more thing."

Haddock turned, his face another notch whiter. "Yeah?"

"Why don't you take your seat again?" Brock said. "This will only take a minute."

Haddock returned to his seat, but his body was rigid as a lamppost.

"Would you mind telling us again what happened *after* Mrs. Davenport left the saloon?" Sensing something in Brock's demeanor, Grace leaned forward.

Haddock must have sensed it too because sweat broke out on his forehead. "Nothing much happened." He pulled out a handkerchief and mopped his head. "Like I said in court, Billy-Joe picked up his winnings and left."

"Picked up his winnings," Brock repeated, emphasizing every word.

"Will . . . will that be all?" Haddock's gaze circled the room like a horse trying to escape a corral.

"Yep, that's it," Brock said.

Haddock stood with an audible sigh and headed for the door.

"Wait!" Jesse jumped up. "You dropped something." He held up a gold coin.

Haddock's hand flew to his vest pocket. Too late, he realized his mistake.

"It's not mine," he said. "I don't own a gold coin."

"Are you certain about that?" Brock asked, standing. "Maybe you better empty your pockets."

Haddock's eyes widened. "My . . . my pockets?" he sputtered. He shot a beseeching look at the sheriff. "He can't order me around, can he?"

Bower shrugged. "Philadelphia lawyers."

The veins on Haddock's neck stuck out like thick blue ropes. He reached into his trouser pocket and threw a money clip with a small wad of bills onto the sheriff's desk.

"Don't forget your vest pockets," Brock said.

Haddock grimaced and ever so slowly emptied the rest. The right-hand pocket of his vest revealed a gold coin.

Grace jumped up. "That's . . . that's Billy-Joe's."

Bower was now on his feet, his casual air abandoned. "Are you sure?"

Jesse picked up the coin and turned it over. "Ma's right. This was his lucky coin." He held it so everyone could see the dent in Lady Liberty put there by an enemy's bullet.

Brock stood directly in front of Mr. Haddock. "Mrs. Davenport testified that her husband had the coin with him the night he was killed. So the question is, how did it end up in your pocket?"

Haddock gaped at him but he didn't say a word.

"Allow me," Brock said. "Stop me if I'm wrong. You were correct in saying that Billy-Joe took his winnings and left. But that was later that night. Earlier, he left his winnings on the table when he went outside to talk to his wife. He lied when he said he lost his pay. The truth is, he was on a winning streak."

Bower rubbed his palms together. "Is there anything you care to add to that, Haddock?"

Realizing he was cornered, Haddock's eyes took on a crazed look. "I . . . I didn't mean to kill him. Honest." He rubbed the sweat off his forehead with the back of his hand. "I needed to pay taxes on my farm or I'd lose it. I asked Billy-Joe for a loan but he refused."

"So you shot him."

"I didn't mean to." He turned to Grace. "It was an accident."

Grace stared at him, speechless. Was she dreaming? Could it be that the nightmare was finally over?

The sheriff seemed to think so. He plucked the key off a nail. "I guess it's time to show you some of our gray bar hospitality."

While the sheriff led Haddock to the jail in back, Grace tried to make sense of all that had happened. "I . . . I can't believe it," she whispered.

"Believe it," Brock said, his voice warm as the summer sun.

"But . . . but how did you know he had the gold coin?"

"I didn't know. Not for sure. But when Jesse pointed out the discrepancy between his testimony and yours, I recalled he kept putting his hand in his pocket during his testimony. So we decided to try a little experiment."

Jesse's eyes shone like two new pennies. "We got the idea from Abraham Lincoln."

"We? We?" Brock teased.

"But why would he keep the coin?" she asked. "It was the only thing that could put him at the scene of the crime."

Brock shook his head. "Who knows? Maybe he thought it would bring him luck. Don't forget, the coin saved your husband's life during the war and he was on a winning streak the night he died."

"The coin didn't save him at the end," she said.

Brock laid his hands on Jesse's shoulders, and that one simple gesture nearly melted her heart. "No, but it helped my partner and me catch his killer."

CHAPTER TWELVE

A WINDSTORM ANNOUNCED THE COMING OF FALL BY bombarding Lone Pine for two days. When the wind finally stopped, it left a layer of dust and pine needles on the porch. Grace wielded the broom and wished that memories of Brock could be swept away as easily as the debris.

He was never far away from her thoughts. Of course, it didn't help that Jesse idolized the man. It was Mr. Moses this and Mr. Moses that. To hear Jesse tell it, Brock was somewhat of a hero in town for catching Billy-Joe's killer and was very much in demand as a lawyer.

"I believe you won the battle of the porch."

"Brock!" She swallowed in an effort to still her pounding heart. "Why are you sneaking up on me like that?"

"Sorry, but you can never be too careful around a lady with a weapon." He closed the distance between them and stopped at the bottom of the porch steps. His smile made her heart race.

"I didn't see you at church Sunday and you haven't been to town. Jesse said you haven't been sleeping well. So I thought maybe this would help." He pulled a newspaper from beneath his arm and held it up for her to read. The headline read: HADDOCK FOUND GUILTY.

Haddock insisted it was an accident, but the jury didn't buy the lie. For that she was grateful, but the verdict brought her no joy. No amount of justice would bring Billy-Joe back or make up for the mistakes of her past.

"Your name has been cleared," he said. "There's no longer any doubt about your innocence."

She smiled. Another prayer answered. "That means that Jesse can hold up his head."

"Jesse always held up his head. He's always been proud of you."

His penetrating gaze made her look away. "And I've always been proud of him."

Brock folded the newspaper and stuffed it into his coat pocket. "Now that it's over, I wonder if perhaps you'd do me the honor of accompanying me to the church social this Saturday."

She leaned the broom against the house. "Not a good idea."

"Why not?"

She narrowed her eyes. Did she really have to spell it out? "You have an election coming up."

"And?"

"And you don't need to be seen with a woman who's . . . used."

His eyebrows shot up. "You're not used, Grace. Far from it."

Hugging herself tight, she battled her raw emotions. "I've had three husbands. If that's not used, I don't know what is."

He pulled off his hat and raked his fingers through his hair. "We both have things in our pasts we regret."

"Me more than you." She moistened her lower lip. "I used to think that a man could fix my problems. That marriage was the only way a woman could survive."

"Marriage is a gift from God," he said.

She scoffed. "Some gift. In any case, my marrying days are over. Husbands ain't caused me nothing but trouble."

His brow knitted. "The trick is to marry for the right reasons. I'd . . ." He cleared his throat. "I'd like a chance to show you what those right reasons might be."

Her heart squeezed tight. "You . . . can't mean that."

"I do mean it, Grace. I've had a lot of time to think about it."

She shook her head and backed toward the door. He placed his hat on his head and his foot on the lower step. "Please, Grace. Hear me out. I want to prove I'm worthy of being the first man you marry out of love. That would make me husband number one in God's eyes."

Her mouth parted and a lump rose in her throat. "And how many votes do you think a wife like me will get you?" Her body trembled along with her voice. "I can tell you right now. None!"

"I don't care about the election—"

"But I do, Brock. This town needs a judge like you. And

what better way to honor your friend's memory? Maybe then you'll forgive yourself for his death."

Pain filled his eyes. "Grace—"

She shook her head and reached for the doorknob. "Please, just go."

CHAPTER THIRTEEN

GRACE GATHERED THE LAST OF THE NEWLY LAID EGGS from the henhouse and walked across the yard. White puffy clouds played peekaboo with the sun. The vanilla smell of Ponderosa filled the air, and a raucous jay called out from the highest branches.

Galloping hooves signaled Jesse's return. Surprised to see him home so early, she set the egg basket on the porch and waited for him to tether his horse.

Something wasn't right; he looked like he'd lost his best friend.

"Jesse?"

Without saying a word, he rushed past her and into the house.

She followed him inside. Finding him facedown on his bed, she sat on the edge of his mattress and rubbed his back.

"What's wrong?"

He answered her in a muffled voice. "Mr. Moses said I can't be his campaign manager anymore."

"Why not?"

"He says he's not running for judge."

She drew her hand away. "But he has to . . . I mean . . ."

"Says it's no use. No one's gonna vote for him anyway."

Her lips parted in dismay. Because of her? Oh please, God, don't let it be because of her. Brock's plan to run for judge and bring law and order to the town was the one good thing that came out of the whole nightmare of her trial. It wouldn't change the past, but maybe—just maybe—it would help lessen some of the pain. It was this hope that made his dream her dream as well.

"I'll talk to him." She hadn't the slightest idea what she could say to change his mind, but she had to try. "Hitch Brownie to the wagon."

Jesse looked up, beaming.

Never had she seen anyone change moods so quickly. She stared at him a moment before rushing out of his room to change.

Arriving in town, Grace left Jesse to park the wagon while she stormed into Brock's office.

He looked up from his desk and didn't seem the least bit surprised to see her. "Morning, Grace."

Ignoring the way the sight of him made her heart leap, she lit into him. "What's this I hear about you not running for judge?"

"I guess Jesse told you."

"How could you?" She stabbed the desk with her finger. "This town needs you. It needs a judge who is fair and cares about justice."

"Yes, it does, but I'm not sure I'm the right person."

Surprised, she drew back. "How can you say that? How can you even think it?"

"I've been talking to people. Not sure I'll get enough votes."

"Because of me?" He didn't answer; he didn't have to. "Why, there's no one more qualified and more capable and more trustworthy and more—" She'd almost added *kind and good and handsome.*

He grinned. "Don't let me stop you."

She folded her arms and glowered at him. "Why do I get the feeling that you and Jesse are up to something?"

He didn't deny it. Instead, his mouth curved and humor warmed the depth of his eyes. "I want to show you something." He stood and walked around his desk. "Outside."

Puzzled, she followed him through the waiting room and out the front door. Much to her shock the street that had been deserted moments earlier was now packed with people. She recognized most but not all from the trial. Some she recognized from church.

She whirled around to face Brock. "What's going on?"

"You'll see." He addressed the crowd. "As you all know, I've been running for judge," he said. "But before I continue with my campaign, I need to know how many votes I can count on."

"You can count on my vote," Jesse said.

"The kid's too young to vote," someone yelled from the back.

"Yeah, well, I'm sure not voting for you," Reverend Fields said, causing Grace to gasp in shock. Jesse covered his mouth to hide his smile. "You aren't married," the reverend went on, "and unless you know the trials of having a wife, you know nothing about law and order." Mrs. Fields gave her husband a playful poke with her elbow, and the churchwomen standing next to her laughed.

"Object-shun," Tall Pete said, but he raised his hand anyway.

"Not married, you say?" Brock locked Grace in his gaze. "What if I was to ask this woman to be my bride? Who would vote for me then?"

Her mouth dropped open. Before she could react, all hands shot up, including the sheriff's and Reverend Fields's.

Just then, a young, thin voice rose. "Extra, extra, read all about it! Philadelphia lawyer to take a wife!"

Brock looked just as surprised as Grace did. Her mind whirled. Acceptance shone from every face peering at her. Overwhelmed, she turned and rushed away.

Brock caught up with her just as she reached her horse and wagon. He grabbed her by the wrist.

She pulled her arm away. "You tricked me!"

"I had nothing to do with the newspaper—"

"I'm not talking about the newspaper." She tossed a nod to the crowd still gathered in the middle of the street. "I'm talking about them. I don't like being tricked, especially to win an election."

He drew back. "Is that what you think this is about? The election?" He turned her around to face the crowd.

"What do you see?" Brock murmured in her ear. When she made no reply, he continued, "I'll tell you what I see. I see people trying to make up for past mistakes. Make up for misjudging you. Make up to Jesse."

Her gaze swung to where her son stood and her heart swelled. Jesse definitely looked like he belonged. This was clearly his town, his home. A warm glow flowed through her.

"They're not voting for me," Brock continued. "They're voting for you. They're voting to make this a more lawful town. A less prejudiced one. *That's* what I wanted you to know." He spun her around in his arms. "Could you find it in your heart to forgive this Philadelphia lawyer?"

She looked up at him and all the hurts of the past melted away in the heat of his gaze. How could she not forgive the man who stood by her side in her darkest hour? "Philadelphia lawyer, no. Colorado judge, yes."

His hold tightened. "Does that mean what I think it means?"

Glancing at the waiting crowd, she drew in a deep breath. She'd made so many mistakes in the past, but only because she'd acted out of fear. It was fear that had made her rush in to all three of her marriages, but this time fear held her back. She couldn't bear to make another devastating mistake.

She swung her gaze to Brock. "You once said that marriage is a gift from God."

He sucked in his breath. "It is. As long as two people love each other and make Him the head of the family."

"Do . . . do you think God means the gift of marriage for the two of us?"

He studied her, and the love shining from his eyes made her want to believe that even someone like her could find true happiness.

"I'm sure of it," he said, his voice husky. "I also believe that loving and cherishing each other will be our gift back to Him."

Loving and cherishing Brock, now that she could do. She reached up and pressed a hand to his cheek. He was real; she wasn't dreaming. "You better watch out. I might take you up on that offer." She blushed.

"Might?" With a glance at the watching crowd, he took her hand in his and pulled her into his office. Kicking the door shut with his foot, he backed her against the wall in full embrace.

He gazed at her intently. "I love you, Grace Davenport, and if you'd like, I'd be happy to put on a good closing argument as to why you should love me back."

She laughed. "That won't be necessary. I already love you," she whispered. "I really, really do!"

His eyes flared as he pulled her close. The moment their lips met, church bells rang out the noon hour—the voice of God, as Reverend Fields called them, the voice of new beginnings.

THE TRAIN WAS LATE ARRIVING IN PHOENIX AND Reverend Gregory Miller was bone tired, no thanks to the four pastors who kept him up during an all-night session with their tales of unlikely couples.

"Yoo-hoo!"

At the sound of the familiar voice, he spun around. Much to his surprise, Elizabeth stood on the other side of the train platform waving not just one arm but both. He blinked. Today she was wearing a knee-high skirt over—*could it be?*—trousers?

Despite her unconventional dress he had to smile when, instead of walking quietly, sedately, ladylike toward him, she ran. Her hat flew off, but no sooner had she stopped to retrieve it than she was running again. Her loose red hair flew every which way, the ribbons on her hat trailing behind.

People stared as she raced by. He had to admit, she was a

sight to behold. She came to a stop in front of him, all rosy-cheeked and out of breath.

"Welcome home."

"Elizabeth, so good to see you. But what are you doing here?"

Clearly surprised by the question, she lifted her chin. "Surely you didn't forget sending a telegram to the church asking me to meet your train?"

"Telegram? What—?" A thought occurred to him. Was it possible that his new friends had sent the telegram in his name?

"Ah, the telegram."

She looked at him funny. "Are you all right?"

"Yes, just tired. It was a long week. We had some late-night sessions, and I didn't get any sleep on the train."

She stared at him for a moment as if waiting for him to . . . what? Grow wings?

"The wagon's parked over there." She sounded hurt or maybe just confused.

"I'll get my baggage."

She hesitated. "You said you wanted to talk."

"I did?"

Her eyes flashed. "Yes, in the telegram that you obviously don't remember sending."

His busybody colleagues would have a laugh if they could see him now, silenced by the woman he loved.

"We can . . . talk." But what more was there to say? He'd already told her why the two of them wouldn't work out. For a man whose job it was to give oratory, he felt oddly out of words.

Her face turned red and her nostrils thinned. "Why do I get the feeling that—?" She stared at him. "Never mind."

He reached for her arm. "Elizabeth, please—"

She pulled away. "Don't say another word. We're done. From now on, I'm . . . I'm attending the Methodist church!"

"You can't mean—" But before he could complete his thought, she turned and stomped away.

As he watched her go, his emotions unraveled like a woolen sweater. He thought about Abram and Sarai and Moses and David and before he knew it, his feet were moving.

"Elizabeth, wait!"

People moved out of his way and turned to stare. He could well imagine what they were thinking: a dignified preacher making a spectacle. Oddly enough, he didn't care.

Nor did he care who saw him take her in his arms.

She stared at him with rounded eyes. "What's come over you?"

"Nothing." *Everything.* Why in the world had it taken him so long to realize what was now as plain as day?

"I want to tell you about some stories I heard. Stories about Maizy and Rylan." He chuckled as he pressed his lips against her forehead. "And Molly and Jack." This time he pecked her cute, little nose. "Then there's Katie and Treb." He dropped a kiss on her silky-smooth cheek. "And last but not least, I want to tell you about Grace and Brock."

She looked confused and he couldn't blame her. "Who . . . who are these people?"

"They're people God brought together." He inhaled her sweet fragrance. "They're people in love, just like you and me."

She glanced around with a worried frown. "If the deacons see us . . . Your reputation—"

"Let them look. If they don't like it, let *them* join the Methodists."

She studied him for a moment as if to make certain he meant what he said. Then with a whoop and a holler, she threw her arms around his neck. His face blazed hot as the burning bush, but that didn't stop him from pulling her close and kissing her pretty pink lips.

Praise be to God—and those new, busybody friends of his—for showing him that even the unlikeliest of couples can find true happiness.

Reading Group Guides

Spitfire Sweetheart

1. Women in the 1800s lived within very strict rules. In *Spitfire Sweetheart* Maizy wearing britches is truly scandalous. These days anything goes. Discuss the pros and cons of being bound by these types of conventions.

2. Rylan is afraid of failing. Despite his tough attitude he is anxious to prove himself to his father, and that motivates his actions. Do you think Rylan took this upon himself or that his father put that pressure on him?

3. Talk about parental pressure to succeed and how children can respond positively and negatively to that pressure. What kind of parent are you? What kind of parents do you have?

4. Maizy's father needs her help around the ranch but he's also ashamed of her for behaving in manly ways—at least

when it gets her in trouble. Talk about how Maizy's father affects her compared to how Rylan's father affects him.

A Love Letter to the Editor

1. Molly is hurt and angered because she was passed over for the position as editor. Was she right to feel this way? Do you think her father had good reasons for the decision he made?

2. Jack isn't put-off by Molly's outspoken ways, but sometimes the amusement and pleasure he feels around her make Molly think he is laughing at her. Have you ever felt that way? How did you handle it?

3. Molly's mother tells her that "love can be quite an adventure." Have past hurts made you try to protect your heart and avoid the adventure?

4. Both Molly and Jack seek the wise counsel of Reverend Lynch. Do you agree with the guidance he gives them? Why or why not?

A Cowboy for Katie

1. In *A Cowboy for Katie*, Katie is determined to fix herself. She is so independent that she literally runs everyone off. Is it possible to be too independent? Discuss reasons why your or someone else would refuse help (e.g., pride, fear, etc.) and why that might not be the best choice.

2. Treb has a plan for his life and believes he's got everything under control. But when his horse dies and leaves him stranded, Treb accepts the job with Katie, fully intending to use the job as a way to get back on track with his plans . . . only God has other plans for Treb. What issues of his past must he face as he helps Katie face her issues?

3. Katie and Treb both think they know what they need, but God is the one with the right plan. They just have to recognize it, overcome their fears, and trust Him. Have you ever had to do this in your own life?

Courting Trouble

1. Brock appears to be ill-suited for the town, but as the story progresses, God's purpose in bringing him to Colorado becomes clear. Have you ever felt that you didn't belong? In what way did this affect your faith and relationship to God?

2. Grace made many mistakes in her life, but she admits she did so out of fear. Has fear ever held you back or caused you to make mistakes you later regretted?

3. Reverend Fields tells Brock that saving Grace might well be his saving grace. What do you think he means by that?

4. Jesse's persistence shows Brock how much he believes in his mother's innocence. In what ways has persistence paid off in your own life?

5. Which character did you most identify with? Why?

Acknowledgments

IT'S AMAZING HOW MANY PEOPLE IT TAKES TO PRODUCE a book. We can't thank our editor, Ami McConnell, enough and the whole Thomas Nelson/HarperCollins Christian Publishing team for the loving care they gave our stories. Also, special thanks to our terrific agent, Natasha Kern, who came up with the idea of us working together. Finally, we want to thank our readers for all the nice things they said about our first group effort, *A Bride for All Seasons*. Four bouquets and a kiss to you all!

—ROBIN, MARY, DEBRA, AND MARGARET

About the Authors

NEW YORK TIMES BEST-SELLING AUTHOR **MARGARET Brownley** has penned more than thirty novels. Her books have won numerous awards, including Readers' Choice and Award of Excellence. She's a former *Romance Writers of American* RITA finalist and has written for a TV soap. Happily married to her real-life hero, Margaret and her husband have three grown children and live in Southern California. www.margaretbrownley.com

DEBRA CLOPTON IS A MULTI-AWARD-WINNING NOVELIST who was first published in 2005 and has more than twenty-two novels to her credit. Along with her writing, Debra helps her husband teach the youth at their local Cowboy Church. Debra is the author of the acclaimed Mule Hollow Matchmaker series, the place readers tell her they wish were real. Her goal is to shine a light toward God while she entertains readers with her words.

BEST-SELLING NOVELIST ROBIN LEE HATCHER IS KNOWN for her heartwarming and emotionally charged stories of faith, courage, and love. The winner of the Christy Award for Excellence in Christian Fiction, the RITA Award for Best Inspirational Romance, the Carol Award, two *Romantic Times* Career Achievement Awards, and the RWA Lifetime Achievement Award, Robin is the author of more than seventy novels.

MARY CONNEALY WRITES ROMANTIC COMEDY WITH cowboys. She is a Carol Award winner, and a RITA, Christy, and Inspirational Reader's Choice finalist. She is the author of the best-selling Kincaid Brides series: *Out of Control, In Too Deep, Over the Edge*; Lassoed in Texas trilogy; Montana Marriages trilogy; and Sophie's Daughters trilogy. Mary is married to a Nebraska rancher and has four grown daughters and two spectacular grandchildren.